CONSUMER CULTURE
AND
SOCIETY

CONSUMER CULTURE
AND
SOCIETY

Wendy Wiedenhoft Murphy
John Carroll University

Los Angeles | London | New Delhi
Singapore | Washington DC | Melbourne

FOR INFORMATION:

SAGE Publications, Inc.
2455 Teller Road
Thousand Oaks, California 91320
E-mail: order@sagepub.com

SAGE Publications Ltd.
1 Oliver's Yard
55 City Road
London, EC1Y 1SP
United Kingdom

SAGE Publications India Pvt. Ltd.
B 1/I 1 Mohan Cooperative Industrial Area
Mathura Road, New Delhi 110 044
India

SAGE Publications Asia-Pacific Pte. Ltd.
3 Church Street
#10–04 Samsung Hub
Singapore 049483

Printed in the United States of America

Library of Congress Cataloging-in-Publication Data

Names: Wiedenhoft, Wendy A., author.

Title: Consumer culture and society / Wendy Wiedenhoft Murphy.

Description: Los Angeles : SAGE, [2017] | Includes bibliographical references and index.

Identifiers: LCCN 2016010157 | ISBN 9781483358154 (pbk. : alk. paper)

Subjects: LCSH: Consumption (Economics)—Social aspects. | Consumption (Economics)—United States—Social aspects. | Consumers. | Consumer behavior.

Classification: LCC HC79.C6 W535 2017 | DDC 306.30973—dc23
LC record available at https://lccn.loc.gov/2016010157

This book is printed on acid-free paper.

Acquisitions Editor: Jeff Lasser
Editorial Assistant: Alex Croell
Production Editor: Veronica Stapleton Hooper
Copy Editor: Gillian Dickens
Typesetter: Hurix Systems Pvt. Ltd.
Proofreader: Lawrence Baker
Indexer: Jean Casalegno
Cover Designer: Candice Harman
Marketing Manager: Kara Kindstrom

MIX
Paper from responsible sources
FSC
www.fsc.org
FSC® C014174

16 17 18 19 20 10 9 8 7 6 5 4 3 2 1

Contents

Foreword and Acknowledgments   xi

About the Author   xv

**Chapter 1. Introduction: Historical Context and
Theoretical Tensions**   1

  Historical Context   2

    Situating the Study of Consumption   2

    Situating the Origins of Mass Consumer

      Society in the United States 4

  Positioning the Concept of Consumption:

  Tensions and Contradictions   7

    Production and Consumption   7

    Freedom and Coercion   10

    Consumers and Citizens   12

  Organization of the Book   14

PART I. CONCEPTUAL FRAMEWORK

**Chapter 2. Objects of Consumption: Commodities and
Mass Consumer Society**   21

  The Production of Commodities   22

    Fordism: Mass Production and Consumption 22

    Post-Fordism: Craft Production and

      Niche Consumption   23

  The Value of Commodities   25

    Use Value and Exchange Value   25

    Sign Value   26

The Meaning of Commodities   28
   Appropriation and Social Relationships   28
   Gifts   30
   The Biography of Commodities   32
Obsolescence and Waste   33
   Smartphones   *36*
The Commoditization of Everything?   37
Conclusion   39

**Chapter 3. Subjects of Consumption: Passive Dupes or
Active Agents?**   **41**
   Emulation, Distinction, or Rebellion?   42
      Veblen: Conspicuous Consumption and Leisure   42
      Bourdieu: Taste, Habitus, and Cultural Capital   44
      The Birmingham School: Bricolage and Resistance   46
   Passive Dupes?   48
      The Frankfurt School and the Culture Industry   48
      Children as Consumers   *51*
   Utility or Hedonism?   53
      Sovereignty and Choice   53
      Desire and Difference: Colin Campbell and
         Postmodernism   56
   Conclusion   58

Chapter 4. The Places and Spaces of Consumption   **59**
   The City, Arcades, and Department Stores   60
   Shopping Malls and Big-Box Stores   63
   Wal-Mart: Killing the Category Killers?   65
      Service Workers   *68*
   Amazon.com and E-Commerce   69
   The Privatization of Public Space   72
   Conclusion   75

**PART II. APPLYING THE CONCEPTUAL
FRAMEWORK: CASE STUDIES**

Chapter 5. Food   **79**
   Food as an Object of Consumption   80
      Industrial Food Chain   80
      Organic Food Chain   82

Local Food Chain   83
Raw Milk   85
Food and the Subjects of Consumption   87
    Class and Status Relations   87
    Ethnic and National Identities   90
Food and the Places of Consumption   91
    Eating In   91
    Dining Out   93
    Supermarkets   95
Conclusion   97

Chapter 6. Tourism   **99**
Tourism and the Objects of Consumption   100
    Economic Development and the Tourism Industry   100
    Cultural Commodification and Objectification:
      Souvenirs and Sex Tourism   101
Tourism and the Subjects of Consumption   105
    Passive Gazers or Embodied Actors 105
    Dark Tourism   107
    Searching for Authenticity or Fun 108
Tourism and the Places of Consumption   110
    Disney World: Authentic or Imagined Fun?   110
    National Parks: Staged or Natural Authenticity?   113
Conclusion   117

Chapter 7. Higher Education   **119**
Higher Education as a Place of Consumption   121
    A Field of Struggle   121
    MOOCs   123
    Corporate Colonization   124
Higher Education as an Object of Consumption   127
    Human Capital and Credentials   128
    Social and Cultural Capital   130
    Evaluating the Product of Higher Education   131
Higher Education and the Subjects of Consumption   132
    Students as Consumers   132
    Obstacles to Future Consumption and
      Becoming an Adult   134
    Disengaged Consumers and Ignorant Citizens   135
Conclusion   136

PART III. ETHICAL CONCERNS AND CONSUMER ACTIVISM

Chapter 8. Political Consumerism and the Consumer Movement   **141**
    Political Consumerism: A Brief History   142
        Consumer Tactics: Boycotts and Buycotts   142
    The Consumer Movement   146
    Political Consumerism: A New Era   147
        The Fair Trade Movement   149
        Culture Jamming   *151*
        Green Consumerism   152
    Conclusion   158

Chapter 9. Credit and Debt   **161**
    Liberalization of Financial Markets and the
        Credit Industry   162
    Debtor-Creditor Relationships   166
        Debtor Default and Settlement   170
        Pawn Shops   *172*
    Debt Forgiveness and Relief   174
    Conclusion   177

Chapter 10. Alternative Forms of Consumption   **179**
    Frugality, Sacrifice, Austerity, and Postmaterialism   180
    The Voluntary Simplicity Movement   182
    Do-It-Yourself Movement   183
    Local Currency Movement   184
        Bitcoin   *186*
    Consumer Cooperatives   187
    Collaborative Consumption and
        the Sharing Economy   188
    Co-Creation, Presumers, and Prosumption:
        Free Consumer Labor   191
    Reduce, Reuse, and Dematerialism   194
    Conclusion   195

Chapter 11. Conclusion: The Globalization of Mass Consumer Culture   **197**
    Globalization and Localization   198

Mecca Cola   202
China: Global Brands and Belonging   203
India: Nationalism and Resistance   207
Conclusion   212

References   **215**
Index   **241**

Foreword and Acknowledgments

My interest in consumer culture and society came about inadvertently when I was randomly assigned to work with a group to present *The Theory of the Leisure Class* in an undergraduate social stratification course. I had never heard of Thorstein Veblen before but found his description of conspicuous consumption—written in 1899—quite relevant to the 1990s. It seemed evident to me that individuals continued to purchase items to display their wealth and status, particularly through brands. However, I was not entirely convinced about his argument that the elite created fashions, which simply trickled down the class hierarchy. On one hand, I thought that what the Frankfurt school called the culture industry was probably more influential than the elite when it came to popularizing consumer goods. On the other hand, I witnessed how certain fashions and styles trickled up from the working class and youth subcultures and became appropriated by the elite and the culture industry. These reflections became the basis of my master's thesis, a semiotic analysis of how Dr. Martens boots trickled up from the working class to youth subcultures to mainstream consumer culture. They also influenced my decision to pursue a doctorate at a university with a strong theory program and at least one faculty member who specialized in consumption. The latter was a challenge as few academics thought consumer culture and society was a serious topic to study at the time. However, I found a home at the University of Maryland–College Park, where I was fortunate to take courses and work on projects with George Ritzer and Richard Harvey Brown. During my doctoral studies, I was introduced to comparative historical sociology and, with the mentoring of Meyer Kestnbaum, was able to successfully bridge my interest in consumer culture with social movements and voluntary associations, resulting in my dissertation on how the American Federation of Labor and the National Consumers League used boycotts and buycotts to politicize consumption during the Progressive Era.

Today, the study of consumer culture and society is thriving across a variety of disciplines, including sociology, history, political science, communications and media studies, anthropology, and economics. The strength of this growth is remarkable given that 20 years ago, few academic books had been published in this area, especially in the United States. Considering the increasing interest in this field of study, I thought it would be an opportune time to write an introductory textbook on consumer culture and society. My primary intention is to introduce undergraduates to the wide array of challenges and possibilities that transpire from living in a mass consumer society. In addition, I have tried to accurately examine and organize the theories and research of a large number of scholars from a variety of disciplines in one place. My hope is that this textbook will encourage others to create and offer more courses on consumer culture and society to maintain the momentum in this field.

I would like to thank my editor at SAGE, Jeff Lasser, for his willingness to take on this project and help me through the entire process—from the initial proposal stage to the completion of the final draft. I would also like to express my appreciation to Veronica Stapleton Hooper for her assistance during the book production process, Gillian Dickens for her careful copyediting, and Alex Croell for her administrative and editorial work. The anonymous reviewers of my proposal, sample chapters, and first draft offered insightful comments that helped make this a better book. In addition, I am grateful to John Carroll University for awarding me a research grant to work on this project and George Ritzer for his letter of support. For the past 5 years, I have been fortunate to co-teach courses on Consumer Culture and Politics and Global Debt and Justice in the honors program and the sociology and political science departments at John Carroll with Mindy Peden, who deserves an extra special shout-out for encouraging me to pursue this project. Several students also deserve acknowledgment, including Katie Kavulic for her extensive annotated bibliography on food, culture, and politics, and Owen Reilly and Sara Sternbach for helping me proof the bibliography. Finally, I would like to thank my mother, who has shared many shopping trips with me over the years, my brother, who has tried to keep me current with digital trends and marketing campaigns, and Jim Murphy, who has patiently listened to me talk about consumer culture and society ever since we were undergraduates.

Publisher's Acknowledgments

SAGE wishes to acknowledge the valuable contributions of the following reviewers.

Aysegul Kesimoglu, City University London

Henry Schwarz, Georgetown University

Jennifer Smith Maguire, University of Leicester School of Management

Jim Snow, Loyola University Maryland

About the Author

Wendy Wiedenhoft Murphy is an Associate Professor of Sociology at John Carroll University. She joined the department in 2003 after completing her doctorate at the University of Maryland. Her specialty areas are sociological theory, consumer culture and society, and environmental justice. She has published work on consumer activism in the *Journal of Consumer Culture and Social Movement Studies*, tourism in *Peace and Conflict Studies*, and the Ulster-Scots diaspora in an edited collection. She is the past director of the Environmental Studies concentration at John Carroll University and has been involved with its summer program on conflict transformation in Northern Ireland. Currently, she is researching the limited but significant and active role of poor consumers in American society and working with George Ritzer on his textbook, *Introduction to Sociology*.

1

Introduction

Historical Context and Theoretical Tensions

O ne of the most visible and salient aspects of contemporary society is **consumption,** or selling, buying, using, and disposing of products and services.

Regardless of income, most of us partake in some type of consumption every day whether it be purchasing a cup of coffee or a new app for our smartphones. Although some forms of consumption are quite tangible, such as buying a car, others are more about consuming experiences, like attending a football game or going to a movie. What we consume conveys not just our preferences but also provides signals to others about our socioeconomic class and status, our gender and sexuality, our race and ethnicity, and our age. These preferences and signals are strongly influenced by advertisers and marketers, who bombard us with images and messages on television and social media platforms on a daily, if not hourly, basis. Our peers also help shape what consumer goods we might purchase, how we use these goods to express belonging or display difference, and where we purchase them. The thought and meaning that goes into our consumer decisions varies, but even those who profess not to care about fashion, style, or novelty are still influenced by consumer culture. Most of us probably know someone who claims that he only purchases clothing that is practical and comfortable, but finding such clothing might take just as much thought, time, and energy as shopping to keep up with the latest trends. Some of us might also know people who think consumption is a trivial activity—a pleasurable hobby for bored housewives and teenagers. This characterized the view of consumption by many academics until quite recently and, as this book will argue, seriously devalues the work, creativity, and care that consumers perform.

Historical Context

Situating the Study of Consumption

As consumption has come to occupy a central part of our everyday lives, it has become increasingly viewed as a subject worthy of the attention of scholars. However, this attention is relatively recent. Historically, what has been called a **productivist bias** informed the field of sociology and other academic disciplines. Production and work were privileged at the expense of consumption not only by classical theorists like Adam Smith and Karl Marx but, until recently, by contemporary examiners of the social world too (Ritzer, Goodman, and Wiedenhoft 2001:410). Starting in the 1960s, this began to change as anthropologists, historians, political scientists, and sociologists started to critically challenge this productivist bias by demonstrating both theoretically and empirically the importance of consumption and consumers in the development of modern society. Miller et al. (1998:1–7) identify three stages of the study of consumption, the first stage starting in the 1960s and ending in the late 1970s with the decline of industrial jobs and traditional working-class culture in Western societies. Academics found that consumption was a clever way to bring culture and interpretation into the social sciences, although it remained linked to production and did not become its own field until the second stage of consumption studies, which lasted from the late 1970s to the early 1990s. During this stage, consumption became understood as a way individuals constructed their identities and was acknowledged as a key component of industrialization, not simply a consequence of it (Slater 1997). Interestingly, one could argue that a **consumerist bias** emerged during this second stage as consumption was often analyzed in isolation from production processes. This was especially the case with studies that emphasized consumer subjectivity and postmodern culture (Campbell 1989; Featherstone 1991; McCracken 1990).

This neglect of production started to be rectified in the early 1990s and continues today during the third stage of consumption studies, which connects the actions of consumers to the treatment of workers and the effects of production and consumption on the environment. The historical development of consumerism, especially in the United States, is a growing area of research (Cohen 2003; Cross 2000; Deutsch 2010; Glickman 1997; McGovern 2006). Ethical and moral considerations are now being addressed more frequently, including the idea that consumers are citizens who can engage in political and social activism through the marketplace (Breen 2004; Glickman 2009; Hilton 2009). Indeed, what some are calling **critical consumer studies** that examine the "contradictions and ruptures within capitalist consumerism in order to discern both the promise and the limits of political action" (Mukherjee and Banet-Weiser 2012) is increasingly characterizing this third stage of consumer studies and perhaps marks the transition to the fourth stage.

Given the growth of consumer studies across numerous disciplines and its institutionalization in academia through journals, conferences, and graduate seminars, it currently appears to be a favorable moment for the introduction of a comprehensive, undergraduate-level textbook on consumption. The impressive breadth of scholarship from anthropologists, economists, historians, market researchers, political scientists, and sociologists makes this a considerable undertaking and inevitably requires some constraints on time and space. In the aim of conciseness, this textbook limits the scope of time and space to mass consumer society in the United States. Although theorists and concepts from earlier time periods will be discussed and some instances of mass consumerism in other countries will be provided, particularly in the concluding chapter, the majority of analysis and examples will focus on the United States, where mass consumerism originated and from which it has spread across the world. Despite the scope conditions of time and space used in this primer, it is my hope that it will offer a preliminary guide to help organize undergraduate courses on consumer culture and society and hopefully encourage the creation of more of them in the future.

The following section of this introductory chapter will provide a brief history of the development of mass consumption during the turn of the twentieth century, including the invention of national brands; the extensive availability of standardized, machine-made products; the use of advertising to create consumer desire; and buying on installment plan credit—strategies of mass consumerism that are so prevalent today that they are often taken for granted by the average American. The next section will highlight several of the main theoretical tensions that have surrounded mass consumption over the years: the oppositions between production and consumption, freedom and coercion, and consumers and citizens. Finally, the concluding section will describe the organization of this book.

Situating the Origins of Mass Consumer Society in the United States

The act of consuming predates modern, industrial society, but it was not until the late nineteenth and early twentieth centuries in the United States that a genuine culture of **mass consumption** commenced. Characterized by the mass production of standardized goods that were relatively inexpensive, nationwide distribution, and brand-name advertising, consumption became a daily activity that was no longer the exclusive domain of the wealthy but open to the masses. From ready-to-wear clothing sold off the racks instead of personally tailored to manufactured food products, like sliced bread, that did not need to be mixed, kneaded, and baked in the home, individuals confronted a variety of novel goods that signified progress, promised convenience, and offered the freedom of individual choice (Benson 1986; Strasser 1989). Between 1880 and 1930, Americans came to "depend on the commercial marketplace, with few feasible alternatives, for the necessities of daily life" (McGovern 2006:10), and by the end of the 1920s, the majority of national income was spent in retail stores on commercial products (Ewen 1976:115). Before 1880, consumption and production were "bound together," and most of the goods that the average American consumed would have been produced by them in their homes (Leach 1993:147). The concept of disposability would have been completely alien to these individuals, who would have repaired and reused the goods they produced instead of throwing them away when they were old or broken (Strasser 1999).

According to Gabriel and Lang (2006:12), "it was not merely the growth of spending power across social classes and strata" but "the experience of *choice* as a generalized social phenomenon" that distinguished mass consumption from earlier forms of purchasing. In addition to the proliferation of choice, "acquisition and consumption as the means of achieving happiness; the cult of the new; the democratization of desire; and money value as the predominant measure of all value in society" became key features of mass consumer culture (Leach 1993:3). Starting with department stores in the cities and spreading into more rural areas through mail-order catalogues, like Montgomery Ward in 1872 and Sears, Roebuck and Company in 1893, tens of thousands of mass consumer goods were available to most Americans if not to purchase then at least to gaze upon. Like mail-order catalogues, the creation of chain stores, such as Woolworth's, which opened in 1879, helped democratize access to the same goods in different locations (Strasser 1989:222). The rise in popularity of installment plans with monthly payments fueled mass consumption, especially the ability to purchase high-priced items like cars, furniture, and appliances. By 1925, almost 75% of cars, 70% of furniture, and 80% of appliances were obtained with this type of credit (Cross 2000:29). Merchants found that extending credit to customers was an economic risk worth taking as customers who used credit in their stores were not only loyal but "apt to buy impulsively and in larger amounts" (Leach 2003:124).

Desire and fantasy were injected into consumer preference by advertisers, who were already promoting a "therapeutic" quality to consumer goods at the turn of the twentieth century (Jackson and Lears 1983). The first advertising agency, N. W. Ayer & Son, opened in 1877, and by 1900, companies were spending $95 million annually on advertising their products (Glickman 1999:3). Some companies, like Colgate toothpaste, used advertising to persuade consumers that they needed a commercial product where one never existed before, while others that had established product categories, like Procter and Gamble's Ivory soap, "put most of their marketing effort into producing demand for a particular brand, not a need for the product itself" (Strasser 1989:17). Prior to the widespread availability of mass-produced products, most people bought items—particularly food—in bulk from barrels, which was not amenable to branding or advertising. But, packaging both raw materials and manufactured goods in cans, bottles, and boxes provided the means to symbolically differentiate one type of cereal or detergent or soup from another, giving rise to **brands** that could be advertised and become easily recognizable (Deutsch 2010; Leach 1993; Strasser 1989). Through national advertising campaigns in newspapers and popular magazines, brands were created not only to confer distinctive qualities and even personalities between comparable mass-produced goods but also to build an implicit trust with consumers that brands would be the same over time and in different stores.

Given the nationwide focus of advertising and distributing mass-produced goods and the progressive reliance by most Americans on them in their daily lives, it is perhaps not surprising that mass consumption engendered a common public culture for "middle and working class, native and immigrant, urban and rural" Americans (McGovern 2006:6). Unlike today, when mass consumerism is often blamed for excessive individualism and narcissism, at the turn of the twentieth century, it was more optimistically viewed by some as providing social cohesion, especially with regard to enlightening the working class and assimilating immi-grants. At the time, economist Simon Patten (1907) argued that workers could be "civilized" if they received higher wages with which they could enjoy a higher standard of living through purchasing mass consumer goods and entertainment. Mass consumption was also a way workers achieved unity and overcame ethnic and racial differences (Cohen 1990). By transforming the notion of "class" into "mass" (Ewen 1976:43), manu-facturers and advertisers effectively masked economic inequality and helped alleviate the potential threat of class conflict in the United States. Indeed, mass consumption became an important component of the ide-ology of the American Dream, conceived of as an inalienable right that was at least hypothetically attainable by anyone regardless of class, race, ethnicity, gender, religion, and age.

By the time mass consumerism came into its prime following World War II, most Americans were familiar and comfortable with the practices that were established during its infancy at the turn of the twentieth century. The shear increase over time in the amount of standardized mass-produced goods, most of them nationwide brands, resulted in even more choices. Advertisers and the mass media expanded their attempts to entice consum-ers with fantasies and desires using new technologies, like the television, in addition to persuading them to "keep up with the Joneses." Retailers and consumers became accustomed to selling and buying with credit, a habit that found its way into the housing market with home mortgage loans from banks that were secured by the federal government. In fact, the post-war suburban housing boom was subsidized substantially by the federal government through the GI Bill to build homes for returning soldiers and their families (Cohen 2003). Many of these homes were prefabricated—the ultimate mass-produced good to enter the market. Of course, these homes needed to be equipped with the latest mass-produced appliances and fur-nishings, their garages housing new garden tools and automobiles, which fueled even more consumption. Today, this logic of consumer acquisition has broadened and become more individualized. Now mass consumer goods are used to equip not so much the household as a unit but the indi-viduals who compose the household, with each person requiring his or her own room, phone, computer, and automobile, when they once were shared with other household members (Lipovetsky 2011:27).

Inevitably, the intensification of mass consumerism over time has raised concerns about problems that have been lurking behind its so-called suc-cess. Some critics have questioned how democratic and inclusive living in a mass consumer society really has been, especially given the racial residential segregation that resulted from federal housing policies and suburbanization and the stubborn persistence of poverty (Cohen 2003). Others point out that mass consumerism has caused serious environmental degradation and psychological insecurities over bodily appearances (Kilbourne 2010). Additional scholars warn that mass consumerism has led to an epidemic of overconsumption triggered by easy access to credit cards and unfulfilling jobs that trap indebted individuals (Schor 1998). The more people work to pay off consumer debt, the less time they have to spend with their family and friends or participating in community activities; furthermore, any free time individuals might have is often spent playing with their consumer toys in the privacy of their homes (Putnam 2000).

Positioning the Concept of Consumption: Tensions and Contradictions

Clearly, the costs and benefits of mass consumerism are subject to debate, but one aspect of consumption in general that the many scholars and commentators agree on is that as a concept, it has been plagued continually by a variety of tensions and contradictions. According to Aldridge (2003:7), the concept of consumption is often depicted in opposition to another concept, like production or citizenship, and "there is usually a latent implication that consumption is inferior to its opposite." These oppositions have given rise to a number of tensions that have supplied rich terrain for theoretical deliberations over the years, proving difficult to resolve. This section will examine three such tensions: production and consumption, freedom and coercion, and consumers and citizens. In the interest of providing a succinct overview of these tensions, the theorists and concepts introduced in this section will be more fully elaborated upon in succeeding chapters.

Production and Consumption

Perhaps the oldest tension surrounding consumption is its relationship with production. Production has been privileged over consumption as a process that is meaningful because it generates employment and wealth, contributing to the economic development of society. Favoring production, an activity that employs labor to give birth to objects over consumption, which is the end or death of production, should be expected given that historically, consumption was associated with waste and destruction. Indeed, not so long ago, the physical ailment of consumption was commonly referred to as the "wasting" disease (Graeber 2011:491). In 1776, Adam Smith notably claimed in the *Wealth of Nations* that "consumption is the sole end and purpose of all production" (1776/1976:625). While his assumption that demand determines supply became a maxim of liberal economic thought, consumption was left as a taken-for-granted end that warranted little explanation because consumers were understood to be rational actors operating to maximize their **utility.** As long as a consumer was sovereign over his or her desires and had the capacity to calculate and pursue them rationally, liberal economists did not really care what these desires were (Slater 1997:54). This narrow focus on utility left little room for investigating other possible motivations that might influence consumer behavior, like emotions, culture, and social relationships (Trentmann 2011:105). Furthermore, positioning consumption as the end of production leaves little incentive to explore what consumers actually do with goods after they have purchased them. According to Firat and Venkatesh (1995:259), "The idea that the consumer is at the end of a process . . . needs to be debunked" because he or she is "a participant in an ongoing, never-ending process of construction."

The celebration of production and workers as opposed to the negative consequences of consumption and consumers is a central theme in the work of two important theorists, Thorstein Veblen's *The Theory of the Leisure Class* and Max Weber's *The Protestant Ethic and the Spirit of Capitalism.* Veblen disparaged what he called **conspicuous consumption,** or the lavish display of wealth through consumer items, as an "unproductive consumption of goods" that was "wasteful" because it did "not serve human life or human well-being on the whole" (1899/1994:69, 97). He also frowned upon **conspicuous leisure,** or the "non-productive consumption of time" (1994:43), and argued that consumption helped destroy the **"instinct of workmanship"** he so admired. Veblen described this instinct as involving "practical expedients, ways and means, devices and contrivances of efficiency and economy, proficiency, creative work and technological mastery of facts . . . a proclivity for taking pains" (Ritzer, Murphy, and Wiedenhoft 2001:203). Weber traces the tension between consumption as frivolous and impulsive and production as sensible and practical back to the asceticism that informed the Protestant ethic and the culture of capitalism. **Asceticism** privileged the values of production over those of consumption, such as "work above leisure, thrift above spending, and deferred over immediate gratification" (Campbell 1999:19). Hedonistically spending money on nonnecessities was viewed as greedy, wasteful, and antithetical to the spirit of capitalism, which stressed making money and investing it wisely to accumulate more money. Efficiency, calculability, frugality, and punctuality were upheld as virtues in addition to individual responsibility and pride in one's work. These characteristics represent what Weber calls an "ethos" that guides one's "conduct of life" in capitalist society (1992). In light of this ethos, the consumption of gratuitous goods would have been "regarded as an arena of superficial activity prompted by ethically dubious motives and directed toward trivial, ephemeral, and essentially worthless goals" (Campbell 1999:20). Before the 2008 recession, one might have wondered if any traces of this former asceticism remained in the United States, but postrecession attitudes toward avoiding debt and saving money have made hedonistically spending money at least temporarily unfashionable.

Another issue surrounding the tension between production and consumption has been the actual separation of the two activities into distinct spheres: the **public sphere** and **private sphere.** As production moved outside of the home and into factories with the advent of industrialization, the construction of a public sphere for men and a private sphere for women emerged (Ewen 1976). The masculine public sphere was situated outside of the home where supposedly more meaningful, wage work occurred, while the nonwage "chores" of cooking, cleaning, childrearing, and consumption were located in the feminine private sphere of the home. As more goods had to be obtained outside of the home at retail stores, women and consumption made advancements in the public sphere, but both remained devalued compared to men and production. During the early twentieth century, women's work as consumers began to be taken more seriously as academics and home economists proclaimed that housework and "the backward art of spending money" could be just as efficient as other types of work and production if women were educated and not so isolated in the private sphere (Frederick 1919; Mitchell 1912).

Over the years, the distinction between the public and private spheres has become ambiguous, especially today with more women working for wages in the public sphere than men (Rosin 2012) and communication technologies making it possible to engage in wage work within the private sphere of the home. However, the separation between production and consumption remains and, some would argue, has grown stronger because of globalization. For example, many of the goods consumed in

Western affluent countries are made in poorer, less developed countries (Harvey 1990; Shannon 1996). This geographic separation makes factory production and workers distant abstractions that many Western consumers are happy to ignore, particularly given the sweatshop working conditions and use of child labor common in many developing countries. At the same time, some are questioning whether the separation of production and consumption has ever been as rigid as we have been led to believe. According to Ritzer and Jurgenson (2010:17), the distinction between production and consumption is a "false binary" because these activities were "never fully distinct." They use the term **prosumption** to describe how consumers engage in work as they consume, such as pumping their own gasoline or clearing the tray off of their table at a restaurant. Likewise, Firat and Venkatesh (1995:245, 260) argue that consumers are producers; they produce identities, personalities, and lifestyles with consumers goods.

Freedom and Coercion

Another key tension surrounding the concept of consumption is whether consumers have the freedom of choice or if their preferences are manipulated by advertisers and the mass media. One characteristic of mass consumer culture is that it equates "freedom with private choice" (Slater 1997:8), which assumes consumers possess sovereignty over their purchasing power. But, some question whether consumers really possess autonomy and if the choices they make embody freedom. Critical theorist Herbert Marcuse argued that choice does not determine freedom, claiming that "free choice among a wide variety of goods and services does not signify freedom if these goods and services sustain social controls over a life of toil and fear" (1964:7–8). Zygmunt Bauman echoes this sentiment when he states that consumers "are not so much free as they have the obligation to choose" (2007:74). In other words, consumption comes to dominate us, and we are coerced into making choices because we do not have the freedom *not* to choose. This coercion is created and coordinated by the cultural agents of mass consumerism, also known as the **culture industry,** like advertisers and the mass media, who tell us that we need certain goods to be happy, when most of these so-called needs are just artificial wants.

Determining a "need" from a "want" is complicated because they are not easily quantifiable and vary across time and place. This produces a unique tension when it comes to deciding whether consumer decisions are free or coerced. Adam Smith defined **needs,** or what he called "human necessities," as "not only the commodities which are indispensably necessary for the support of life, but whatever the custom of the country renders it for creditable people, even of the lowest order, to be without" (Schudson 1999:343). Likewise, Karl Marx separated **necessities,** goods that were used habitually by the working class, from **luxuries,** or goods used exclusively by the bourgeoisie (Schudson 1999:344). Thus, the difference between a "need" and a "want" is relative to societal customs, habits, and even socioeconomic class. While these factors remain important, needs are almost entirely subsumed by wants in a mass consumer society, where the majority of consumers have the financial means to purchase goods other than those necessary for survival. According to Daniel Bell (1976:22), "Wants are psychological, not biological, and are by their nature unlimited." A mass consumer society is by definition one dominated by the logic of want or what Marcuse (1964) called **false needs**—and they do appear to be unlimited, which can make consumer choices appear overwhelming.

Taking into account the vast array of mass consumer goods on the market today, it is no wonder that many consumers feel subjugated by what Waldman (1999) calls the "tyranny of choice." Instead of feeling empowered by so many options, we feel anxious. Did we make the "right" choice when we decided to buy the black pair of shoes instead of the red ones? Too many options also might encourage consumers to take too much time to finally make a decision—if they end up making one at all. According to Ritzer (2010), our consumer daydreams can quickly turn into consumer nightmares when we are confronted by too many options or even too many people in crowded retail spaces, forcing some consumers to retreat without purchasing anything. The nightmare for other consumers comes when they receive their monthly credit card statement and realize they are in debt. Instead of retreating and buying nothing or choosing to buy the black pair of shoes instead of the red ones, they decided to buy the black pair of shoes, the red pair of shoes, a brown pair of shoes, and a purple pair of shoes because they did not feel comfortable with selecting just one color (Schor 1998; Vyse 2008).

The dilemmas surrounding the proliferation of choice are not confined to the individual but also society. Waldman (1999:364) argues that too many choices can weaken social bonds, resulting in social fragmentation because people share "fewer and fewer common experiences." For example, when there were only three commercial television networks, ABC, NBC, and CBS, Americans were more likely to be watching the same shows at the same scheduled time, creating a common media culture. However, today, the wide variety of television programs available from multiple media sources at any time, such as cable, Netflix, and Hulu, makes it increasingly doubtful that tens of millions of Americans are watching the same show simultaneously. In 1983, 106 million Americans watched the *M*A*S*H* finale, and in 1998, 76.3 million watched the *Seinfeld* finale, while in 2013, only 10.3 million watched the *Breaking Bad* finale (Lowry 1998; Pomerantz 2013). While this increased freedom to choose what, when, and even where we watch television programs may result in social fragmentation, one could argue that it produces less coercion as consumers are no longer exclusively controlled by the prior dominance of the big three networks.

Consumers and Citizens

Mass consumerism is not just a "moral doctrine" that likens consumption with the good life but also a "political ideology" that has been employed to justify the superiority of capitalism over communism (Gabriel and Lang 2006:9). Alleged democratic access to plentiful mass-produced goods was equated with progress, peace, equality, and a civilized society. Werner Sombart commented in 1906 that one reason why socialism would not gain much popularity in the United States was because plenty of "roast beef and apple pie" subdued socioeconomic class hostilities (Cross 2000:17). Richard Nixon echoed Sombart's sentiments when he visited the Soviet Union in 1959, boasting to Nikita Khrushchev that the average American wage worker could attain home ownership, which he felt "would diffuse the most dangerous potential of class conflict" (May 1999:298). According to McGovern, "Long before the Cold War's contrasts of capitalism and communism made 'underdeveloped' synonymous with 'underconsuming,' China and Russia frequently served as Madison Avenue's examples of nations whose ignorance of advertising and material desire kept them in semibarbarity" (McGovern 2006:27–28). Even today, government-controlled goods and services are often decried in the United States as being "socialist" and poor in quality or inefficient. Citizens are warned that their democratic consumer freedom could be encroached upon if the government extends its reach into the economy, forcing them to wait in lines for rationed goods at government-owned stores with nonexistent customer service.

The political ideology of mass consumerism has provoked a debate over whether the freedom of choice by consumers in a capitalist economy should be understood as the equivalent of the freedom of choice by citizens in a democratic state. On one hand, an individual consumer does not have a constitutionally protected "right" to vote with one's purchasing power like a citizen does with her or his political power at the ballot box. Furthermore, monetary constraints, including household income and access to credit, are not distributed equally, making the democratic nature of consumer "votes" problematic. On the other hand, consumption has provided "opportunities for participation that transcended suffrage rights or political ideologies" (Cross 2000:2). Before women had the right to vote at the ballot box, they could—and did—use their purchasing power to make their voices heard and influence public policy (Wiedenhoft 2006). Likewise, disenfranchised African Americans used consumption as a site of protest against Jim Crow laws and other forms of institutional racism (Glickman 2009). Thus, if a state is not responding to the demands of its citizens, then they can turn to the realm of consumption to try to and incite social change.

Another concern regarding the tension between the role and power of consumers and citizens is if mass consumerism threatens the stability of political democracy, causing individuals to value the possession and protection of private ownership over public goods and civic engagement. John Kenneth Galbraith perhaps expressed this best in *The Affluent Society*, arguing that lavish spending on private goods was restricting the resources available for public goods and services. He gives the example of Americans privileging the importance of their cars at the expense of the condition of the roads they drive on, demonstrating how our personal interests as consumers often outweigh our public interests as citizens (1958:110). According to Galbraith, Americans need to achieve a social balance between private and public expenditures, or "privately produced goods and services and those of the state" (1958:201).

This social balance has yet to be realized, and the scale of power has shifted away from state spending and toward privatization since the emergence of **neoliberalism** in 1980s. The rise of unregulated markets and the dominance of corporate power, coupled with individual self-reliance and fiscal responsibility, have slowly dismantled the welfare state, prompting some to argue that states need to adjust how they interact with their citizens. Instead "of treating them as passive clients, public services should treat citizens as active, informed customers" (Trentmann 2011:99).

Furthermore, neoliberalism appears to have increased consumer power through **commodity activism,** making it "utterly unsurprising to participate in social activism by buying something" (Banet-Weiser and Mukherjee 2012:1). Instead of working through the state as citizens to try to achieve justice against corporate malfeasance, many consumers are now taking their demands directly to corporations through withholding their purchasing power. At a time when corporations are increasingly crossing national borders to avoid labor laws, environmental regulations, and taxes, consumer power that has the same geographic capability seems especially critical for corporate accountability (Barnett et al. 2011).

But as Schudson (2007) reminds us, citizens are not always motivated to do what is best for the public good, nor are all consumer actions motivated by self-interest. Even though we tend to elevate the ideal of citizenship over consumer identities, most of us are both citizens and consumers—they are not "invidious distinctions" (Schudson 2007:238). Besides, it would be a mistake to assume that consumption is causing people to turn away from traditional forms of political action. Instead, it is possible that politics is too "time-consuming, alternatively boring and scary . . . and often makes people feel ineffectual, not empowered" (Schudson 2007:238). Trentmann (2011:107) agrees with Schudson, arguing that some people have given up on formal political institutions and traditional modes of engagement because they feel powerless and no longer trust politicians. Consequently, recognizing that consumption can be a form of political action—one that consumers have the opportunity to participate in daily—might represent "a movement away from institutional and formal modes of engagement . . . grounded in the belief that day-to-day action might be a more effective way to achieve political ends by using the market to influence public policy" (Shah et al. 2007:219). The dilemma is how to harness the power of consumers, but not at the expense of our democratic rights as citizens.

Organization of the Book

The tensions described above will be further explored in various chapters throughout this book, which is organized into three broad parts. The first part uses a conceptual framework developed by Ritzer, Goodman, and Wiedenhoft (2001) to examine three dimensions of consumption: the objects of consumption, the subjects of consumption, and the places of consumption.

The part begins with Chapter 2, which discusses the objects of consumption, focusing on their production through the industrial processes of Fordism and post-Fordism; their use, exchange, and sign values; their meanings in connection to gifts and social relationships; and their biographies, particularly how they "die" through planned obsolescence and become waste. This chapter concludes with the controversy over the social implications of more goods and services being commodified. Chapter 3 highlights the theoretical debates surrounding the subjects of consumption, or consumers. This chapter discusses various explanations for what influences consumer behavior. Do we consume to emulate others or to try to differentiate ourselves from them? Are we manipulated into buying goods we do not need by the mass media? Perhaps we purchase certain goods because they are useful or allow us to fulfill our desires instantaneously. Chapter 4 provides a more historical narrative of the places of consumption, or where we consume, beginning in the city and the creation of department stores and moving into the suburbs with the construction of shopping malls and big-box stores. A detailed examination of the bricks-and-mortar dominance of Wal-Mart and the e-commerce ascendancy of Amazon.com will be offered as both have changed the contemporary landscape of consumption considerably. Chapter 4 concludes with an analysis of the increasing privatization of public space.

The next part of the book will apply the conceptual framework from the first part of the book to three case studies: food, tourism, and education. While each of these cases has been popularized by the mass media—most newspapers and magazines have food and travel sections—they also have come to occupy their own disciplinary niches within academia. One can now earn a degree in food or tourism and hospitality studies at universities across the world. Therefore, the aim in this part of the book is not to review the entirety of these fields but to attempt to make some provocative interdisciplinary connections that introduce readers to a range of themes and issues. It should be noted that these case studies were selected because of my own interest in them. Students should be encouraged to use the conceptual framework from the first part to examine additional cases studies, such as fashion, music, religion, or social media.

Part II begins with Chapter 5, which examines food as an object of consumption through the production practices of three food chains, the industrial, the organic, and the local. Next, how and why consumers use food to signify class and status relationships and ethnic and national identifications is discussed, followed by a look at the different dynamics involved when consumers eat at home compared to dining out.

Chapter 5 concludes with a history of where most Americans purchase food, the supermarket. Tourism is the focus of Chapter 6, and it begins by addressing economic development and the tourism industry, followed by the objectification of culture and people through souvenirs and sex tourism. Tourists as subjects of consumption are studied in regards to whether they are passive gazers or embodied agents and if they are traveling to discover authenticity or just have fun. The chapter then compares and contrasts two seemingly opposite tourist destinations, Disney World and the U.S. national parks, questioning if the experiences that they offer are really that different. Chapter 7 applies the conceptual framework of the objects, subjects, and places of consumption to higher education. Higher education in the United States has become commodified, and overwhelmingly, only the wealthiest students are able to afford the costly tuition without the support of student loans. As an object of consumption, higher education is no longer about learning so much as earning a credential that signifies its recipient possesses the human capital to perform a specific job or the cultural capital to fit into the organizational structure of the modern workplace. As students and their parents are increasingly viewed as consumers, places of higher education are starting to resemble corporations competing for students with glossy marketing campaigns and lavish amenities like state-of-the-art recreational facilities. The places of higher education constitute a field of stratified positions as different types of institutions from private elite colleges, public nonprofit universities, community colleges, and for-profit universities compete for prestige, which in turn affects what kinds of students they can most likely recruit.

The third part of this book deals with ethical issues associated with mass consumerism and various forms of consumer activism that have been organized to challenge problems associate with it, such as environmental degradation, greed and materialism, and alienation. Chapter 8 explores political consumerism and some of the tactics that have been used to guide consumer purchasing power, like boycotts and buycotts. The fair trade movement and green consumerism are examples of contemporary political consumerism that are addressed in addition to some limits of using market-based strategies for achieving social change. The consumer movement is also described, including its similarities to and differences from political consumerism. Chapter 9 explains the role of consumer debt in the maintenance of a mass consumer society, situating its rise within the liberalization of financial markets in the 1980s and the increasing power of the banking industry. The relationship between debtors and creditors is discussed—who is most to blame for indebtedness? Is charging interest to debtors fair? Why do debtors choose to pay certain forms of debt back to their creditors and not others? Debt forgiveness and relief are explored as possible solutions to both sovereign debt and personal debt. Chapter 10 describes a variety of alternative forms of consumption that aim to challenge problems associated with mass consumerism. Some, such as the voluntary simplicity movement and do-it-yourself movement, ask individuals to be frugal and sacrifice many of the conveniences of mass consumerism to achieve environmental sustainability or overcome alienation. Others, like collaborative consumption initiatives, encourage consumers to share items instead of owning them or use local currency to support local businesses and strengthen community ties. Some alternative forms of consumption require that consumers freely give their labor to help create new products for the market or make social media platforms, like Facebook, actually function. These so-called prosumption activities may be viewed as liberating or exploitative, depending on the context and level of consumer autonomy. Many alternative consumers embrace a degrowth or dematerialism ideology, which suggests that a continued emphasis on economic growth and material possessions at the expense of social and environmental justice will lead to more poverty and the destruction of nature.

The final chapter of the book explores the expansion of mass consumer culture on a global scale, including whether it is being imposed on other countries as a form of cultural imperialism or if they are adapting or localizing it to accommodate their own norms and values. The development of mass consumer culture in China and India is analyzed in some detail, with emphasis on how global influences are currently shaping what particular aspects of mass consumer culture each is actively adopting or rejecting. The conclusion of this final chapter contemplates why many Americans are so quick to critique mass consumer culture and hope to prevent it from spreading to developing countries, while at the same time people residing in these countries—and indeed low-income people within the United States—need more consumer options to improve their standard of living.

As noted above, this book is an introductory text written for an undergraduate audience. Important concepts that are defined within the text have been marked in bold, so that they can be easily identified. Readers will find definitions of concepts, descriptions of theories, and discussions of research rather succinct but hopefully accessible. Each chapter contains a box that connects a case study to themes covered within that chapter. Questions about each case study are also contained with these boxes to encourage critical discussions. In an attempt to achieve balance, I have tried to remain neutral on controversies surrounding consumer culture and invite readers to reach their own conclusions. I further invite readers to use this book as a guide to explore topics, actors, and places that have been omitted.

PART I

Conceptual Framework

2

Objects of Consumption

Commodities and Mass Consumer Society

Contemporary consumer society "is characterized by commodities—it is awash with them, it would be impossible to escape them, even if one wanted to" (Fiske 1989:11). **Commodities** are "part of the physical world that has been defined, classified, and appropriated by humans" (van Binsbergen 2005:45). They are "objects of economic value" and are generally thought of as constituting the material culture of mass consumer societies (Appadurai 1986:3, 5). As such, commodities have the ability to "reflect the whole social organization of capitalism at any historical and geographic point in its development" (Lee 1993:119). Examining how and why particular objects and services become commodities and how commodities change over time can help us understand the transformation of social institutions, like the economy and the family, and social relationships. For example, children in the United States today are more likely to play with commoditized toys than they were in the past. This change could signal a change in the family, such as increasing dual-income and single-parent households. Perhaps it is more convenient and less time-consuming for parents to purchase toys for their children than to make them by hand. If these toys are labeled

"Made in China," this might indicate that the economy has changed over time as well, becoming more global in scope.

So, where do all these commodities come from? Why are they considered valuable? What do they mean? Where do they go when we dispose of them? Why are more goods and services becoming commodities? This chapter begins by discussing the production of commodities in mass consumer society and explaining the three values of commodities: use value, exchange value, and sign value. It continues by exploring the meaning of commodities and how they can be used to develop the self and maintain social relationships, particularly in the case of gifts. The biography of commodities is then explained, followed by a discussion of planned obsolescence and waste. The chapter concludes by looking at the various goods and services that have become commodities over time and identifies some challenges that this has created.

The Production of Commodities[1]

Fordism: Mass Production and Consumption

The Fordist mode of mass production emerged in the United States during the turn of the twentieth century when Henry Ford established **scientific management techniques** in his automobile factories. Based on the work of Frederick Taylor, these production techniques were based on the principle of the assembly line: worker efficiency could be increased if each component of the production process was broken down into unskilled, repetitive tasks. Equipped with the knowledge of motion sequence and timing, managers had the ability to measure and predict productivity levels with precision and implement a rigid quota system to discipline and control workers. Not only was the workforce standardized under Fordism, but so were the commodities produced, resulting in a large quantity of relatively inexpensive homogeneous goods that needed to be consumed (Ewen 1976; Lee 1993).

Recognizing that workers needed to be able to purchase all of the goods being produced by the Fordist production process, Henry Ford instituted a fixed wage of $5 per day for his workers. As other manufacturers began to imitate Ford, an industrial workforce began to emerge that earned enough in wages to support a stable, mass consumer market.

---

[1] Parts of this section were previously published in *Encyclopedia of Social Theory,* Volume II. Edited by George Ritzer. Thousand Oaks, CA: Sage, 2005, pp. 282–83.

"Fordism engendered a complete structural transformation of *the whole way of life*" (Lee 1993:73), requiring, in the words of department store merchant Edward Filene, the masses "to behave like human beings in a mass production world" (Ewen 1976:54). It was not just products but consumers themselves that needed to be produced. Individuals needed to be socialized, mainly by advertisers, that consumption could ameliorate "boredom and social entrapment" and was a legitimate way to spend their leisure time (Ewen 1976:86). Furthermore, new places to purchase consumer goods needed to be constructed. While Fordism was dehumanizing on the factory floor, it could be romanticized on the department store floor with the working class being able to actively participate in the mass consumer economy.

Post-Fordism: Craft Production and Niche Consumption

The Fordist mode of production operated relatively well in an era dominated by large-scale, capital-intensive industry. However, by the 1980s, Fordism began to be challenged by a number of critics who suggested that it was too rigid for the economic growth of advanced industrial societies. Michale Piore and Charles Sabel argue in *The Second Industrial Divide* (1984) that two seemingly contradictory developments were beginning to make Fordism obsolete: the reemergence of craft production and the introduction of new technologies in the manufacturing sector. Both developments were viewed as a result of the changing tastes and demands of consumers and the rise of segmented marketing techniques. Most important, both of these developments are characterized by **flexible specialization** methods, including "small-batch production runs and high levels of product differentiation" (Lee 1993:109). This new type of economic organization, referred to as post-Fordism (Amin 1994; Lash and Urry 1994), requires skilled workers to engage in craft production or perform technological jobs. Piore and Sable suggest that they have more autonomy than those working under Fordism. Post-Fordist consumers not only have a wider variety of commodities to consume but are able to select more distinctive commodities that express their specific interests and lifestyles. Post-Fordist consumers are increasingly able to personalize or customize the commodities they purchase, such as the NIKEiD tennis shoe, which allows consumers to select their preference of sole cushioning, shoe width, the colors of the upper and lower shoe, the mesh, the laces, and even the swoosh, in addition to their own logo or "iD" that is printed on the tongue top.

Not all critiques of Fordism are as optimistic of the potential of post-Fordism as described by Piore and Sabel. David Harvey claims in *The Condition of Postmodernity* (1990) that workers in a post-Fordist world may have more flexibility in terms of part-time and temporary employment but that this flexibility is jeopardized by less job security and few benefits. Harvey refers to the economic processes that are undermining Fordism as **flexible accumulation,** which is characterized by high levels of structural unemployment, fluctuating job skills, a large service sector, stagnant wage levels, and the decline of trade unions. **Time-space compression** is also typical of the post-Fordist world where information technologies allow us to communicate over a large area of space in a short amount of time. In addition, the production process itself has become increasingly global, comprising a multitude of transnational **commodity chains** through which goods are designed, manufactured, assembled, distributed, and consumed across the world (Gereffi, Korzeniewicz, and Korzeniewicz 1994). Today, a Ford automobile may be designed in one country, assembled in another country from parts manufactured in dozens of other counties, and distributed and sold to consumers in yet another country. Indeed, consumer culture itself has been globalized, as discussed in the concluding chapter of this book.

Cultural intermediaries, creative workers who help produce culture and act as "taste makers," are especially important actors in a post-Fordist society (Maguire 2014:20). Bourdieu describes cultural intermediaries in terms of occupations in "a new economy . . . whose functioning depends as much on the production of needs and consumers as on the production of goods" (1984:310, quoted in Maguire 2014:18). They create designs, brands, and advertisements to guide consumers through the post-Fordist landscape, signaling what is "cool" or legitimate based on their expertise (Maguire 2014). Sassatelli (2007:49) describes how cultural intermediaries act to aestheticize ordinary objects—many of which are in fact mass produced, like kitchen chairs at Ikea and salad bowls at Pottery Barn. However, many consumers overlook the mass standardization of these objects because they seem cleverly personalized to represent their niche lifestyles. The Internet and social media have facilitated the reach of cultural intermediaries, who can share their favorite music on Spotify, recipes on Pinterest, fashion on YouTube, and videos on Facebook with millions of followers around the world. At the same time, this reach may undermine the legitimacy of cultural intermediaries, if in fact new technologies allow everyone to try to become taste makers.

Even though elements of post-Fordism have emerged in recent years, "there has been no historical break with Fordism" (Ritzer 2013:49). Ritzer reminds us that many of the places where we consume, including fast-food restaurants, shopping malls, and big-box retail stores, are organized according to the Fordist principles of efficiency, calculability, and predictability. But, post-Fordist places of consumption also exist, including farmers' markets, family-owned diners, and local gift stores, providing consumers a way to avoid Fordist establishments. Most consumers have few problems navigating between Fordism and post-Fordism, shopping at a local farmers' market for fresh produce and at the chain grocery store for cans of processed soup. Mass-produced commodities coexist side-by-side with craft-produced commodities, such as the cans of Budweiser next to the bottles of Bells Two-Hearted Ale at my local beverage store. Recently, Target experimented with "The Shops at Target," which feature the products of five specialty shops from across the country for six weeks at select locations. The Shops offer Target customers easy access to novel, boutique products, while at the same time they can continue to purchase mass paper towels and laundry detergent (Wilson 2012).

The Value of Commodities

Use Value and Exchange Value

Adam Smith, in *The Wealth of Nations* (1776/1976), identified two characteristics of a commodity: use value and exchange value. At their most fundamental level, commodities have a **use value** or the ability to satisfy a human desire. Wheat, for example, satisfies a particular desire that glass cannot. However, when wheat and glass are traded in a market, they become commodities with values that can be exchanged, and in the process, each commodity comes to possess not only a use value but also an exchange value. While use value refers to the physical or material dimension of a commodity, **exchange value** refers to its social dimension because the actual value of the commodity is "never an inherent property of objects, but is a judgment made about them by subjects" (Appadurai 1986:3). According to Smith, these judgments are expressed in the price of a commodity, which provides a quantitative measure through which commodities can be monetarily exchanged for one another. While one might think of monetary exchange as impersonal, it is embedded—for better or worse—in social relationships (Simmel 1907/1990; Zelizer 1997). For example, if one is part of group that is purchasing rounds of drinks at a pub, then one is expected to not only pay for a round but also stay and participate in the group, such as exchanging conversation over the rounds of the drinks (Staudenmeier 2012). While some might cringe at the social obligation of reciprocity involved in buying rounds, other people who frequent pubs find this activity enjoyable.

Karl Marx (1867/1967) captured the more sinister side to the social dimension of exchange value, uncovering how in a capitalist society, labor becomes a commodity. Workers must sell their labor to producers in exchange for a wage to survive and purchase basic necessities. In this process, workers become alienated because they no longer own their labor power or the products they make and suffer from exploitation because they are not paid for the surplus labor that they produce. Indeed, Marx claimed that the exchange value of commodities should be thought of as "definite quantities of congealed labour time" (1859/1970). In other words, when we purchase an automobile, we are actually purchasing all of the labor time sold by the workers who made it. However, Marx was aware that neither workers nor consumers thought of commodities in this manner. Instead, we "fetishize" commodities as they magically appear in the marketplace for our consumption divorced from the workers who produce them. Marx referred to this as **commodity fetishism** and argued that in capitalist societies, commodities reify human relationships into relations between objects: "men are degraded to the status of objects, and objects receive human attributes" (Avineri 1968:118). By giving personalities to our commodities and dehumanizing each other and ourselves, we end up alienated and allow commodities to control us. According to Marx, "The *devaluation* of the world of men is in direct proportion to the *increasing value* of the world of things" (1932/1992:323). Put simply, Marx believed that the more we value commodities, the less we value human beings.

Sign Value

Price is not the only judgment that matters in determining the value of a commodity. Indeed, the price of an object need not correlate with its utility, so exchange value does not necessarily indicate how useful an object may be. In the words of Adam Smith, "Nothing is more useful than water; but it will purchase scarce anything; scarce anything can be exchanged for it. A diamond, on the contrary, has scarce value in use: but a very great quantity

of other goods may frequently be had in exchange for it" (1776/1976:33)
So, if not simply price, what makes a diamond more valuable than water?
Some theorists argue that objects are valuable because of what they signify
(Baudrillard 1975, 1981, 1998; Debord 1994; Fiske 1989; Gottdiener 1995).
The **sign value** of a commodity refers to its meaning in relation to other
commodities. A commodity often derives meaning from its binary opposition, or what it is not. For example, generic jeans signify nature, work, and
the West, while designer jeans signify culture, leisure, and the East (Fiske
1989). We know what a generic jean is because it is not a designer jean. In
short, a commodity is meaningful because it is different from another commodity and therefore signifies or communicates a different message. As
such, commodities may be understood as comprising a code or "information system" (Douglas and Isherwood 1996). According to Jean Baudrillard,
"Certain objects are the carriers of indexed social significations, of a social
and cultural hierarchy . . . they constitute a code" (1981:37). For example,
Smith's diamond is valuable not just because it is expensive but because
it signifies social status in relation to water, which does not. Compared to
water, a diamond is considered a **positional good** because it is scarce, making it highly desirable to those who wish to display their socioeconomic
standing in society (Hirsch 1978/2015). Of course, unbeknownst to many
consumers, the scarcity of diamonds is artificially created by the diamond
industry, which ensures their exchange value remains competitively high
compared to other gemstones.

Applying **semiotics,** the study of signs, to commodities can capture
the more sophisticated and sometimes amusing aspects of consumption
compared to limiting ourselves to use and exchange values. For example,
we can study what McCracken calls the **Diderot effect,** or how consumers
attempt to maintain harmony and consistency through the commodities
they purchase (1990:118). McCracken tells the story of the French philosopher Denis Diderot (1713–1784), who, upon receiving a new, elegant robe,
felt compelled to replace all the old items in his room with new, elegant
goods to match his new robe. In other words, all of his personal objects of
consumption had to be "unified" in order for him to feel comfortable. While
many of us may not feel the need to unify our outfits with an entire room,
most of us are probably familiar with the desire to match our shoes, with
our pants, with our shirts, with our coats to look and feel "put together"
and display a cohesive identity. In semiotic terms, we want our "signifiers"
to represent their "signifieds" and be unified within a consistent code so
that others clearly understand what message we are trying to communicate.

However, signifiers can come to have a life of their own and become freed from any signified. When this happens, commodities as pure signifiers become **spectacles,** dominated by the logic of appearance over utility or price (Debord 1994). W. F. Haug (1986) refers to this phenomenon as **commodity aesthetics** and describes how commodities are purchased simply because they are attractively packaged. Perfume, for example, is sometimes purchased not to be used or for how good it smells but because of the stylish bottle it is in. Logos and brands are other examples of how we purchase signifiers. It is not the actual athletic shoe that we are purchasing but the Nike swoosh. In contemporary mass consumer society, "successful corporations must primarily produce brands, as opposed to products" (Klein 1999:3). Taken to the extreme, "the sign no longer designates anything at all" and refers "back only to other signs" (Baudrillard 1975:128). This is perhaps most recognizable when we purchase immaterial commodities, like apps for our iPhones, because we are literally consuming images or appearances. Baudrillard's suggestion that signs are losing their referents in the real world may sound absurd, but with the rise of digital technology and media, some view virtual reality as a dominant social force in our "real" lives. However, even though the consumption of images may be increasing and many of us are shopping in cyberspace, material commodities have yet to disappear and sign value has not completely destroyed use and exchange value.

The Meaning of Commodities

Appropriation and Social Relationships

While a commodity may derive meaning from its relationship with other commodities as sign value proposes, semiotics can limit our understanding of commodities by privileging object-to-object relations over subject-to-object relations. One way that individuals develop a relationship with an object is through appropriation. **Appropriation** is "the process by which a person establishes a relationship of identity with an object, makes it a possession" (Carrier 1995:10). Consumers use possessions to contribute to and reflect their identities, or construct **extended selves** (Belk 1988:139). For example, a person might wear a sports jersey with his favorite team's logo to express his extended self. Other people assemble collections of commodities, such as comic books or bobble heads, to define their extended selves (Belk 1988:154). Consumers often use objects, including commodities, to differentiate themselves from others and express their individuality or to integrate themselves with others and exhibit their shared similarities. Psychologically, both differentiation and integration are critical components of developing one's self-identity. Adolescents often appropriate objects to differentiate themselves from their parents and other adults, while older adults identify with possessions that represent integration or belonging (Csikszentmihalyi and Rochberg-Halton 1981:38, 119). "Objects have a determining effect on the self" as they enable or constrain our thoughts and practices, and through interacting with objects, we learn social norms and culturally acceptable ways to use things (Csikszentmihalyi and Rochberg-Halton 1981:50–51, 53). For example, toy dolls, like the Tamagotchi, can teach children nurturing skills. The Tamagotchi toy is a small, electronic "pet" that children need to take virtual care of in order for it to "survive," such as washing it, giving it food, and playing with it. If a child ignores the toy, it electronically "dies" and a new pet needs to be activated or "hatched." Unlike a real pet, the life span of a Tamagotchi is only 26 to 32 days in length, even with virtual nurturing. Bloch and Lemish (1999) suggest that the Tamagotchi socializes children to understand a social norm of capitalist culture, where many of our commodities and our social connections are disposable.

Commodities and mass consumer goods do not necessarily have to result in alienation, as Marx argued, but can "create the context of close social networks and normative mechanisms promoting solidarity and sociability" (Miller 1987:199). Put differently, consumer goods can "make and maintain social relationships" (Douglas and Isherwood 1996:39). Interestingly, feeling close or comforted by consumer goods does not inevitably imply we are materialistic or antisocial. Anthropologist Daniel Miller found in his recent 17-month study of 30 people who lived on an ordinary street in South London that "usually the closer our relationships are with objects, the closer our relationships are with other people" (2008:1). A socially isolated person on the street had an empty house, while a socially connected person had a house full of stuff.

Miller's study resonates with findings from Mihaly Csikszentmihalyi and Eugene Rochberg-Halton's classic study on the meaning of household objects, whose sample consisted of 300 people in 82 families residing in a major metropolitan area. They selected to interview subjects in their homes because they wanted to be able to observe and discuss the objects that were part of their everyday lives, including televisions, carpets, sports equipment, vehicles, furniture, trophies, visual art, and candlesticks among the 41 object categories they identified. The meanings associated with these objects were diverse. For instance, furniture was valued because it was an heirloom, books because they were associated with ethnicity, appliances because of their use value, and stereos because they allowed respondents to release stress. Some objects were valued because they were received as gifts from friends or inherited from a relative or enjoyed in the company of one's spouse and children. In sum, not only were objects found to have an intrinsic use value, but how they were acquired or if they could be shared with others was also meaningful (Csikszentmihalyi and Rochberg-Halton 1981:268–76).

Gifts

The acquisition of objects through gift-giving is a particularly explicit way to understand how social relationships are represented by objects. Gifts are "bound to people," and they "bear the identity of the giver and of the relationships between the giver and receiver" (Carrier 1995:24). Anthropologist Marcel Mauss provided one of the first and arguably most famous accounts of how gift exchange functions in preindustrial societies in his book *The Gift* (1923/1967). According to Mauss, **gift exchange** is based on the concept of reciprocity; thus, gifts are never free because the receiver of a gift is obligated at some point in time to give a gift back to the gift-giver. To reject a gift is to reject a relationship with the gift-giver, which is not really an option in many societies as "to do so would show fear of having to repay" and the "loss of dignity" (Mauss 1923/1967:39–40). Social status plays a significant role in gift exchange because the gift-giver must be careful not to give a gift to someone so poor that to reciprocate would be an extreme burden or so rich and powerful that he or she will refuse the gift and humiliate the gift-giver (Graeber 2011a).

While gifts may be thought of as the opposite of commodities—gifts are sometimes characterized as "durable and personal" and commodities as "transient and impersonal" (Carrier 1995:18)—this is not always the case. Indeed, Appadurai (1986:11–13) reminds us that Georg Simmel thought of both gift and commodity exchanges as involving calculation, even if the sociality associated with each varied, and that Pierre Bourdieu viewed gift exchange as one specific way that commodities circulate in society. Gift-giving in capitalist societies is clearly different from gift-giving in the preindustrial societies described by Mauss not only because many gifts are themselves commodities but also because gift exchange is voluntary and does not necessarily require reciprocity (Belk 1979; Carrier 1995:22). However, gifts continue to bond us with other people in capitalist societies, even if they are commodities, and rituals surrounding gift-giving still often involve reciprocity. Many of us have experienced embarrassment when we forgot to give a gift to a friend on her birthday when she has given us one on ours or have felt uncomfortable when a person we do not consider close to us gives us a gift. Furthermore, the idea that a gift is "priceless" and should represent our social relationships instead of economic ones remains even if the gift is a commodity (Carrier 1995:150). Therefore, even in capitalist societies, it is often "the thought that counts" in regards to gift-giving, not how much a gift costs; a two-carat diamond ring can express just as much love between the gift-giver and receiver as a plastic candy ring. As Daniel Miller (1998) found in his ethnography on shopping, purchasing even mundane items, like school clothes or groceries, for others can be a manifestation of love between wives and husbands, mothers and children.

Monetizing gifts poses an interesting challenge to how durable and personal they are, especially because the recipient knows exactly how much they cost. Are cash and gift cards impersonal and thoughtless gifts? One might argue that cash or a gift card is the perfect gift because it provides the recipients freedom to choose what they want and conveys that the gift-giver knows that this will make the recipients happier than if they were to receive something that the gift-giver selected. A grandchild might prefer that his grandparents give him a gift card instead of an article of clothing that they selected. However, receiving a gift card from a close friend might seem impersonal because the recipient might feel that this person did not want to take the time to find an appropriate gift. Thus, even with gift cards or cash, social relationships matter in regards to gift exchange. In her study of the social meaning of money, Vivian Zelizer found that people "cared deeply about differentiating money as a gift; they did so by decorating, inventing, segregating, and restricting currencies. What mattered was to mark standardized currency in some unmistakable way that would allow the same legal tender used in other impersonal transactions to be bestowed as a sentimental gift" (1997:114). For example, cash might be wrapped up in a gift box or a gift card might be placed in a homemade ornament. Thus, monetized gifts do not necessarily indicate impersonal or weaker social relations between givers and receivers. The fact that more people request gift cards than any other item for holidays and that people spent more than $90 billion on gift cards between 1998 and 2010 suggests that they have become an important gift in contemporary society (Sandel 2012:104–5).

The Biography of Commodities

It is not just how we acquire a good that matters when studying a commodity but also the origin of where exactly it came from and who made it. Investigating and discovering the entire biography of a commodity is a way to **de-fetishize** it and help consumers understand the environmental and social significance of the raw materials and labor power used to make the goods that they purchase. Is the coffee we drink every morning funding a genocidal dictatorship or protecting the habit of endangered birds or helping workers earn a fair wage (Pendergrast 2010)? Did the cow that made the cream I use in my coffee wade in a stream, making it warm and muddy, threatening the life of salmon and trout (Ryan and Durning 1997:11)? The biography of a particular commodity can also help consumers understand societal history and social change. Aaron Bobrow-Strain (2013) situates the introduction of mass-produced white bread in the United States with social issues, including immigration, public health, class inequality, and the rise of multinational corporations. Pietra Rivoli's (2009) study of a T-shirt that she purchased at a Walgreen's in Fort Lauderdale, Florida, illuminates the political and economic dimensions of globalization. The cotton used to make her T-shirt was grown in the United States with the aid of polluting herbicides and the protection of government subsidies but had to travel to China to be made into a T-shirt with the labor of young women in sweatshops. Her T-shirt then had to be imported back into the United States, where until 2009 it was subject to a quota system in an effort to protect textile workers in the United States. She discovers that if she were to donate her T-shirt at the Salvation Army, it would most likely be exported out of the United States and resold by local merchants at an African market. This last chapter of a commodity's biography—where it ends up after the original purchaser disposes it—is an especially hidden aspect of a commodity's life. While many consumers care about how the objects they buy were made, most of us have no idea what happens to them once we donate them to charity or throw them away in our garbage bins.

Obsolescence and Waste

In 1959, *Time* magazine published an article about the growing wastefulness that was becoming to characterize the American lifestyle:

> The force that gives the U.S. economy its pep is being generated more and more in the teeming aisles of the nation's stores. . . . U.S. consumers no longer hold on to suits, coats, and dresses as if they were heirlooms . . . furniture, refrigerators, rugs—all once bought to last for years or life—are now replaced with register-tingling regularity. (Packard 1970:36)

According to Vance Packard (1970), by the late 1950s, the large quantity of mass-produced goods in America constituted economic growth, and societal progress was being measured by how many of these goods we threw away. Advertisers and marketers had been promoting hedonism and a "throwaway ethic" over the asceticism and frugality that typified the Protestant work ethic since the early 1900s (Packard 1970:139; Weber 1992) and encouraging Americans to "spend, don't mend" like the characters in Aldous Huxley's *Brave New World* (1932/2006). By the 1950s, reusing and recycling consumer goods became associated with poverty and backwardness (Strasser 1999:200). America's solution to overproduction was "not producing less, but selling more," and one of the main tactics used to get consumers to keep spending was, and continues to be, planned obsolescence (Slade 2006:9).

Planned obsolescence refers to the "assortment of techniques used to artificially limit the durability of a manufactured good in order to stimulate repetitive consumption" (Slade 2006:5). According to Packard (1970:46–47), there are three different ways to make commodities obsolescent: (1) obsolescence of function, or when new products function better than old ones; (2) obsolescence of quality, or when a product is designed to break or wear out in a short amount of time; and (3) obsolescence of desirability, or when a product's design is no longer fashionable. According to Slade, all three types of obsolescence are a "uniquely American invention" and constitute "the very concept of disposability itself" (2006:3–4). The production and consumption of disposable products coincided with the establishment of Fordism at the beginning of the twentieth century, when "more and more things were made and sold with an understanding that they would soon be worthless or obsolete" (Strasser 1999:187). From the creation of the disposable razor by Gillette in 1901 to General Motors introducing new models of cars annually, the principle of obsolescence was firmly entrenched in

American culture by the 1950s (Packard 1970; Slade 2006). Before the twentieth century, the concept of consumer waste did not exist as almost all "garbage" was reused and often resold to be repurposed, such as using meat bones to make buttons. Some cities even relied on scavenger pigs to clean up the food refuse that households dumped from their windows into the streets (Strasser 1999). Today, most of us rarely question the role of obsolescence in the commodities we purchase, replacing computers and smartphones sometimes more than once a year. The majority of these products are not broken when we replace them but lack the innovative features or sleeker designs of new models. Put simply, function and desirability tend to dominate our repetitive consumption. However, quality obsolescence is not uncommon. For example, I recently purchased a new dishwasher and was advised not to buy the warranty for it because it was less expensive to replace it with a new one than pay to have it repaired when it inevitably breaks down.

If Packard was alarmed by the vast amount of waste caused by obsolescence in 1970 when he wrote *The Waste Makers,* he would be appalled by how much more we throw away today. According to the Environmental Protection Agency (EPA), in 2013, Americans generated 254 million tons of garbage with the average American generating 4.4 pounds per day of municipal solid waste (www.epa.gov/waste/nonhaz/municipal). One increasingly problematic development is our disposal of hazardous waste, particularly **e-waste,** or electronic waste. "Electronic components have extremely short lives. In the United States, cell phones built to last five years are retired after only eighteen months of use . . . [and] in 2005 more than 100 million cell phones were discarded in the U.S." (Slade 2006:261). The EPA estimates that in 2009, 438 million electronic devices were sold in the United States, 5 million short tons were in storage, and 2.37 million short tons were ready for "end-of-life management" (EPA 2011). The end-of-life management of electronic products is especially troublesome because most contain toxic materials, including lead in computer monitors and circuit boards, arsenic and cadmium in cell phones, and mercury in flat-screen televisions and laptop computers. Even though it is illegal to dispose of electronic devices through municipal garbage collection in many states in the United States, they often end up in landfills where they can contaminate soil and water or are incinerated and pollute the air. Often discarded electronic devices are exported to developing countries, where they are either dumped or dismantled for parts, which is extremely hazardous because people are not protected from the toxic chemicals contained in these devices. The Basel Convention (1989) bans the global export of toxic and hazardous waste; however, the United States has refused to ratify it because of contention over how the treaty defines waste. For example, the U.S. government considers mercury a traded metal, not a toxic waste (Clapp 2002:171). Approximately 25% of the 2.37 million short tons of electronic equipment ready for end-of-life management is recycled in the United States (EPA 2011). Interestingly, some of this recycling takes place in federal prisons as part of government-run work programs, exposing prison workers to hazardous chemicals and creating "toxic sweatshops" (Jackson, Shuman, and Dayaneni 2006). However, most e-waste is exported for the purpose of recycling, which is permitted by the Basel Convention.

Concerns about waste, disposability, and obsolescence like those expressed by *Time* magazine in 1959 continue to remain strong and have been most popularly portrayed in the animated Disney-Pixar movie *WALL-E* (2008), which depicts the Earth as uninhabitable for humans because of excess garbage. WALL-E, the trash compactor robot, spends his days on Earth compacting garbage and collecting junk that humans threw away years ago before they had to leave the planet. Fortunately, many innovations in waste management are being implemented that hopefully will prevent humans from completely destroying the Earth. Recycling plastic, paper, aluminum, and cardboard has become mandatory in many communities, and convenient curbside collection makes this easy for residents. Businesses are increasingly participating in **extended producer responsibility** (EPR), which requires them to manage the life cycle of the products they produce, most significantly the end-of-life costs. While voluntary in the United States, several European countries have enacted EPR laws that stipulate producers must take back their products when they have reached the end of their life cycle. EPR provides an incentive for businesses to produce and design products "for easy reuse, repair, and recycle" (Clapp 2002:175) and avoid using hazardous and toxic chemicals, which are harder to manage at the end of life. Some EPR practices are associated with the concepts of **cradle-to-cradle** and **zero waste,** which aim for all products to be reusable and ultimately waste free (Braungart and McDonough 2002). For instance, Nike takes back used athletic shoes (regardless of brand) and shreds the rubber and foam into flooring for gyms (Royte 2005:256).

Smartphones

One contemporary object of consumption that most people claim they cannot live without is a smartphone. Smartphones have become appendages of our bodies that travel with us from our homes to our cars to our classrooms and workplaces. We feel the need to keep them on the tables of restaurants when we eat, and some of us cannot leave them behind even when we need to use the bathroom. We use them as social crutches, sometimes to help us initiate conversations with others and other times to help us ignore those around us. We talk to them as if they were another person, asking them for driving directions or weather reports. Like a child, we buy things for them, including new apps and accessories, such as jeweled case covers. We trust them with our memory, storing our contact lists, phone books, and photographs. Some of us even bestow personalities upon our smartphones by giving them names or describing them with human attributes. Smartphones have become truly part of many people's extended selves—forgetting to leave the house without them can induce anxiety, and losing them can cause real despair.

Most smartphone owners do not reflect on how dependent they are on their smartphones, much less how these objects of consumption were produced or where they go when they are discarded. Furthermore, many are unaware of the hazardous chemicals they contain. Smartphones contain minerals, like gold, tin, tungsten, and tantalum. Often, these minerals are sold to finance conflicts in the countries where they are extracted, like the Democratic Republic of Congo. Child labor is used in some countries to mine for these minerals. Many smartphones are assembled by workers in China, who receive low wages and are forced to work long hours to keep pace with the introduction of new versions. Discarded smartphones usually end up in China, where they are recycled or disassembled by people who are exposed to the toxic chemicals they contain. Some health officials and consumers advocates wonder if smartphone users are at an increased risk of health problems from repeated exposure to radiofrequency energy (Woyke 2014).

Questions

1. What objects of consumption do you consider essential to your extended self? Why? Have you ever lost or purposely disengaged with these objects? If yes, describe this experience.

2. Select an object of consumption and research its biography from its birth, or production, to its demise, or disposal. Do your findings make you think differently about this object of consumption, such as its environmental impacts or the workers who produced it? Why or why not?

3. Have you ever bestowed a personality on an object of consumption, such as giving it a name or using human attributes to describe it? How do advertisers use this technique to try to persuade us to purchase one brand over another?

The Commoditization of Everything?

Commoditization "is the tendency to preferentially develop things most suited to functioning as commodities . . . as the answer to each and every type of human want and need" (Manno 2002:70). While we should not think of commodities as static because some objects may be treated as commodities at one point in time but not another (Kopytoff 1986), historically the trend in capitalist societies has been toward commoditizing more and more aspects of our everyday lives from child care to food preparation. According to political philosopher Michael Sandel (2012:3–4), money can buy practically everything today, including prison cell upgrades, services of surrogate mothers, access to carpool lanes while driving solo, and the right to emit carbon dioxide into the air. Our intimate lives and relationships are even being commoditized. Sociologist Arlie Hochschild argues that now we are outsourcing not just work but our own selves, particularly our emotions. Personal services have commoditized a variety of intimate activities that seemed unimaginable in the past, like hiring a professional potty trainer or paying Rent-a-Friend for someone to hang out with at a pub or gym. Love coaches help clients with relationships, match.com can help you find the perfect date, a romance concierge can arrange a wedding proposal, and "wantologists" can advise you if they really want more stuff (Hochschild 2012:10–11). I recently received a flyer in the mail advertising "Rent-a-Husband" to hire someone to complete chores around the house. By and large, the entire life cycle of an individual is up for sale today: we can pay someone to help us find a spouse, arrange our marriage proposal, plan our wedding, care for our child, counsel us when our marriage hits a rough patch, care for us when we are old, and even pay someone to maintain our gravesite when we are dead.

So, what is the problem with commoditizing everything? For those who can afford it, commoditizing more goods and services should make life easier. But, reducing use value and sign value to exchange value can be corrosive, changing morals and social norms and "crowding out nonmarket values worth caring about" (Sandel 2012:8–9). For example, Sandel wonders if paying underachieving children $2 for each book they read will prevent them from acquiring a passion for reading for its own sake (61). He questions the fairness of being able to pay to "jump the queue" in airport security and worries about how the commoditization of health care and education will lead to increasing inequality. The commoditization of the human body itself raises ethical concerns regarding the dominance of market values in our society. Should a person be able to pay for a human kidney if she can afford it and find a willing seller? If no, why is it acceptable to purchase another person's ova or sperm? Is it okay to purchase sex if both buyer and seller freely negotiate the price? These are just a few questions we should ask ourselves when debating how comfortable we are with the increasing commoditization of our society (Kopytoff 1986:85–86).

The commoditization of public goods and services is another way in which market values may be trumping nonmarket values and contributing to inequality. According to economist John Kenneth Galbraith (1958), we need a social balance between public and private spending if we hope to achieve some semblance of equality in our society. As citizens, we expect the government to provide certain services without direct payment, including services provided by police and fire departments, public schools, post offices, libraries, and garbage collectors. However, as governments face shrinking budgets and citizens continue to vote against higher taxes, many of these services are in jeopardy of becoming commoditized. Some cities have started to charge citizens for garbage collection services, and others make citizens pay when the fire department responds to their house fires. Libraries are forced to shorten their hours of operation, and the post office is considering eliminating Saturday delivery, decreasing the quality of the public services available to citizens. When the public sector suffers, the private sector is happy to intervene and make a profit. If your library is closed on Sundays, then you can go to Barnes & Noble to purchase the book you want. If the number of police officers in your city has been reduced due to budget cuts, then you can purchase a home security system to feel safe, or if you have the financial resources, you can hire private security guards. In sum, commoditization may result in not just inequality but also threaten democracy.

Conclusion

Commodities can lead to a homogeneous, impersonal world where everything, including personal identity and social relationships, is determined by exchange value and evaluated by price. They can disguise the labor power and environmental costs that went into their production, resulting in alienation and unsustainability. But, commodities can also signify love and help build social relationships. As material objects, commodities can "provide immense specificity, but potentially also extreme fragmentation" (Miller 1987:78). The challenge of modern society is to try to minimize what Georg Simmel (1903/1971) called the **tragedy of culture,** which occurs when "the spread of objective [material] culture has outstripped the capacity of the subject to absorb it" (Miller 1987:77). While Simmel was referring not just to commodities but cultural objects in general, the rise and triumph of a mass consumer society increasingly puts us in jeopardy of experiencing the tragedy of culture. There are so many commodities that it is impossible for one person to master them all. Indeed, it is difficult for one person to possess the capacity to absorb or fully know even one genre of one particular kind of commodity, such as jazz music or romance novels or designer handbags. The challenge for those of us living in mass consumer societies is to try to exert some control over all the objects of consumption that we encounter every day and not allow them to overwhelm and control us.

Some consumers are attempting to de-commoditize their lives through the voluntary simplicity movement or exert more control over commodities through the do-it-yourself movement or share commodities to save money and unburden themselves from the responsibilities of owning certain commodities, all described in Chapter 9 of this book. The rapid diffusion of digital technologies is an especially interesting development when considering the future of material commodities and waste. Although electronic devices are required to take advantage of digital technologies, like streaming movies and music and playing video games, the need to own material copies of movie DVDs and music CDs becomes less important. Of course, the life cycle of electronic devices tends to be so short, which may defeat the potential de-commoditization effects of digital technologies. Finally, some recent studies have found that experiences, not objects, tend to make people happier. American consumers seem to be following this advice as they are increasingly using their disposable income to dine out, travel, and attend yoga or other exercise classes instead of purchasing durable household items (Tabuchi 2015). Time will tell if consuming experiences will result in less waste and a more sustainable society.

3

Subjects of Consumption

Passive Dupes or Active Agents?

Who exactly is purchasing all of the commodities produced in mass consumer society—and, more important, why? Social theorists have been debating the various motivations for why we consume since the inception of mass consumer society. Some claim that consumers are **passive dupes,** manipulated by advertisers and marketers into buying whatever they are selling, while others believe that consumers are **active agents,** creatively using commodities to express their tastes and lifestyles. Some theorists argue that commodities are used to control individuals, while others suggest that consumers manipulate commodities to express their class, status, and lifestyle. A few theorists even assert that consumers can use commodities to resist and even rebel against mass consumer society. Others debate whether consumers are rational, sovereign decision makers when they select and purchase consumer goods or if they act irrationally, pursuing pleasure as they attempt to fulfill their daydreams and fantasies. Are consumers victims or rebels, rational utilizers or hedonistic pleasure seekers (Gabriel and Lang 2006)? This chapter will explore the various types of consumers that can be found in mass consumer society.

Emulation, Distinction, or Rebellion?

Veblen: Conspicuous Consumption and Leisure

American social economist Thorstein Veblen, writing at the turn of the twentieth century, established the framework for a critique of mass consumer society. In his book *The Theory of the Leisure Class* (1899), he argued that **conspicuous consumption,** or the lavish display of wealth, was the motivating force of consumer behavior for the leisure or upper class. He quite abhorred this behavior, describing it as wasteful and an "unproductive consumption of goods," because it did "not serve human life or human well-being on the whole" (1899/1994:69, 97). While Veblen was most critical of the leisure class for establishing conspicuous consumption as a way to demonstrate their class and status, he stated that "no class of society, not even the most abjectly poor, foregoes all customary conspicuous consumption" (1899/1994:85). However, the classes below the leisure class were motivated by **emulation.** Veblen suggested that the leisure class created standards of tastes and fashion trends, which the lower classes would then copy. Once this happened, the leisure class would have to invent new trends to differentiate themselves from the classes below them—what Veblen referred to as making invidious distinctions based on their social standing. In the words of Georg Simmel,

> Just as soon as the lower classes begin to copy their style, thereby crossing the line of demarcation the upper classes have drawn and destroying the uniformity of their coherence, the upper classes turn away from this style and adopt a new one, which in its turn differentiates them from the masses; and thus the game goes merrily on. (1904/1957:136)

This process has been referred to as **trickle-down theory** and, according to Veblen, each class emulated or copied the class right above it in the class hierarchy; thus, the upper middle class emulated the leisure class, while the middle class emulated the upper-middle class and so forth (Ritzer, Murphy, and Wiedenhoft 2001).

Veblen also frowned upon what he called **conspicuous leisure,** or the "non-productive consumption of time," and believed that the "instinct" to work rather than to consume was what needed to be more fully developed for the common good of society (1899/1994:43, 33). Conspicuous leisure allowed the upper class to develop refined manners, etiquette, and tastes, which differentiated it from other classes, who had to work to survive and did not have the time to cultivate an appreciation for the opera or fine art or travel to Europe to experience other cultures. Knowing how to dress in the most current fashion or what fork to use during a specific course at dinner were signs that one was a member of the leisure class. Veblen argued that over time, due to the changes in "the means of communication and the mobility of the population," conspicuous consumption would come to trump conspicuous leisure because an individual would become exposed "to the observation of many persons who have no other means of judging his reputability than the display of goods" (1899/1994:86).

Veblen's theory of conspicuous consumption continues to be relevant today—many of us use commodities to display our socioeconomic class position. However, today conspicuous consumption revolves around displaying brand logos and upscale spending. According to sociologist Juliet Schor (1998:47), "A whole group of consumer goods that were once neutral symbolically are now highly recognizable," such as athletic shoes, T-shirts, and even bottled water. These branded or logoed everyday commodities are conspicuously consumed alongside luxury, designer brands. Indeed, the whole idea of a designer logo points to "the importance of visibility" in mass consumer society (Schor 1998:46). Furthermore, people are willing to spend more on items that they can visibly display. For example, in one study, women were found to spend more on expensive lipstick, which they could apply in public, than on facial cleanser, eye shadow, or mascara that are usually used in private (Schor 1998:50).

Another significant change regarding how we conspicuously consume involves who we are trying to emulate. "Today a person is more likely to be making comparisons with, or choose as a 'reference group,' people whose incomes are three, four, or five times his or her own" (Schor 1998:4). Instead of trying to emulate the class directly above us in the class hierarchy or "keeping up with the Joneses" next door, we are now participating in **upscale spending** and trying to copy the consumption patterns of the rich and famous, particularly celebrities. "Keeping up with the Kardashians" by watching their television show or following their Twitter feeds makes their celebrity lifestyle feel accessible to the average fan. The problem with upscale spending is that keeping up with the rich and famous is becoming more and more difficult as income and wealth inequality increases in the United States. To participate in upscale spending, more Americans are falling into credit card debt and working longer hours, leaving them unhappy and unsatisfied (Schor 1998:14, 19).

Bourdieu: Taste, Habitus, and Cultural Capital

Although Veblen argued that conspicuous consumption would become more popular than conspicuous leisure as a means to display one's wealth, leisure has not completely disappeared as a device that distinguishes the elite from the masses. Given that U.S. workers fail to take around 429 million paid vacation days per year, those who do take time off of work continue to distinguish themselves as members of the elite (Fisher 2015). On one hand, consumers can display their wealth by taking lengthy vacations to expensive destinations, demonstrating that they have enough money to either take time off of work or do not have to work at all. On the other hand, "cultivation of the aesthetic faculty" still "requires time and application" (Veblen 1899/1994:74). A certain amount of "leisure" is necessary to learn manners and etiquette, as well as develop an appreciation for classical music, expressionist art, and caviar.

French sociologist Pierre Bourdieu investigated the relationship between class and taste in his work *Distinction: A Social Critique of the Judgment of Taste* (1984) and found that although economic capital is strongly correlated with taste, it does not determine it. Cultural capital also plays a role. **Cultural capital** is *"widely shared, high status cultural signals (attitudes, preferences, formal knowledge, behaviors, goods and credentials used for social and cultural exclusion)"* and is "used by dominant groups to mark cultural distance and proximity, monopolize privilege, and exclude and recruit new occupants of high status positions" (Lamont and Lareau 1988:156, 158). Cultural capital is shaped by what Bourdieu calls **habitus,** our mental dispositions or "schemes of perception" (1984:2), that we acquire through socialization, most generally through the institutions of the family and education. The elite attend the same schools, live in the same neighborhoods, and often marry each other, acting as gatekeepers as to who will be allowed access. While it is possible for a person not born into the elite to gain access to their privileged world, it can be difficult for this person to fit in if he or she does not possess enough cultural capital. For example, in the popular movie *Pretty Woman* (1990), the prostitute character played by Julia Roberts tries to buy new clothes on Rodeo Drive and is laughed out of the store because she is dressed indecently. Even though she has enough money to purchase these new, expensive clothes, she does not look like she belongs in the store. Thus, a person cannot buy his or her way into the elite—economic capital is not enough to confer membership. Throughout the movie, her character is continually coached on the proper manners and etiquette to fit into the world of her high-status "john." However, she often experiences what Bourdieu refers to as hysteresis when she self-consciously reflects how she does not easily fit into the upper class; what takes her concentration and patience to perform comes naturally to the elite (Bourdieu 1984:209).

In practice, we are not always aware that our habitus is shaping our taste, creating predictable consumption patterns, and reproducing class distinctions unless we experience hysteresis or are consciously trying to increase our cultural capital, such as a Midwestern working-class student attending an Ivy League university. We just "like what we like" and "act how we act" without spending a lot of time contemplating why this is the case. But, even though the preference for French wine over soda pop with a meal seems harmless, it could in fact account for why someone receives a job offer or is asked out on a second date. According to Bourdieu, taste is "one of the most vital stakes in the struggles fought in the field of the dominant class and the field of cultural production" (1984:11) and contributes to creating and reproducing structural class inequality. Indeed, taste, habitus, and cultural capital can affect our life chances. A child raised in a family that reads books, engages in conversation using a large vocabulary, and encourages artistic and musical creativity will be better prepared for and more likely to succeed in school than a child raised in a family that does not—and success in school translates not only to higher cultural capital but higher economic capital as well. This creates a privileged position for the next generation, who will be raised with high cultural and economic capital and use these "nonmerit resources" to reproduce class distinctions (McNamee and Miller 2009:79). Chapter 7 discusses the relationship between economic and cultural capital and higher education in the United States in more detail.

While Bourdieu examined taste in French society during the 1960s and 1970s, more recent research on taste in the United States has found that over time, elite or highbrow taste has changed from "snobbish exclusion" to "omnivorous appropriation" (Peterson and Kern 1996:900). Some reasons for this change include greater geographic migration and social class mobility, exposure to mass media, an increase in tolerance, and a devaluation of the arts as "markers of exclusion" (Peterson and Kern 1996:905). **Omnivore taste** is characterized as eclectic and diverse, embracing both high- and lowbrow culture. Today's elite listen to both classical and country music, as well as attend art gallery openings and professional football games. In contrast, today's lower classes have "singular" or "limited" tastes" (Khan 2012). This can be observed in food preferences, which are elaborated upon in Chapter 5. A British study found that a variety of ethnic cuisines were consumed by those with high-status occupations to display "specialized knowledge with a cosmopolitan orientation" (Warde, Martens, and Olsen 1999:123). Knowing how to appreciate different ingredients and spices, pronounce certain ethnic dishes, or eat with chopsticks have become signs of class distinction associated with being cultured and sophisticated. Meanwhile in the United States, lower classes are rebelling against yuppie food trends and government dietary guidelines to eat more fruits and vegetables by consuming Wonder white bread and Spam canned meat (Bobrow-Strain 2013:163).

The Birmingham School: Bricolage and Resistance

One could argue that a certain amount of "leisure" is not just necessary to acquire high cultural capital but any kind of cultural capital, including what is considered lowbrow, countercultural, or subcultural. It is possible for individuals to create their own style or fashion, not just emulate the class above them, engage in upscale spending, or conform to the taste of the dominant classes. Scholars at the Centre for Contemporary Cultural Studies (1964) at Birmingham University in England—often referred to as the Birmingham school—focused on how working-class, youth subcultures, such as the mods, teddy boys, skinheads, and punks, created distinctive styles as a means of resistance to the dominant culture's norms and values (Hall and Jefferson 1975; Hebdige 1979; McRobbie 1991; Willis 1978). According to Dick Hebdige, style is a form of **bricolage** or "structured improvisation" and is "basically the way in which commodities are *used* in subculture which mark the subculture off from more orthodox cultural formations" (1979:103–4; de Certeau 1984). For example, punks used safety pins as jewelry and skinheads appropriated Dr. Marten boots as part of their "uniform." By subverting the intended use of mass-produced commodities, youth subcultures also transformed their meanings, engaging in "semiotic guerilla warfare" with the dominant culture (Hebdige 1979:105). In this process, youth subcultures demonstrated that they could be creative agents, not passive or manipulated dupes.

The fact that groups outside of the elite can instigate their own styles and fashions challenges the cultural hegemony or power of the elite, indicating that they do not have absolute control to make others conform to their norms and values (Clarke et al. 1975:11–12). Furthermore, the fact that these nonelite styles and fashions are occasionally emulated by the elite challenges the trickle-down model of conspicuous consumption. Styles and fashions can **trickle up** from social or class locations below the elite. From Levi Blue Jeans to Converse One Stars, styles from the working class and from youth subcultures have trickled up the class hierarchy. Today, some multinational corporations like Reebok even hire people to go out on the streets and **coolhunt,** discovering what is cool by observing what certain youths are wearing. These street styles are then incorporated into new designs and sold back to both the elite and the masses. Using coolhunters accelerates the trickle-up process. New styles are introduced by companies every few months instead of every few years because "the act of discovering what's cool is what causes cool to move on" (Gladwell 1997).

The trickle-up and coolhunt movement of style and fashion suggests that class differentiation is not the sole motivation for conspicuous consumption. While class remains one variable that explains why individuals consume, it is not the sole determinant. Sociologist Herbert Blumer argued that instead of class differentiation, consumption, particularly fashion, was driven by **collective selection,** or a shared, societal mood or attitude. Collective selection suggests that the elite do not so much create fashion but follow it like everyone else; thus, fashion does not so much trickle down as disseminate horizontally from a variety of groups. According to Blumer, *"The fashion mechanism appears not in response to a need of class differentiation and class emulation but in response to be in fashion . . . to express new tastes which are emerging in a changing world* (1969:281; Davis 1992). Today, cool may be replacing class as "the central determinant of social prestige" (Heath and Potter 2004:200) and may be what is informing the collective mood of mass consumer society.

Just as the elite were forced to create new styles to differentiate themselves from the classes below it in Veblen's trickle-down theory, cool people must create new styles to differentiate themselves once companies have co-opted them. According to Hebdige (1979:94), when subcultural signs, like dress or music, are converted into mass-produced objects, a process of **recuperation** takes place. For example, when punks use safety pins as earrings, a company can recuperate or reclaim the safety pin by intentionally producing and marketing them as earrings. Often businesses will practice **co-optation,** copying styles from subcultures or countercultures, subverting their rebellious meanings, and making them palatable for mass society. Co-optation is a way of "neutralizing" countercultural dissent or resistance to mass consumer society, demonstrating that capitalism is quite capable of tolerating subversion, particularly if it can be commoditized (Heath and Potter 2004:34–35). Perhaps, as Thomas Frank argues in his book *The Conquest of Cool* (1997), commerce and countercultures are not so much enemies but allies in a battle against conformity. However hard countercultures try to oppose mass consumer culture and conformity, they seem doomed to participate in a game that they cannot win. Corporations recuperate and co-opt their styles, forcing subcultures to create new styles, which will then be recuperated and co-opted. Therefore, these subcultures are inevitably providing fuel for the engine of mass consumer society, which they oppose. As Dick Hebdige (1979:96) states, "Youth cultural styles may begin by issuing symbolic challenges, but they must inevitably end by establishing new sets of conventions." Thus, the question arises as to how much agency consumers really possess when it comes to resisting mass consumer society. Does bricolage or subverting the intended meanings and uses of consumer goods constitute rebellion if it does not change the dynamics of mass consumer society?

Passive Dupes?

The Frankfurt School and the Culture Industry

The argument that mass consumer society has the power to absorb and commoditize rebellion, revolt, dissent, and subversion can be traced back to the scholars of the Frankfurt School for Social Research (1923), including Theodor Adorno, Walter Benjamin, Max Horkheimer, and Herbert Marcuse. The Frankfurt school developed what is known as **critical theory,** which questions whether scientific rationality and technology represents progress and liberation or stultification and repression. They situate culture, not the economy, as the primary source of social control in mass consumer society, claiming that cultural control is more invisible as it alters our consciousness and makes us passive, uncritical consumers (Ritzer 2009). The **culture industry,** including advertisers, marketers, and television, movie, and music producers and entertainers, creates **false needs** for consumer goods that we neither want nor need, yet we purchase anyway, which results in our own repression (Horkheimer and Adorno 1993; Marcuse 1964:4–5). However, we do not comprehend that we are repressed because the culture industry manipulates us into thinking that buying another frivolous pair of designer shoes or watching three hours of professional football every Sunday fulfills our true needs and desires. The culture industry has created a society where "people recognize themselves in their commodities; they find their soul in their automobile, hi-fi set, split-level home, kitchen equipment" and have anchored social control in "the new needs which it has produced" (Marcuse 1964:9).

According to Marcuse, pursuing false needs over true needs has resulted in the loss of critical thinking capabilities in mass consumer society, creating what he calls **one-dimensionality** (1964:10–11). Individuals can no longer think for themselves or oppose what the culture industry tells them to do because they have lost the ability to reason. If Apple tells us we need the newest version of its iPhone to be smarter, we stand in line outside one of its retail stores overnight to be the first customer who can buy it without thinking about how much this corporation and its technology are controlling our lives.

The Frankfurt school was concerned with not only how the culture industry indoctrinates consumers but also how it creates a standardized and homogeneous society. In particular, they were dismayed by how the culture industry "forces together the sphere of high and low art," which resulted in the dominance of popular or mass culture (Adorno 1991:85). Horkheimer and Adorno (1993:133, 125) call popular television shows and movies "rubbish," based on predictable, "ready-made clichés" that could "be slotted in anywhere." Mass culture requires little creativity to produce and little imagination to consume. Indeed, part of the attraction of mass culture is that it provides an escape from thinking about the real world, much less changing it. According to Horkheimer and Adorno (1993:144), "The liberation which amusement promises is freedom from thought." They thought that high art was desecrated when it became commoditized or democratized. The fact that most individuals, regardless of class or education level, can listen to an opera or visit an art museum does not necessarily mean that they can appreciate or understand high art. Democratization has not elevated art but turned it into a commodity to be consumed by the masses. Thus, art no longer captures the abstract ideals of beauty or truth but is just another amusement produced by the culture industry to keep us pacified and entertained. Fordist production techniques of standardization further debase the true purpose of art. Walter Benjamin thought that the ability of some technologies, like film and photography, to mass reproduce art led to its disenchantment. Mass reproduction resulted, he argued, in the loss of "the aura of the work of art," robbing it of its authenticity (1969:221, quoted in Shull 2005:62).

Just as capitalist mass production alienates workers, capitalist mass consumption alienates consumers. Marcuse contended "Free choice among a wide variety of goods and services does not signify freedom if these goods and services sustain social controls over a life of toil and fear—that is, if they sustain alienation" (1964:7–8). Adorno (1991:85) agrees, claiming that "the customer is not king, as the culture industry would have us believe, not its subject but its object." As an object, the consumer is classified, organized, and labeled and "something is produced for all so that none may escape" (Horkheimer and Adorno 1993:123). Take, for example, one dominant actor in the culture industry, advertisers. They spend over $200 billion every year in the United States (Klein 1999:11) in an attempt to convince consumers that they have the freedom of choice, such as having a Burger King hamburger "Your Way" or that they have the power of sovereignty if they drive a Ford because "Everything We Do Is Driven by You." The false freedom and power that advertisers and the culture industry in general promote turn consumers into "helpless victims to what is offered [to] them" (Horkheimer and Adorno 1993:123); however, consumers suffer from false consciousness because they do not understand that they are victims. They think that the choice between one hundred different types of cereal in a grocery store is true freedom and do not contemplate the fact that they really are not free *not* to choose or that the one hundred different types of cereal are produced by a small handful of corporations. In sum, the Frankfurt school would agree that "our increasingly market-saturated life spaces make us dumber, lazier, fatter, more selfish, less-skilled, more adolescent, less politically potent, more wasteful, and less happy than we should be" (Dawson 2005:2).

Children as Consumers

One consumer demographic that is particularly vulnerable to the manipulative powers of the culture industry is children. Historically, children were not constructed as consumers until the 1930s, when manufacturers, advertisers, and merchandisers started to view them as a primary market. Consumer goods, like clothing, began to be created according to the preferences of children, instead of their parents, and some stores reconfigured their sales floors to be more child-friendly (Cook 2004:2–3). Today, children are completely entrenched in consumer culture. Retail stores like Gap Kids and Toys-R-Us, cable channels like Nickelodeon and the Disney Channel, and food items like Fruit Roll-ups and McDonald's Happy Meals, have all been created to take advantage of this prized segment of the marketplace. While many children may not have much money of their own, most possess the power to influence the purchasing power of their households—even if this power entails simply nagging their parents.

The development of children into consumers can be understood as empowering because it provides a way for them to be recognized as having individual identities and perhaps even autonomy in terms of making decisions in the marketplace. But, turning children into consumers can also be considered exploitative, socializing them early into a culture that emphasizes that the acquisition of material goods is a means to happiness and a symbol of success. Further exploitative practices include marketing unhealthy foods, like surgary cereals and soft drinks, to children; forcing them to watch commercials in public schools during Channel One broadcasts; exposing them to violence in popular video games; and fabricating unrealistic body images in dolls (Buckingham 2011; Cook 2004; Schor 2004).

But, do children always strictly follow the ways that the culture industry dictates to them regarding how they should play with their toys, eat their food, or wear their clothes? In her ethnography of how black, mostly low-income children confront consumer culture, Elizabeth Chin (2001) found that some children do not passively adhere to meanings imposed on consumer goods by advertisers. For example, several girls in her study who played with a white Barbie doll braided her long, blonde hair to imitate their own hairstyles. They also actively critiqued how she was a stereotype of dominant white society, instead of being overweight, pregnant, or the victim of abuse, which corresponded to images and experiences in their own community.

(Continued)

(Continued)

In addition, children do not necessarily act in greedy or selfish ways in their role as consumers. When children in her study were given money to spend, many purchased practical goods that they needed, shared goods that they purchased with their siblings and friends, and bought things not just for themselves but also gifts for their caregivers.

Questions

1. Do you think that advertising that targets children should be banned? Why or why not? If it is, how do you think this might change the future of consumer culture?

2. Many cable, satellite, and streaming channels provide programming for children, such as ABC Family, the Disney Channel, and Nickelodeon. Watch a program on one of these channels and write down your observations on how they construct children as consumers.

3. Defend this statement: Children are not necessarily passive victims of consumer culture but possess some agency. Provide a specific example to support your defense.

Frankfurt school theorists have been criticized for being too elitist in their judgment of popular or mass culture and giving too much power to the culture industry and too little power to the consumer. While the culture industry possesses a large amount of control over production and consumption, it does not, as the Birmingham school demonstrates, have absolute control. Furthermore, the Frankfurt school neglects what consumers "make of what they 'absorb,' receive, and pay for" (de Certeau 1984:31). An individual may watch hours of television, but "it remains to be asked what the consumer *makes* of these images" (de Certeau 1984:31). Are we just watching television passively, or are we interacting with it by yelling at the screen when a referee makes what we think is a bad call? Are we watching television alone or with our family? Are we unconsciously tempted by the fast food shown on an ad, or are we actively making fun of the manipulative tactics used in these ads? Are we even watching television at all—or is it on in the background as we eat dinner or do our homework? Finally, the Frankfurt school did not anticipate how consumers could become active participants in the production of culture. With the advent of the digital economy, the number of individuals involved in creative work is growing (Johnson 2015). People can now more easily self-publish their own books, direct their own music videos, and sell their own handmade jewelry using new digital platforms like YouTube and Etsy. While these activities may not challenge the hegemony of the culture industry at large, they do highlight how individuals can be active producers instead of passive victims in a mass consumer society.

Utility or Hedonism?

Some theorists frame their understandings about why we consume through the lens of utility and hedonism, as well as debate whether or not consumers are rational decision makers or hedonistic pleasure seekers. Are consumers motivated to consume to maximize their utility or to fulfill their fantasies? Do we carefully calculate each purchase to ensure that we obtain the greatest quantity of goods for the lowest prices, or do we lavishly indulge our desires when we consume? Either way, theorists who stress either utility or hedonism challenge the "class-based status-driven models" of consumption proposed by Veblen, Bourdieu, the Birmingham school, and the Frankfurt school (Schor 2007:19). Instead of trying to display socioeconomic class positions with conspicuous consumption or reproduce class distinctions with cultural capital, consumers are viewed as seeking to exercise their individual preferences or express their individuality. Furthermore, unlike the Frankfurt school, both the utility and hedonism approaches view consumers as agents, not dupes—even if we might act irrationally, we still possess autonomy.

Sovereignty and Choice

The idea that consumers are rational decision makers seeking to maximize their **utility,** or preferences, is a standard assumption in classical economic thought. Liberal economic theorists argue that preference formation is determined by prices and income (Pietrykowski 2009:3) and "refrain from making any judgments about the substantive needs and desires of individuals" (Slater 1997:46). Indeed, the consumption of utility "allows no distinction between good and bad, essential and nonessential, needs and wants" (Slater 1997:49); thus, utility has nothing to say about the "substantive content of [a consumer's] preferences" (Knox 2005:384).

Utility as a motivation for consumer behavior depends on **consumer sovereignty,** or "the notion that consumers are the best judges of their own welfare and that their economic choices are effective in advancing their self-interests" (Redmond 2000:177). At the heart of consumer sovereignty is the concept of choice, particularly the notions that choice is free, that it increases economic growth and efficiency, and that it is better to live in a society that values choice than one that does not (Gabriel and Lang 2006:26). Interestingly, the concept of consumer sovereignty has been used throughout the years to try to equate economic markets with democracy. Just as citizens have the right to vote for their choice of political candidate, consumers can exercise their "right to choose" by voting with their wallets and pocketbooks for or against certain products (Schwartzkopf 2011:110). If consumers have this kind of power, then it means that they can effectively control production; products that do not sell will not make a profit for the producer and subsequently will cease to be manufactured (Knox 2005). Chapter 8 explores the political potential of consumer activism, including the different tactics that consumers can use to try to achieve social change.

The agency and power of consumers from the perspective of consumer sovereignty is clearly at odds with the passive victims portrayed by the Frankfurt school. The economist Gary Becker argues that instead of manipulating consumers, "advertising conveys information to consumers" and that they "receive a greater perceived input in terms of utility from advertised goods than from others" (Redmond 2000:181). But, others question whether the choice emphasized by liberal economists is really free if consumers lack basic information about the goods they purchase and the choice between similar items is "only choice in a marginal sense." The ideology of choice can also be used to deceive consumers and remove responsibility from those who produce consumer goods and services (Gabriel and Lang 2006:26). For example, a corporation might produce and distribute an unhealthy product, like soda, or an ineffective product, like wrinkle cream. When consumers who drink soda become obese or consumers who use wrinkle cream continue to have wrinkles, the corporation can reply "but we didn't force you to purchase these items—it was your free choice, so we are not to be blamed for your weight gain or wrinkles." While government regulations can protect consumers from some defective and unsafe products, the belief in *caveat emptor* (buyer beware) makes it difficult to conceive of consumers as victims in societies where the ideology of consumer sovereignty is strong. Indeed, far from challenging the logic of choice, many states have applied it to justify the privatization of government goods and service, like public utilities (Gabriel and Lang 2006:41). In the United States, the logic of choice is being used to try to validate the privatization of Social Security, rationalize vouchers for education, and create fear of establishing a government-run health care system. As governments embrace the logic of choice, they begin to view and treat their citizens more and more like consumers.

Others question if utility can really capture the dynamics of consumer behavior. Rational consumers have been described as "undersocialized" because it is assumed that they do not take social or cultural factors into account when they decide to purchase an item (Redmond 2000:185). It seems that the consumer has "achieved sovereignty at the cost of becoming an isolated rational individual whose tastes are given" (Winch 2006:32). Are consumers really just shopping to fulfill their individual preferences determined by price and income, or are they being influenced by their neighbors or celebrities or the culture industry? Some theorists wonder if consumer sovereignty is just an ideology promoted by corporations to make us feel empowered. Schor notes that it is interesting that the growing power of corporations in recent years "has been accompanied by an ideology that posits the reverse—that the consumer is king and the corporation is at his or her mercy" (2007:28). Others acknowledge that while consumers may be able to practice sovereignty in the marketplace, they do not necessarily exercise their freedom of choice to maximize their utility. Some consumers "vote" for social justice by purchasing fair trade coffee, which usually costs more than mass-produced coffee. Furthermore, focusing on consumer sovereignty, choice, and utility does not explain what consumers actually *do* with the goods that they purchase, so these motivations for consumer behavior end at the point of sale.

Perhaps the most problematic aspect of how consumer sovereignty and choice is typically analyzed is its neglect of poor consumers, who because of their limited incomes and where they live do not have the freedom to always act rationally in the marketplace. If poor consumers are acknowledged at all, it is often to morally critique what they purchase, especially if they are using welfare funds on items not deemed necessities. Given that approximately 14.5% of all Americans are currently living below the poverty line and many more may be classified as living in relative poverty, poor consumers constitute a notable segment of the market, even if they might not have a large amount of discretionary income. Because of limited options, people who reside in low-income areas are forced to pay on average 41% more for similar goods and services as those who live in more affluent areas (Hill 2002:214). According to Andreasen, poor consumers suffer from "sources of outrageous consumer exploitation," especially at the hands of questionable credit lenders (1975:26, quoted in Hill 2007:78). The lack of legitimate banks in their neighborhoods makes it difficult for poor consumers to obtain conventional loans, positioning them as targets for predatory lending practices that involve high interest rates and late fees. James Baldwin best described the difficulty of poor consumers to maximize their utility when he wrote that "anyone who has ever struggled with poverty knows how extremely expensive it is to be poor" (Sturdivant 1969:1, quoted in Hill 2002:214).

Desire and Difference: Colin Campbell and Postmodernism

Instead of our individual preferences being determined by rational calculations, like price and income, some theorists suggest that consumers can—and should—have fun and "seek to reclaim pleasure, not least physical, sensuous pleasure, from sanctimonious moralizing and the grim heritage of the Protestant ethic which said 'Work! Work! Work!'" (Gabriel and Lang 2006:97). Rather than delaying our gratifications and saving money, we should celebrate the fact the mass consumer society provides us the means to satisfy our pleasures and needs instantaneously. In *The Romantic Ethic and the Spirit of Modern Consumerism* (1989:60), Colin Campbell argues that individuals are motivated to consume not because of status competition but because they want to fulfill their fantasies and daydreams. Campbell makes a distinction between pleasure and utility as motivations for consumer behavior, which typically have been equated in economic theory. He suggests that utility should be understood as the satisfaction of needs, while pleasure represents the satisfaction of desire and sensation. For example,

> Food and drink can provide pleasure via the senses without any being ingested, as is the case with the aroma of a steak or the bouquet of a wine, whilst the body's need for the nourishment may be met by a process of direct injection which bypasses the taste buds entirely. (Campbell 1989:61–62)

While the injection of nourishment may satisfy our utility or need for food, it does nothing to satisfy the pleasure associated with the desire of consuming food. Campbell makes a further distinction between **traditional**

hedonism that is based on physical pleasure and **modern self-illusory hedonism,** which is based on emotional experiences like daydreaming. According to Campbell, modern consumers long "to experience in reality those pleasures created in the imagination, a longing which results in the ceaseless consumption of novelty" (1989:205). This quest for novelty keeps the consumption cycle in motion because when consumers purchase goods to fulfill fantasies, they are inevitably disappointed, so they must construct new fantasies to fulfill and find new goods to purchase. The inevitable disappointment that occurs once we have purchased a new pair of shoes or worn them for a while does not seem to dampen our hedonistic desire to seek to experience pleasure for its own sake or fantasize about purchasing a new pair of shoes (Slater 1997:96).

While Campbell situates his study of consumption in eighteenth-century England, other theorists have focused on the role that pleasure plays in contemporary society. In particular, postmodern theorists celebrate the "liberatory" aspects of consumption, including its "emancipatory potential" (Firat and Venkatesh 1995:239). A **postmodern world** is characterized by play and fragmentation with individuals who are free to experiment with a variety of identities and lifestyles. Above all else, the postmodern consumers want to fulfill their desire to express difference and "make lifestyle a life project" (Lyotard 1984; Featherstone 1991:86). Instead of wanting to keep up with the Joneses, postmodern consumers want to be different from them (Rutherford 1990:11, quoted in Gabriel and Lang 2006:37). According to Firat and Venkatesh (1995:253), in a postmodern world "the individual is freed from seeking or conforming to one sense or experience of being; the disenchantment from having to find consistent reason in every act, in every moment, is transcended, and the liberty to live each moment to its fullest emotional peak . . . is regained." In other words, a postmodern consumer can be a Goth one day and a Preppy the next day without feeling like she is being unfaithful to some stable identity. After all, the postmodern world is one big game, of which the postmodern consumer is "hyper-aware" (Slater 1997:197). The superficial trumps the profound in a postmodern world where appearance reigns supreme and "a decentered selfhood has become a plurality of intermittent, disconnected, recognition-seeking spectacles of self-presentation" (Langman 1992:40). Thus, from a postmodern perspective, a person really can be what he or she wears.

While the postmodern consumer appears to be a refreshing, engaged actor compared to the dull, passive dupes of the Frankfurt school or the calculated, decision makers portrayed by liberal economists, the fragmented world that the postmodern consumer encounters may threaten to offer a schizophrenic experience of disconnection and incoherence (Jameson 1984). For some, this can be experienced more as a nightmare than fun. Furthermore, consumers may be fulfilling their fantasies in a more calculating than irrational manner. Mike Featherstone (1991:86) suggests that **calculated hedonism,** a combination of a calculus of style and an aestheticization of rationality, best characterizes postmodern consumer behavior. Rather than trying to dichotomize pleasure and rational decision making, we should attempt to understand how they work together in contemporary consumer culture. According to Zygmunt Bauman, "Reality, as the consumer experiences it, is a pursuit of pleasure. Freedom is about the choice between greater and lesser satisfaction, and rationality is about choosing the first over the second" (1992:50). However, just as choice may be promoted by the culture industry and corporations to make us feel empowered, so might be the pleasure and liberation experienced by the postmodern consumer. Therefore, postmodern consumer liberation—if it exists at all—might be "institutionally authorized by market-mediated institutions" (Arnould 2007:100). Our postmodern play and fantasies may be more structured than we realize.

Conclusion

In sum, much of the controversy surrounding what motivates consumer behavior revolves around the broad theme of whether consumers possess agency or are passive dupes. If one assumes consumers possess agency, then the next question concerns the purpose of this agency: do consumers exercise their sovereignty to achieve utility or to fulfill fantasies or to rebel? If one assumes consumers are passive dupes, then one must examine if consumers are being manipulated to conform to the norms and values established by the upper class or by the culture industry. Taking exclusive sides in this controversy is problematic because, on one hand, a strong agency approach often fails to acknowledge that agency may be "constructed *by* producers, rather than being deployed against them" (Schor 2007:24–25). On the other hand, a strong dupes approach ignores the various ways individuals construct identities and create meaning with consumer goods as well as find pleasure in consumer activities like shopping or watching television. Perhaps Yiannis Gabriel and Tim Lang best summarize the consumer as "unmanageable" because "as consumers we can be irrational, incoherent and inconsistent, just as we can be rational, planned, and organized" (Gabriel and Lang 2006:4).

4

The Places and Spaces of Consumption

Compared to the objects and subjects of consumption, the places and spaces of consumption have only recently begun to be analyzed with the same rigor (Ritzer, Goodman, and Wiedenhoft 2001). This oversight may be attributed to the fact that individuals were involved with consumption far before there were permanent, physical buildings established solely for this activity. Prior to the establishment of places exclusively devoted to mass consumption, individuals engaged in self-production and barter and may have attended the occasional fair (Williams 1982). Consumers might have traveled to a market to purchase food and clothing, but these were often temporary vendor stalls located in more densely populated urban areas. In large cities, vendors often hawked goods from pushcarts and wagons on street corners or in central squares and parks. Not only were many early markets not fixed in space, but prices were not either. Consumers had to haggle, making of consumption rather inefficient and unpredictable (Deutsch 2010). It was not so much these markets but the city itself that was the earliest place of consumption—and it was a public space, free and accessible to anyone regardless of socioeconomic class. Permanent places of consumption were eventually constructed, including the dreamlike worlds of the Parisian arcades and department stores. Large retail stores became "central features of downtown life" by the late 1800s, and as they became fixed in space, they established one-price systems that eliminated the need for merchants and consumers to bargain over the price of goods (Strasser 1989:207). Profits were achieved by setting prices at levels that moved a high volume of goods quickly. Detailed recordkeeping, including the invention of the cash register and sales slips, and departmentalization allowed mass merchants to easily audit which goods were most popular (Strasser 1989).

This chapter will provide a historical narrative of the places of consumption, beginning with cities, arcades, and department stores and moving to the suburbs with the development of shopping malls and big-box stores. The Wal-Mart effect will be explored in addition to how Amazon.com and e-commerce are influencing current consumption patterns. Finally, the concern over how many places of consumption have privatized public space will be addressed. A central theme discussed in this chapter is how places of consumption lose their enchantment over time as they become dominated by the principles of formally rationality, or **McDonaldization.** The main principles of McDonaldization include efficiency or speed, calculability or quantification, standardization or sameness, and technological control of workers and consumers (Ritzer 2013). When places of consumption start to become disenchanted, they either lose their market share to new places of consumption or have to try to reinvent their magic by employing strategies that make them appear new and exciting again. In the words of George Ritzer (2010), they must figure out how to re-enchant a disenchanted world.

The City, Arcades, and Department Stores

According to Georg Simmel (1903/1971), the city was the center of capitalist economic activity and culture, which radiated so much "nervous stimulation" that individuals were forced to adopt a **blasé attitude** of indifference to survive. Yet, despite the calculating and predictable culture of the city—and capitalism itself—people continued to attempt to maintain their autonomy by trying to differentiate themselves from one another. The city allowed for this to a certain extent, cultivating individuality over the confining conformity of a small town. However, the price to pay for this autonomy was increasing specialization, a consequence of what Simmel called the **tragedy of culture.** The city contained simply too much—too much art, too much technology—that individuals could only hope to control a small part of it. From a consumption angle, the question was how to shock all of these metropolitans out of their blasé attitudes and entice them to consume and express their individuality through fantasy. Was there space in the city to break free from its culture of formal rationality or at least feel as if one had escaped it? According to Walter Benjamin, the Parisian arcades of the early 1800s were constructed to provide just such an experience. The **arcades** were shops that were enclosed by glass to create a dream world where consumers could browse, window shop, and enjoy urban street life, while being protected from its harsh elements. Interestingly, the very technology that created the culture of formal rationality was used to create these dream worlds, but its fusion with art made this cold and calculating technology appear "phantasmagoric," or entertaining, and capable of enticing individuals to become consumers and purchase their desires. Indeed, one did not even have to purchase goods to enjoy the arcades. For example, the **flâneur** was a man of leisure who strolled around the arcades to window shop and experience extravagance.

The Parisian arcades set the stage for the next, more phantasmagoric place of consumption: the department store. **Department stores** by definition offer a large variety of merchandise organized into specialty departments under one roof. The first department stores were unique not simply because of the sheer quantity of goods they offered but because their policies were "consumercentric." Department stores were one of the first places of consumption to offer fixed prices—often advertised in newspapers—so that consumers would not have to engage in the time-consuming practice of haggling over the cost of each individual item that they wanted to purchase. Catering to the whims of consumers, department stores established the "no questions asked" policy of merchandise exchanges and refunds, money-back guarantees on purchased products, and free delivery. Some even offered cooking and knitting classes, provided tailoring and alteration services, and operated as "Saturday bankers," cashing checks when banks were traditionally closed. In addition, personal attention by sales clerks became an unquestioned expectation of loyal customers (Rosenberg 1985; Leach 1993).

The first department store, Bon Marché, opened in Paris in 1852, followed in 1862 by Cast Iron Palace, the first department store in New York City. John Wanamaker's Grand Depot in Philadelphia was established in 1876, becoming the largest, single-floor department store in the world with 129 concentric counters surrounding a central ballroom. In Chicago, Marshall Field topped Wanamaker's as the largest department store in the world when he added a 20-story men's store in 1917 across the street from his existing 12-story structure erected in 1907. Macy's department store soon took over this title when it came to occupy an entire city block and stand 30 stories tall in 1924. Like the Parisian arcades that preceded them, department stores created "dream worlds" (Williams 1982) with extravagant displays and spectacular atriums. They implemented new technologies to create spaces that appeared to be enchanting to the consumer but were carefully planned and managed. The sensational array of goods displayed in department stores depended on the mass production of consumer goods, especially ready-to-wear clothing. Reliable distribution methods were necessary to continually restock merchandise. Elevators and escalators were installed to provide comfort and convenience as well as methodically navigate consumers through different departments. Pneumatic tube systems were installed to efficiently handle the high volume of cash transactions until credit became popular. Installment payment plans were offered to tempt consumers to immediately gratify their desires. Thus, a hidden, formally rationalized system supported the enchanting façade of the department store (Ritzer 2010).

Although department stores catered to an overwhelmingly bourgeois consumer base, they did not close their doors to working-class consumers who wanted a glimpse of luxury. Everyone, regardless of socioeconomic class, was encouraged to become flâneurs, wandering from department to department, fantasizing about the novel array of goods on display without being obliged to spend any money at all. Marshall Field extended this practice to the city sidewalk, installing spectacular window displays to create consumer desire. According to Leach (1993:63), glass was used by department stores to democratize desire while "dedemocratizing access to goods." Displaying goods under the protection of glass counters or windows allowed all classes of consumers to gaze at luxurious products, even if they could not physically touch them or financially afford them. While poorer consumers were welcome to gaze at expensive goods, department stores created bargain basements with marked-down goods and cheap imitation of products for sale on the upper levels so that they could capitalize on the purchasing power of all classes of consumers (Leach 1993). Luxury was democratized not only with the mass production of cheap, imitation goods but also the expansion of credit. Department stores institutionalized **installment plans,** which permitted consumers to pay a certain percentage of money down, paying the remainder off over consecutive weeks. This permitted consumers to "possess images of wealth without actually having a large income" (Williams 1982:92).

In addition to democratizing desire and opening up a space for the working class to become participants (even if it was limited) in consumer culture, department stores created a privileged space for women (Reekie 1993). Places of consumption "offered a public sphere in which women tested their political and economic authority" (Deutsch 2010:10). Although men certainly consumed goods, they were viewed as too rational to be tempted into buying something that they did not really need. Store managers did not think that most men had the time to waste spending hours wandering through a variety of departments; conventional wisdom held that most men would feel uncomfortable walking through women's departments. Women, on the other hand, were stereotypically viewed as not only having the time to shop but also possessing an irrationality that could be managed through desire. The department store became the female public sphere, replacing the church (Miller 1994). Like the church, the department store was a place where middle-class women could legitimately be alone in the city. Their access to this part of the public sphere was ironically a consequence of their domestic duty to take care of the private sphere. While women could fantasize about the latest fashions, much of their shopping revolved around purchasing necessities for their household. This expectation added to the burden of lower- and working-class women who had to not just consume for themselves and their families but also work in the public sphere. Females who worked as sales clerks in department stores had the additional worry of having to maintain a fashionable wardrobe on low wages (Benson 1986). As a result, hidden within these dream worlds of consumption were tangible gender and class inequalities.

Shopping Malls and Big-Box Stores

The creation of new places and spaces of consumption in the postwar era, especially the enclosed, suburban shopping mall, marked both the success and the eventual downfall of the traditional department store. Mall developers courted the large department stores to anchor their shopping centers, many offering them low or no rent in exchange for bringing in prized foot traffic. Shopping malls became an integral part of the suburbs by the 1950s, which changed the physical arrangement of American commercial life (Cohen 2003). The major triumph of shopping malls was bringing department stores to the suburbs from the cities, eliminating the need for suburbanites to drive into the city and be forced to experience the alleged dangers of "unenclosed reality" (Kowinski 1985:353). Suburban malls attempted to re-create the urban environment in an enclosed, safe, and clean space (Gottdiener 2001), offering free and convenient parking, providing late shopping hours, and becoming destinations for the whole family to enjoy. These new suburban spaces seemed more enchanted than the dirty and unpredictable space of the city. And unlike the early department stores, the inclusion of men in this space of consumption made evenings and week-ends the busiest times to shop (Cohen 2003:279).

Early shopping malls mimicked a "dumbbell" architectural model with department stores as the anchors to force consumers to walk through the interior of the mall and hopefully be tempted to shop at smaller, specialty stores. But when department stores moved to the suburbs, they began creating national chains, losing much of their distinctiveness. No longer rooted in a local city culture, chain department stores became increasingly McDonaldized (Ritzer 2013). Efficiency, calculation, and predictability have made these former dream worlds disenchanted. Their physical architecture and the homogeneous products that they offer for sale do little to distinguish one department store chain from another. Frequent sales reduce prices but at the expense of personal service. Recent depart-ment store mergers have increased their disenchantment, particularly the mega-merger of about 950 May department stores in 2005 by Federated Department Stores. Most of the former May department stores, such as Lazarus, Rich's, Hecht's, and Kaufman's, were renamed Federated's most popular chain, Macy's, losing what little regional distinctiveness that they once possessed. Furthermore, the smaller, specialty stores in the interior of shopping malls have robbed the department store of its actual depart-ments. Consumers can now shop at Victoria Secret for lingerie or Foot Locker for athletic apparel instead of searching for these departments at J. C. Penney or Bloomingdale's. While early shopping malls may have needed department stores to attract consumers, contemporary shop-ping malls have created dream worlds that include hotels, restaurants, rollercoasters, water parks, and even indoor lakes (Urry 2002). Clearly, to enchant consumers today, spaces of consumption must go beyond lavish window displays and offer the opportunity to gaze upon luxuri-ous objects of consumption. In fact, it may no longer be the objects of consumption that attract consumers to shopping malls but experiences.

The rise of "big-box" stores, like Home Depot, Staples, and Best Buy, has also contributed to the decline of department stores in recent years.

Big-box stores are freestanding spaces that specialize in selling large quantities of a distinct category of merchandise at low prices. Dubbed "**category killers**" (Spector 2005), big-box stores seek to monopolize the market of a specific category and have literally taken the "departments" out of the department store. For example, department stores dominated the market for toys until Toys-R-Us was established. Since the birth of big-box stores, department stores have steadily eliminated a number of their departments, including toys, home furnishings, and electronics. Unlike department stores, big-box stores self-consciously embrace the disenchanting elements of McDonaldization as part of their competitive advantage. These sites of consumption lure the bargain hunter with their warehouse-like settings, lack of personal service, and, most important, low prices.

Enclosed shopping malls seem to be following a similar fate as department stores. Although firmly rooted in suburbia, many are now owned and operated by international conglomerates, like Westfield, and appear less enchanted than the new, outdoor shopping "**festival marketplaces**" or "multiuse malls" that are being created (Cohen 2004; Hannigan 1998). Unlike the traditional enclosed spaces, these new outdoor sites of consumption are places where people can reside, work, shop, eat, and play. While most of the stores and restaurants that comprise these outdoor sites of consumption are national chains, the Main Street look of these new places of consumption makes them feel more enchanting and unique. Interestingly, enclosed shopping store owners are trying to compete with the festival marketplaces by courting big-box stores, including Target and Costco, to become new anchors. In the process, some of these big-box stores are transforming themselves from low-maintenance warehouses to lifestyle centers, incorporating some of the elements that once made department stores so enchanting to consumers like cafes and even daycare facilities. However, department stores are not being invited to relocate to festival marketplaces. Their replacement as anchors by big-box stores at enclosed shopping malls has pushed some department stores to experiment with freestanding stores, independent of the city and shopping malls they once dominated.

Wal-Mart: Killing the Category Killers?

Currently, one of the most significance places of consumption is Wal-Mart, and its ability to encourage **hyperconsumption**, or overconsumption, through combining low prices and a wide variety of merchandise under one roof.

Indeed, this superstore is able to create enchantment through its use of **implosion,** or the "disappearance of boundaries" (Ritzer 2010:120). For example, Wal-Mart has imploded the grocery store, the hardware store, the pet store, the electronic store, the book store, and the clothing store all under one roof. This massive de-differentiation has helped Wal-Mart become the ultimate category killer, challenging even the dominance of big-box stores by collapsing their specific categories into one supercenter. Paradoxically, the growth of the supercenter may be reinventing the department store, albeit without the pomp and circumstance. Like the early department stores, Wal-Mart supercenters are enormous (an average of 187,000 square feet) and composed of a variety of departments; however, its ascetic décor makes this space a world apart from the extravagant spectacles that department stores once were. In place of the ornate architecture and luxurious display cases of the early cathedrals of consumption, Wal-Mart more closely imitates an unembellished Protestant church. In doing so, Wal-Mart has taken the bargains out of the basement of the early department stores, putting them front and center of its retail empire. In doing so, it seems to be suggesting that lower- and working-class consumers should be positioned prominently as well.

The first Wal-Mart was opened in 1962 by founder Sam Walton, whose business philosophy was to "sell stuff that people need every day just a little cheaper than everyone else" and "sell it at a low price all the time" (Fishman 2006:8). He correctly predicted that this philosophy would have customers flocking to his stores. Today, Americans spend $35 million every hour at Wal-Mart stores, and more than 100,000,000 of them shop at one weekly. Ninety percent of all Americans live within 15 miles of a Wal-Mart, and a staggering 93% of American households shop at a Wal-Mart at least once a year, the average spending $2,060.36 annually (Fishman 2006:4,6). This is precisely how Wal-Mart is able to make a profit even though it sells products at such low prices—by selling to a lot of people a lot of the time. Wal-Mart's niche is **discount retailing,** or making profit "on low markups by selling large volume of goods in no-frill stores with self-service" (Moreton 2009:27). While discounters were traditionally based in urban areas with dense populations, Walton introduced this type of shopping experience to rural areas with populations as low as 5,000 (Moreton 2009:27).

The Wal-Mart effect, or the way that Wal-Mart has transformed both the global marketplace and local communities, has had a major influence on how we work and how we consume (Fishman 2006). In 2002, Wal-Mart replaced General Motors to become the largest employer in the world, signaling the demise of blue-collar jobs and the ascendancy of the service sector. It is no longer manufacturers but retailers who are the source of power in contemporary consumer society. Today, retailers dominate supply chain initiatives and no longer have to rely on manufacturers' brand-name products as many have invented their own private labels that have become increasingly successful (Thain and Bradley 2012). For example, Wal-Mart created its private label, equate, allowing it the opportunity to become its own supplier and compete with the more well-known national brands. Wal-Mart also institutionalized the practice of using barcodes on every product and demanding that its vendors do so as well, building a digital warehouse that can collect and analyze data on all the products purchased in Wal-Mart stores. Considering that Wal-Mart controls more than half of all world trade, these data are crucial for setting prices and coordinating global commodity chains starting in the factory, traveling by container to the warehouse, and ending on the store shelf (Lichtenstein 2010). According to Thain and Bradley (2012:18), the introduction of UPC scanning and its universal adoption is the primary reason that power has transferred to retailers like Wal-Mart from manufacturers. Wal-Mart has also been able to influence how products are packaged, forcing all of its suppliers to change their practices if they want their goods to be sold at its stores. The reason that deodorant is no longer sold in cardboard packages anywhere anymore is because Wal-Mart told its suppliers it did not want that type of packaging (Fishman 2006).

In addition, Wal-Mart has influenced why we consume, transforming shopping into a family value. Women, in particular, shop there to procure necessities for their families, not hedonistically indulge their personal desires. The ascetic and orderly landscape of the typical Wal-Mart store enhances the feeling that consumers are shopping there not to fulfill their daydreams and fantasies but to provide a service for others (Moreton 2009). Overwhelmingly, Wal-Mart employees are female sales clerks (72%) who, according to Moreton (2009), foster an ethos of family and service. Unlike the early department stores, workers and customers tend to be from the same socioeconomic class, especially in more rural Wal-Mart locations (Moreton 2009:77). In fact, 42% of all purchases made at Wal-Mart stores are by individuals living in households making less than $40,000 per year (http://www.statisticbrain.com/wal-mart-company-statistics/). Wal-Mart has convinced its loyal patrons not only that their shopping is important for the care of their families but that it is providing a service to them in helping them achieve this care through offering low prices. Thus, part of the enchantment of Wal-Mart stores derives from how it cleverly has combined "Main Street values and the efficiencies of the huge corporation" (Moreton 2009:6).

Service Workers

Places of consumption could not function without the labor of service and retail workers, yet they are often treated as dispensable by both their employers and consumers. In the United States, service and retail workers are paid some of the lowest wages in the labor force, frequently working part-time and receiving no benefits. Many are forced to comply with on-call scheduling practices that give them little notice of whether or not they will even be permitted to work their shifts. While the owners of retail stores like Target, Gap, and Urban Outfitters can profit from on-call scheduling by not calling in workers when shopping traffic is slow, the workers themselves are left without the guarantee of wages for securely scheduled working hours (Weber 2015). Other retailers, like Starbucks, require service workers to close their stores late in the evening and then open them early in the morning, otherwise known as "clopening." With some stores closing as late as 11 p.m. and opening as early as 6 a.m., workers who "clopen" are asked to sacrifice their sleep in order to keep their jobs. Even more intrusive on employees' time, some places of consumption are now open on major holidays, like Thanksgiving. Although some individuals might prefer to work on such days, others are compelled to work instead of spending time with their friends and family.

In addition to low wages and job insecurity, retail and service workers are vulnerable to becoming victims of crime when they work in certain places of consumption. For example, more restaurant workers were murdered on the job than police officers in the United States in 1998, and fast-food restaurants are more likely to be robbed than banks. Since most robberies at fast-food restaurants occur early in the morning or late at night, those who must "clopen" these places of consumption may not be sacrificing just their sleep but also their lives. Instead of being victims, some retail and service workers might be tempted to become criminals themselves given their low wages, lack of respect, and easy access to cash and credit card numbers. One study found that the typical restaurant worker steals $218 per year, excluding food (Scholsser 2001:83–84).

Besides engaging in the physical demands of retail and service work, such as standing for long hours at a time, retail and services workers are obliged to perform what is called **emotional labor**. Emotional labor refers to how service and retail workers must manage their emotions when dealing with customers. This frequently involves faking emotions, such as smiling when one is not especially happy or acting calm when one is really anxious, as part of one's job requirements. Often these workers are not even permitted to express their own thoughts, forced to follow prescribed scripts that they must use when interacting with customers. The emotional labor required for some jobs becomes so overwhelming for some workers that they become detached and cynical, while others find it increasingly difficult to discern their work emotions from their true emotions (Hochschild 1983; Kivisto and Pittman 2010).

Questions

1. Do you think that places of consumption should be open on national holidays, like Thanksgiving? Why or why not? Be sure to provide the perspectives of both service workers and consumers in your answer.

2. Select a place of consumption and observe the interactions that occur between customers and service workers. Do these interactions appear scripted and controlled or genuine and spontaneous? If any kinds of emotions are displayed by workers and/or customers, how would you characterize them? How might customers help make the labor of service workers more meaningful?

3. Why do you think that places of consumption, such as movie theaters and fast-food restaurants, are sites of violence? What can be done to help protect both workers and consumers from this violence?

Amazon.com and E-Commerce

Amazon.com has taken implosion one step further than Wal-Mart by erasing the boundary between home and store via e-commerce or online shopping. Taking Sam Walton's business philosophy to the Internet, Amazon .com offers low prices and a wide variety of goods coupled with the convenience of 1-Click software that allows consumers to purchase products with just one click. This has shifted consumer gratification to the "act of making a purchase rather than taking possession of the thing you have bought" (Zukin 2004:234). Started by Jeff Bezos in 1995, the keys to Amazon.com's success are (1) its digital inventory, which is limitless; (2) its digital customer service, which is customized at the individual level; and (3) its prices, which are almost always the lowest—on average 15% lower than Wal-Mart. Using digital technology, Amazon.com can magically "reconfigure [its] virtual store based on daily or even hourly sales trends and individual customers' past buying behavior" (Thain and Bradley 2012:221). Personalized offers, customer reviews, free shipping on orders over $35, and the ability to virtually look inside products, like the table of contents of a book, are more strategies that Amazon.com has invented to make Internet shopping especially enchanting to consumers (Stone 2013; Thain and Bradley 2012). By reducing **transaction time** or the "brief interval from idea to purchase," Amazon.com and other e-commerce websites have made it much easier for consumers to spend their money by using on-screen prompts to **upsell,** or persuade us to put more into our virtual shopping carts (Vyse 2008:106; Zukin 2004:235–37). Jeff Boaz's proposal to use drones in the future to deliver orders placed on Amazon.com to customer's doorsteps within hours of purchasing is likely to make this virtual shopping experience even more magical.

Despite the fact that Amazon.com is the largest Internet company and cleared $61 billion in sales in 2012, its growth and operating profit margins have been relatively weak (Stone 2013). The company actually lost money in 2012, but its stock record reached a record high (Streitfeld 2013). Yet its popularly is undeniable as it had 137 million customers who made 900 million purchase orders from 320 billion monthly visits to its website in 2010 (Thain and Bradley 2012:220). Amazon.com is anticipating that its current popularity will build customer loyalty and translate into profits in the future, even if some of the enchanting features that make it popular, particularly free shipping and low prices, have resulted in the company losing money (Stone 2013). Future profits will likely be realized through raising shipping costs (which the company did in 2013 by raising the price for free shipping on orders from $25 to $35) and prices (Streitfeld 2013) in addition to its success at conquering brick-and-mortar discount stores. "While the chains shrink, Amazon grows," according to Brandt (2011). Like Wal-Mart, Amazon.com has been challenging the dominance of big-box stores. Chain bookstores in particular have been an easy prey for this category killer. For example, in 2010, Amazon.com's fourth quarter revenues grew by 36% to $12.95 billion and its profits increased 8% to $416 million, while during this same time period, Barnes & Noble's revenue grew by only 7% to $2.3 billion and its profits dropped 25% to $61 million (Brandt 2011:150). The big-box bookstore Borders was buried by Amazon .com in February 2011 when it filed for bankruptcy. With its endless supply of digital videos and music that can be easily streamed and watched on demand, Amazon.com has virtually killed most music and video rental stores. Hollywood Video closed in 2010, and Blockbuster has shuttered most of its physical stores to imitate Amazon.com's digital format.

According to J. P. Morgan, global e-commerce sales reached $820 trillion in 2012 and are increasing at a compound annual growth rate of 19.4.

While the 2010 online sales of the world's 100 largest retailers accounted for only 6.6% of their total sales on average, they are experiencing a trend of increasing online growth and decreasing traditional store-based transactions (Thain and Bradley 2012:216–17). Brick-and-mortar stores are trying to compete with e-commerce with a variety of consumer-friendly services. Wal-Mart, for example, allows customers to order items online and then pick them up at its stores in designated lockers. This is an important advantage considering that Wal-Mart has over 4,000 stores, some that are open 24 hours a day. Furthermore, Wal-Mart provides the opportunity for consumers without credit cards or bank accounts to place online orders and then pay from them in cash when they pick them up, catering to its lower income customers (Miller 2013). Wal-Mart has also created a mobile app that offers digital coupons to customers when they enter its stores and enables them to scan items as they are shopping for quick self-checkout. It is testing an app that directs consumers to where items they want are located. Shopping malls are also trying to make themselves "Internet proof" by offering more services for sale, like ceramic painting and cake decorating classes (Clifford 2012). Some are putting sensors in their parking lots and garages that allow customers to use their smartphones to easily find open spots and help them find their cars after a long day of shopping (Trop 2013).

Small brick-and-mortar businesses are also taking advantage of e-commerce, using online websites, like Boutiika, that help consumers find specialty boutiques and let them place products on hold to pick up or be delivered to their homes via a same-day courier service (Zimmerman 2013). Other strategies that small businesses are using to compete with Amazon.com and other e-commerce supersites include giving products in their stores different model names and labels to prevent shoppers from comparing prices online, carrying exclusive products, building relationships through devoted customer service, and refusing to sell products that can be found elsewhere at cheaper prices so as not to make potential customers perceive that all the products they offer are too expensive. Still, it is difficult for these small stores to truly challenge online supersites, like Amazon.com, Walmart.com, and Target.com, which combined received 70% of all e-commerce dollars spent during the 2013 holiday shopping season (Clifford and Miller 2012). Some small businesses have elected to not even try and, instead of embracing e-commerce, are fighting back against practices like **showrooming,** which is when consumers try on clothes in a physical store to find their right size but go home to order them online at a cheaper price (Goltz 2013). One small business owner has started a "Buy It Where You Try It" campaign to try to raise consumer awareness about how showrooming threatens the survival of local businesses (Clifford and Miller 2012).

Ironically, as many brick-and-mortar stores attempt to increase their presence online, Amazon.com is increasing its physical presence by building more warehouses to expedite its shipping. It has also placed lockers at physical stores, including 7-Eleven, Staples, and RadioShack, where customers can pick up items that they have ordered online (Miller and Clifford 2013). Amazon.com argues that instead of destroying small brick-and-mortar businesses, it is actually helping them by allowing them to sell products on its website through its Marketplace program. While businesses that participate in this program have to pay a percentage of their revenues to Amazon.com, they are able to take advantage of its large customer base, its 1-Click technology and search engines, and its assertive marketing (Clifford and Miller 2012). In sum, e-commerce is not eliminating all the physical places of consumption and cannot exist at the moment in a virtual vacuum free from the constraints of the material world. For instance, in the United States, consumers buy more than 90% of all their purchases offline (Himmelman 2013).

The Privatization of Public Space

One disturbing trend that all of the sites of consumption discussed in this chapter share is that they contribute to the increasing privatization of public space. According to Cohen (2004:70), "The most important public place," the shopping mall, "is now private." Shopping malls have attempted to become not just places of consumption but also of civic life in the suburbs, offering recreational activities, musical concerts, and meeting spaces for community organizations; some even include post offices, beauty salons, banks, and chapels (Cohen 2003:263). Even though shopping may be "one of the few activities that still bring all classes of people" (Zukin 2004:63) and malls are the "only place that many Americans encounter strangers" (Cohen 2004:70), it is important to recognize that these spaces are managed, monitored, and controlled by private entities, including security. It is not a stretch to claim that these places of consumption are contemporary **Panopticons,** disciplining consumers to behave in particular ways through constant surveillance. This surveillance is not just to protect the owners of the places of consumption from losing profits through shoplifting or vandalism but also to monitor the movements of consumers, tracking how they navigate these spaces and what they put in (and sometimes take out) of their shopping carts. Stores as varied as Nordstrom, Family Dollar, and Cabela's are testing technology that tracks customers' movements through Wi-Fi signals on their smartphones, stating that the data it collects will help them change store layouts and offer customized coupons (Clifford and Hardy 2013). At the register, purchases are recorded and stored, with preferences sorted and categorized to predict future purchases. Some stores are even using facial recognition technology on customers with the motive of offering them better, more personalized services (Singer 2014).

The increasing privatization of public space is not surprising, especially in suburbia, where concerns about safety are often exaggerated. Less recognized is that it is funded by federal government subsidies. From backing home mortgage loans to building the highways to transport suburbanites, public subsidies gave rise to private space that became segregated by socioeconomic class and race (Cohen 2003; Hayden 2006). Government mortgage guarantees to private lenders through the Federal Housing Administration (FHA) resulted in a real estate boom after World War II and made the suburban house one of the pivotal objects of consumption, constituting an essential component of the American Dream (Vyse 2008). However, this dream was not easily obtainable for everyone, especially people of color. The FHA supported **redlining** policies by banks, which explicitly stated that people of color brought down property values and encouraged **white flight** from the cities and older, inner-ring suburbs to the new, outer-ring suburbs. As the suburbs became increasingly white and affluent, the cities became increasingly black and poor with limited tax bases to provide funding for critical resources, such as quality public schools and efficient public transportation.

Over time, like the suburbs where they are located, shopping malls have become stratified by class and race. Some cater to the upper-middle class, while others cater to the working class; however, all exclude the poor and those without access to automobiles, an aspect that has come to define the scope of privatized public space (Cohen 2003:288). Thus, unlike the early department stores in cities where all classes had access to the space (although not to all of the items for sale), newer spaces of consumption are especially exclusionary. **Consumer racism** is also experienced in these privatized spaces of consumption. People of color are often racially profiled by sales clerks and store security guards, who they suspect are more likely to shoplift or use fraudulent credit cards than white consumers. One survey found that 86% of African Americans believed that they had been treated differently in retail stores because of their race, while another study confirmed this belief, finding that they wait longer for customer service than whites (Williams, Henderson, and Harris 2005).

While consumers might have an expectation that enclosed spaces of consumption are private spaces that are often physically patrolled by private security guards, they may be less aware of this in the new festival marketplaces that more closely simulate traditional public squares and downtowns with their "New Urbanist" style (Cohen 2004:77). With their sidewalks, outdoor cafes, and green spaces, not to mention names that usually include the word *park, village,* or *commons,* it is not surprising that people might believe that these seemingly free spaces are inclusive and democratic. However, like their enclosed cousins, these newer shopping malls are environments that ensure "safety, cleanliness, and order" and are "carefully designed to exclude any source of discomfort" (Cohen 2004:69, 75). While all shopping malls may "represent membership of a community of consumers" and permit the consumer to be "recognized as a citizen in contemporary society," they do not tolerate public debate or protest (Urry 2002:133). These "domesticated" spaces are family-friendly and safe (Miller et al. 1998:92) with the power to remove any people or ideas that threaten their image.

Consumers might also be more likely to ignore the Panopticon effect of Internet shopping. The freedom of shopping anywhere has been coupled with a decrease of privacy as our **cookie crumbs,** or navigational browsing histories, are carefully tracked, stored, and analyzed by marketers and advertisers. Indeed, some of our cookies magically appear to us on a variety of websites to entice us to consume products that we recently looked at or put in our virtual shopping carts but did not purchase. Amazon.com is planning on using these data to predict our future purchases through what it calls **anticipatory shopping.** According to Welch (2014), "It may box and ship products that it expects customers in a specific area will want, based on previous orders and other factors it gleans from its customers' shopping patterns, even before they place an online order." Furthermore, shopping online in our homes may feel private and secure, but digital thieves can steal our identity almost as easily as the marketers can track our purchases. Clearly, surveillance is pervasive in all of the places of consumption we enter, even the seemingly private space of our homes. Perhaps this constant gaze and lack of privacy provide a sense of security for contemporary shoppers, who also seem to prefer the security offered in privatized places of consumption.

Conclusion

Consumers may be growing wary of implosion. Supercenters are becoming so big that consumers are forced to waste time as they navigate these enormous spaces just to find one specific item. Even though the Internet does "minimize the social space of shopping," it ironically does not actually save us time, even though most consumers think it does (Thain and Bradley 2012:218; Zukin 2004:244). Turning homes into sites of consumption through the Internets makes shopping an isolating experience for some consumers, and the invasive presence of technology causes others feel like they are trapped in an **iron cage** of formal rationality. According to Ritzer (2013), the process of McDonaldization inevitably results in irrationality, such as long lines at fast-food drive-thru windows and the dehumanization of workers and consumers who are encouraged to engage in scripted interactions. Furthermore, the hyperconsumption that is supported in these places of consumption has resulted in financial debt and bankruptcy for many consumers (Vyse 2008).

But, it would be unwise to attribute overarching power to the new places of consumption. **Localization,** or how ordinary people experience everyday life in specific locations, is an important process to consider in the places of consumption described in this chapter (Watson 2006:9). According to Watson (2000:131), "Local citizens have appropriated private property and converted it into public space," including privately owned places of consumption. For example, some elderly consumers subvert the principles of McDonaldization at fast-food restaurants by turning them into de facto senior community centers, hanging out in them for hours at a time to socialize or read a book (Torres 2014). Miller et al. (1998:3–4) remind us that consumption spaces are not mere "passive backdrops" but spaces with "their own properties which could intervene in the construction of difference." Zukin (2005:265) argues that individuals can reappropriate the new spaces of consumption and that they offer a space that allows the possibility of "discussion and debate." Places of consumption can and have been used as sites of protests, whether it be negotiating gender roles in grocery stores (Deutsch 2010) or boycotting Wal-Mart for unfair labor practices (Dreier 2013). Indeed, these **third places** that are neither our homes nor our workplaces have served an important role in the creation and maintenance of civil society insofar as they have been inclusive, like coffee shops and taverns (Oldenberg 1989; Outram 2013). Finally, it would be remiss to acknowledge that many people simply enjoy places of consumption because they are fun, which is also why some of them find pleasure in being prosumers (Ritzer and Jugrenson 2010).

PART II

Applying the Conceptual Framework

Case Studies

5

Food

While seemingly ordinary and part of our daily routines, food occupies a unique position in the realm of consumption. Clearly, we all need to consume food to survive; however, our choice of what food to consume, when to consume it, and where to consume it is riddled with political, cultural, and social implications. The social significance of food can be understood from a structuralist or materialist perspective (Wood 1995). **Structuralists,** such as Roland Barthes, Mary Douglas, and Claude Levi-Strauss, posit that the symbolic meaning of food is produced from relational differences. Food, according to structuralists, is like a language with its own grammar or code. For example, Levi-Strauss (1964) argued that food could be understood in general terms of binary oppositions, such as food that is raw as opposed to food that is cooked. Mary Douglas preferred to examine how food is "the medium through which a system of relationships within the family is expressed" (Wood 1995:13). Power relations within the family, for instance, are exposed by what member is served first or receives the largest portion. **Materialists** study the historical development of food customs and tastes. Stephen Mennell's work demonstrates that over time, the variety of food we can choose to consume has increased, resulting in the growth of **culinary pluralism**. Norbert Elias focused more on how we eat, connecting the evolution of mealtime etiquette to the self-restraint that was characteristic of what he called the civilizing process (Ashley et al. 2005; Wood 1995).

This chapter will incorporate both structuralist and materialist perspectives in analyzing food as an object, the subjects who consume food, and the places where we shop for, prepare, and eat food. First, the production of food will be explained through three specific food systems: the industrial, the organic, and the local. Next, the use of food by individuals to display their identities will be explored, particularly in relation to social status or lifestyle and economic class. The importance of using food to create and maintain group boundaries and gender relations in the family will be addressed as well. Finally, where we buy, prepare, and eat our food will be discussed. The social implications of eating in compared to dining out will be considered in addition to the development of the supermarket.

Food as an Object of Consumption

Industrial Food Chain

"Any food whose provenance is so complex or obscure that it requires expert help to ascertain" is part of the industrial food chain (Pollan 2006:17). According to Pollan, the industrial food chain tries to "obscure the histories of foods it produces by processing them to such an extent that they appear as pure products of culture instead of nature" (2006:115). For example, one would be hard-pressed to find any resemblance between a chicken nugget and a real chicken breast or thigh. As Pollan states, the chicken nugget is just a "boneless abstraction" that is completely divorced from the animal it is named after not just by its appearance but also because of the 38 ingredients it contains, only one of which is chicken (2006:113–14). It is tempting to use quotations when discussing industrial "food" because of the synthetic ingredients that constitute it, such as tertiary butylhydroquinone (TBHQ), a form of butane that is frequently sprayed on processed food or the boxes it comes in to preserve freshness. In addition to chemicals, corn is a key ingredient of the industrial food chain. Corn and its derivatives are used in almost all processed food, often in the form of high-fructose corn syrup found in soda, ketchup, cereal, and bread (Pollan 2006). If processed food is mostly made up of corn and synthetic chemicals, then what makes it taste so good to so many consumers? According to Moss, the industrial food chain carefully combines salt, sugar, and fat to create bliss points that "send consumers over the moon" (2013:xxv). The corporations that control the industrial food chain are addicted to salt, sugar, and fat because these ingredients are cheap and they can be cleverly adjusted to meet shifting dietary trends. For example, when fat became their nemesis, these corporations reduced the amount of fat and increased the amount of sugar and salt in their processed foods without changing the taste.

Corn is used not only to produce processed food but also to feed cattle and other animals that are raised in **concentrated animal feed operations** (CAFOs) and supply humans with meat and dairy products. CAFOs are essentially animal factories, some warehousing hundreds of thousands of animals in cramped quarters where they often cannot move. Not surprisingly, this concentration of animals is not particularly healthy for animals or the humans who eventually consume them. This is exasperated by feeding cattle a diet of corn, which they cannot digest very well and weakens their immune systems, requiring that they be given antibiotics. In addition, many of these animals are given growth hormones to promote faster growth and speed up their "production." Many of these cattle carry *Escherichia coli*, and any bacterial contamination that remains after slaughter must be irradiated to disinfect the meat. Thus, humans who consume this meat are exposed to not only hormones and antibiotics but also possible side effects of irradiation. Corn-fed meat contains higher levels of saturated fat, which can lead to numerous health problems, particularly heart disease (Pollan 2006:70–82). Besides these public health concerns, CAFOs are viewed by many as an especially inhumane way to treat animals as profits and efficiency are prioritized over care and comfort.

The industrial food chain is controlled by **agribusiness,** which in the words of Harvard business professor John H. Davis, who helped coin this term in the 1950s, has made modern agriculture "inseparable from the business firms which manufacture production supplies and which market farm products" (Hamilton 2009:23). Agribusiness in North America is dominated by three firms—ConAgra/DuPont, Cargill/Monsanto, and Novartis/ADM—which have monopoly-like control over the vertical integration of production, owning inputs, including fertilizers and seeds; farms; grain collection and milling; production and processing of beef, pork, and poultry; and supermarket shelves. Agribusiness also has concentrated control within each of these inputs. For example, only four companies control almost 70% of the North American seed corn market and 80% of beef packing in the United States (Halweil 2000:20). Agribusiness operates via the logic of an economy of size, producing large quantities of relatively inexpensive food. However, this economy of size is not entirely rational. On one hand, the staple crops that dominate agribusiness—corn and soybeans—are subsidized by the federal government. In 2012, these subsidies topped $2.7 billion for corn and $1.5 billion for soybeans (http://farm.ewg.org).

On the other hand, in order for farmers to make any profit at all, they must keep increasing agricultural yields, which results in cheaper prices—and lower profits. This creates a variety of irrational outcomes, including overproduction, an increasing number of farmers losing their land and declaring bankruptcy, and environmental degradation due to the large quantity of fertilizer needed to grow crops in overused soil (Pollan 2006:53–54). Of course, these irrationalities can be understood as **negative externalities,** costs that are incurred by the public, not agribusiness.

Organic Food Chain

Unlike the industrial food chain, the organic food chain is based on natural inputs instead of chemical ones and allows "more information to pass along the food chain between the produce and the consumer" (Pollan 2006:136). Historically, the organic food chain started out as a countercultural movement founded on the ideals of "food, health, and soil" and was strongly opposed to the practices of agribusiness, especially synthetic fertilizers, pesticides, and ingredients (Fromartz 2006:12). The spark that revolutionized the organic food movement from the fringes to the mainstream was the Alar pesticide scare in 1989. Alar was a pesticide sprayed on apples that was found to turn into a carcinogen when heated to make juice and applesauce, products that were consumed in large quantities by children (Fromartz 2006:4). The Environmental Protection Agency (EPA) quickly banned Alar, and in 1990, the federal government passed the Organic Food and Production Act (OFPA) to regulate the certification and labeling of organic food and products. Now valued at $11 billion, the organic food chain is the fastest growing sector of the U.S. food economy (Pollan 2006; Fromartz 2006). Some of the most significant standards for organic food established by the OFPA include that (1) no pesticides are used on crops; (2) livestock is fed organic food, cannot be given growth hormones, or be raised in overcrowded conditions and can only be given antibiotics if they are sick; and (3) organic food cannot be packaged in anything that contains synthetic chemicals or preservatives. Interestingly, the organic label does not specify any human health benefits, which was found in one survey to be the most important motivation for 70% to 80% of organic shoppers (Fromartz 2006:240).

Absurdly, industrial food corporations were key players in the creation of the OFPA, which is why it did not go far enough in prohibiting all additives and synthetic ingredients. This is one reason why it is possible to have a certified organic Twinkie. Processed organic food needs synthetics, which is why 38 synthetic ingredients have been approved for use, but these nonorganic ingredients can only constitute 5% of a product to be certified as organic. A product can be labeled "made with organic ingredients" if at least 70% of these ingredients are organic. The inclusion of synthetic ingredients is significant because processed organic food products, including snack foods and drinks, account for almost one-third of total organic food sales (Fromartz 2006:205–6). Furthermore, some of the language of the OFPA is not well defined, like "access to pasture." Thousands of chickens, for example, may be housed together, but if they have access to a door that permits them to use open land, then they may be labeled organic, even if none of them ever use the door (Pollan 2006:154–57). This issue was particularly contentious regarding dairy cows because of the popularity of organic milk. Opponents of dairy cows primarily raised in CAFOs but granted occasional access to grass argued that labeling their milk organic was an insult to the principles of the organic food movement; they eventually won a battle to change "access to pasture" to "grazing on pasture during the growing season" (Fromartz 2006:233).

Some critiques argue that what started out as a subcultural movement has become an agribusiness, with some firms monopolizing specific segments of the organic market. Earthbound Farm produces 80% of all organic lettuce sold in the United States, and Horizon controls 50% of the organic dairy market (Pollan 2006). Moreover, agribusinesses associated with the industrial food chain are becoming players in the organic market. General Mills owns Cascadian Farm, and ConAgra and ADM now have organic brands (Pollan 2006). Many followers of the organic movement view corporate monopolization and agribusiness co-opting of organic as destroying the ideals it was based on, especially the ethical concerns with healthy food and sustainable farming (Hahn and Bruner 2012; Strom 2012). As organic food has made its way into the mainstream American supermarket, many consumers who purchase it do not really care about where it came from or how it was grown (Hahn and Bruner 2012). Indeed, some argue that the organic food chain is increasingly characterized by a **moralistic hedonism,** which attracts mostly affluent and educated consumers interested in health and nutrition with aesthetically pleasing packaging and stores, like Whole Foods (Fromartz 2006:238).

Local Food Chain

The local food chain aims to go beyond the organic one by emphasizing food that is produced, distributed, and consumed on a small-scale, regional basis. Local food is "rooted in a perennial polyculture," grown on small farms that practice biodiversity and use few mechanical inputs (Pollan 2006:198). Instead of synthetic chemicals and corn, the local food chain is founded on solar power and grass (Pollan 2006). The local food chain favors transparency and community—knowing who grows food, where and how food is grown, and forming collaborative relationships, such as a local brewery using ingredients that customers forage in the woods to make craft beer (Beckham 2014). Schrank suggests that the local food chain is characterized by **commodity de-fetishization,** "a process that requires transparency, honest information, and an affinity between producers and consumers" (2014:157). While participants in the local food movement, or **locavores,** are not opposed to organic food, some are skeptical of how environmentally friendly it really is given the fossil fuel necessary to transport it. Others are more libertarian in ideology and do not trust government agencies or want to be bound by federal regulations for organic certification (Pollan 2006). According to Pollan, "Local food, as opposed to organic, implies a new economy as well as a new agriculture—new social and economic relationships as well as ecological ones (2006:257). Compared to the industrial and organic food chains, the local food chain resists economic growth at the expense of nature and community and aims for local **food sovereignty,** which is achieved when individuals have control over the production of their own food and food choices, not distant actors. Schrank argues that "localism is all about looking inward in the market instead of outward and expanding" and building "cultural and economic integration with the surrounding community" (2014:151).

The local food chain is constrained by seasonality and availability. Certain foods are only available locally during specific times of the year, and it can be difficult for consumers to find as it is mainly available at farms, farmers' markets, through becoming a member of a community-supported agriculture (CSA) program, or dining at a local restaurant that serves food made with local ingredients. But these challenges are part of the reason that consumers support and find enjoyment in the local food chain. From getting to know the farmer who grows their food to learning how to can tomatoes to sharing recipes with their neighbors, locavores are discovering that participating in the local food chain is a rewarding way to spend their time and money (Moore 2006). Outlets to purchase local food are growing, especially farmers' markets, which have increased from 1,755 in 1994 to 8,144 in 2013 (http://www.ams.usda.gov/AMSv1.0/ams.fetchTemplateData.do? template=TemplateS&leftNav=WholesaleandFarmersMarkets&page=WF MFarmersMarketGrowth&description=Farmers%20Market%20Growth).

Membership in CSAs has also increased in the United States, with more than 12,000 farms offering such programs in 2007 (http://www.nal.usda .gov/afsic/pubs/csa/csa.shtml). CSAs require members to purchase shares in a farm, usually between $200 and $500, and in return receive a weekly box of seasonal produce that they pick up at a predetermined location, often a church or library in their community. CSA farmers often invite members to visit the farm itself and host tours and tastings for educational and social purposes (Thompson and Coskuner-Balli 2007). Some CSA programs have expanded their offerings to include meats, cheeses, eggs, nuts, honey, soap, and other locally made goods, which allow them to operate into the winter months. The twist with CSAs is that members do not get to decide what is in their weekly allotment, and there is no guarantee that they will receive anything at all if produce is destroyed because of flooding, droughts, or pests.

Raw Milk

In the word of food critic and activist Michael Pollan (2006), "Eating is a political act." This is perhaps most evident when purchasing a specific food product that is against the law, like raw milk. Raw milk is unpasteurized, containing bacteria that some governments maintain endanger public health. In particular, fecal matter is often present in raw milk, which can contaminate it with deadly bacteria like *E. coli*, *Listeria*, and salmonella. In the United States, the Federal Drug Administration (FDA) prohibits the interstate sale and distribution of raw milk, while many individual states ban the sale of raw milk within its borders. Consumers who desire to drink raw milk in some states can join a herd-sharing program, which requires that they purchase a share of a cow, thereby owning the milk that they consume.

Advocates of raw milk argue that pasteurization kills not just harmful bacteria but also beneficial bacteria that may actually make us healthier. Although lacking solid scientific evidence to support their claims, raw milk advocates believe that people who consume raw milk suffer from fewer allergies and digestive issues, including lactose intolerance. More generally, raw milk advocates argue that government food safety policies have resulted in food becoming overly processed. Furthermore, these regulations overwhelmingly support the industrial food chain over organic and local ones and might even encourage unsanitary practices in the industrial food chain. For example, raw milk

(Continued)

(Continued)

cows are usually grass fed and pasture raised, which means they often have fewer pathogens and therefore do not need antibiotics to keep them healthy or pasteurization to make their milk safe for human consumption. Industrial dairy cows are often confined inside manure-filled quarters and fed inexpensive grain-based diets, which they cannot naturally digest easily and weaken their overall health. However, industrial dairy farmers do not have to worry about the health of their livestock because pasteurization can "clean" their dirty practices (Goodyear 2012; Johnson 2008).

Perhaps more revealing than specific food products that the FDA has banned are those that it deems safe that other countries have either prohibited or restricted. Australia and New Zealand both prohibit farm-raised salmon because of the excessive use of antibiotics needed to raise them. The European Union and Japan both ban brominated vegetable oil (BVO), a flame retardant, that is used as an emulsifier in processed citrus beverages. However, due to consumer pressure over potential health risks, both Coca-Cola and Pepsi have agreed to voluntarily stop using BVO in their beverages in the near future (Associated Press 2014). Genetically modified foods are either prohibited or restricted in many countries and must be labeled. The FDA refuses to even label genetically modified foods, much less ban them, because it considers them to be the nutritional equivalent of its natural counterparts. Without mandatory labeling, this puts American consumers at a disadvantage if they want to avoid genetically modified foods. It also displays the bias of the FDA toward the industrial food chain, which primarily consists of genetically modified foods that are patented and thereby owned by agribusiness.

Questions

1. Weighing the pros and cons of raw milk, would you be willing to try it? Why or why not? If you have consumed raw milk, discuss how it is different from or similar to pasteurized milk.

2. Given its implicit support for the industrial food chain, how much oversight should the government have over our food choices? Why?

3. Do you think mandatory labeling of genetically modified foods should be required in the United States? Would knowing that the cereal you eat every morning or the salmon that you eat for dinner is genetically modified dissuade you from eating it? Why or why not?

The local food chain is promoted by advocates of the **slow food movement** (Pietrykowski 2004). Founded in 1986 by Italian Carlo Petrini to protest the opening of a McDonald's restaurant near Rome's Spanish Steps, slow food "seeks to establish a universal society based on 'educated pleasure'" by supporting local, traditional food and artisan products (Lindholm and Lie 2013:56). Symbolized by a snail, slow food supporters emphasize that our fast-paced world is making us too stressed and anxious and that by slowing down, we can learn how to reconnect not just with the food we eat but with each other as well (Honoré 2004; Tam 2008). Slow food also embraces **eco-gastronomy** or the idea that "eating well can, and should, go hand in hand with protecting the environment" and that meals should be leisurely adventures in culinary flavors to be prepared and consumed with others (Honoré 2004:59). Currently, there are over 100,000 official members of the slow food movement in over 100 countries; however, these members tend to be upper-middle-class Caucasians who live in metropolitan areas. Many argue that the slow food movement and the local food chain that it supports needs to be more inclusive and reach out to lower-income individuals and people of color. Prices, preparation, storage, distribution, and lack of knowledge are just a few issues that have been recognized as being barriers of entry to the local food chain for those with limited financial resources (Donati 2005; localFoodconnection.org; Parkins and Craig 2009). These issues affect not just individuals but also the government programs that serve them, including cafeteria lunches at public schools and where food stamps can be used (localFoodconnection.org). As the next section of this chapter discusses, socioeconomic class is one of many boundaries created and reproduced by our access to food and our food preferences.

Food and the Subjects of Consumption

Class and Status Relations

According to Sidney Mintz, food is a "symbolic marker of membership . . . groups characteristically employ food to draw lines, confirm statuses, and separate those who do, and do not, belong" (2002:26). One's food preferences or taste are a reflection of socioeconomic class and cultural capital (Bourdieu 1984). "Food consumption, like other forms of consumption, is a site of class struggle in which the middle classes have a better opportunity to capitalize on their assets" (Ashley et al. 2005:66).

It is not just what we eat but how we eat it that signals class distinctions. Manners are one way "how social prestige and power are negotiated between people," reflecting "what is acceptable and proper" (Finkelstein 1989:127). According to Elias, manners were an important part of the **civilizing process,** or how we internalize social expectations and convert them into "self restraints" (2000:230). For instance, class is produced and reproduced through meals. According to Bourdieu, working-class meals emphasize quantity with food that can be served with spoons and without strict measurements, like soup. An "economy of comfort" is accomplished through serving all the food for the meal simultaneously and assuming that each person will use the same plate throughout the meal. In contrast, middle-class families have strict rules on portion size and stress-delayed gratification by serving courses that are sequenced, requiring a variety of plates and utensils to be used throughout the meal (Wood 1995:20–21).

Ashley et al. argue that members of the middle class today are most distinguished by the variety of foods that they consume in addition to how they consume them, using their economic and cultural capital to become **cultural omnivores** (2005:70). These cultural omnivores confidently negotiate the "cultural spaces of gourmet food" that are coming to define the contemporary foodscape and equally enjoy eating working-class fare and haute cuisine (Johnston and Baumann 2010:2). According to Johnston and Baumann, these **foodies** are members of a food culture that is democratic in regard to exploration and access but exclusionary because a certain level of economic capital is required to fully participate. Anyone can go into a Whole Foods Market to browse at the wide selection of gourmet cheeses and wines, but few can afford the high price of these goods—at least on a weekly or monthly basis. Indeed, one study found that the equivalent food bought at Wal-Mart cost $340 less than at Whole Foods (Johnston and Baumann 2010:28). However, this is not to deny that gourmet food is inaccessible to the majority of consumers to enjoy at least occasionally, like a cup of Starbuck's coffee (Johnston and Baumann 2010:27). Silverstein and Fiske (2008) argue that premium products today are more widely available than in the past and that the majority of consumers trade up or spend more on premium products that matter to them regardless of income. If you care about organic milk but not organic laundry detergent, then you will trade up for the organic milk but purchase lower priced, nonorganic laundry detergent. Thus, it is not uncommon to find higher-income people shopping for bulk toilet paper at Wal-Mart or middle-income purchasing organic apples at Whole Foods.

Social class also plays a role in the decision to focus on nutrition or efficiency when making food choices. According to Koch and Sprague (2014:243), professional, middle-class mothers prioritize purchasing healthy food, while working-class and part-time working mothers are more concerned with saving money. The problem is that "efficient shopping isn't necessarily healthy" as lower priced food items are often processed with high fat, salt, and sugar content (Koch 2012:108). While the price of processed foods supplied by the industrial food chain has decreased since the 1980s, the price of fresh fruits and vegetables has increased 40% (Nestle 2013:95). **Food deserts** or "areas where there is little or no access to healthy and affordable food" are a structural obstacle preventing many lower-class individuals from purchasing nutritious food in the neighborhoods where they reside (Karpyn and Treuhaft 2010:7). According to the U.S. Department of Agriculture (USDA), approximately 23.5 million Americans resided in food deserts in 2009, mostly those living in low-income areas, communities of color, or rural locations (Karpyn and Treuhaft 2010:7). Lower-income zip codes have 30% more convenient/corner/liquor stores than middle-class zip codes, few transportation options to reach stores with healthy food items, and more fast-food restaurants in urban areas (Karpyn and Treuhaft 2010:8; LeGreco, Greene, and Shaw 2014). Many people who live in food deserts suffer from **food insecurity** because they do not have a consistent supply of food or know when they will eat their next meal (Silverbush and Jacobson 2013). Households receiving federal government food aid through the Supplemental Nutrition Assistance Program (SNAP) increased from 12.7 million to 18.6 million between 2008 and 2010, but the average monthly benefit is only $289.61 per household or approximately $3 per day per individual (Koch 2012:105). While it makes sense for SNAP recipients to buy inexpensive vegetables like cabbage and potatoes or dry beans in bulk, if they live in food deserts, they may not have the option. Furthermore, even if less expensive nutritional foods are available, it takes time and knowledge to prepare them, which they may not possess (LeGreco, Greene, and Shaw 2014).

One must be cautious when positioning food deserts as a problem determined by access to supermarkets. Alkon et al. surveyed 581 poor individuals who live in urban food deserts and found that proximity to a supermarket was less important than the price of food when making food choices. They argue that focusing on access to supermarkets ignores the **foodways** of the poor, or the "cultural and social practices that affect our food consumption, including how and what communities eat, where and how they shop, and what motivates their food preferences" (Alkon et al. 2012:127). In particular, they found that poor people have relatively strong culinary skills and cook at home an average of five days per week. In addition, poor people value sharing food and often eat with friends and family, which challenges the individualist act of eating promoted by the USDA's food pyramid. Finally, the poor people they interviewed left their neighborhoods at least once a month to shop at supermarkets and used their social networks to overcome transportation obstacles.

Ethnic and National Identities

Food symbolizes not only socioeconomic class but also ethnic and national identities. According to Barthes, "Food has properties that allow people to have daily involvement in their national past," such as the French through eating steak and *pomme frites* (Wood 1995:15). Rituals surrounding the consumption of food, like the British Sunday lunch, function to produce and maintain ethnic and national identities. National cuisines can cultivate feelings of unity and a sense of belonging or an **imagined community** that helps to connect citizens to a particular nation-state (Ashley et al. 2005:71, 79). These sentiments may even transcend national borders and help immigrants in the diaspora preserve their ties to their homelands. Using food to construct ethnic and national identities fosters not just feelings of inclusion but also difference as food acts to mark group boundaries (Gabaccia 2000). For example, eating pork signifies to others that one is not Jewish or Muslim. In the words of Douglas, "The social act of sharing a meal both maintains and disrupts significant group boundaries" (Guptill, Copelton, and Lucal 2013:35).

While ethnic and national cuisines can be difficult to change entirely (Mintz 2002), the food choices and preferences available to individuals are becoming increasingly hybrid as a result of immigration, international travel, and global capitalism. Individuals in different nations are appropriating cultural goods, like food, music, and art, from each other and in the process making these goods their own. Although the British are attached to their national cuisine of roast beef and fish and chips, they are more likely to eat tikka masala on a daily basis, transforming it into a British dish (Ashley et al. 2005:79). Likewise, children in China who have grown up with McDonald's do not view it as American but as part of their own culture (Watson 2000). Indeed, Probyn (1998:161) argues that on a global scale, McDonald's is "shaping and fueling a climate of good citizenship" as it provides a "universality" that connects people together across different nations. Even though the food options between different nations seem to be decreasing or becoming more homogeneous, the menu of food choices within different nations is continuing to expand. So, while almost every country in the world has a McDonald's, it is only one of a wide variety of restaurants to choose to eat at. As Cowen (2004) explains, diversity within societies is increasing, while diversity across societies is decreasing. Thus, in regards to food choices, globalization has not resulted in **cultural imperialism** or the cultural norms and values of one society dominating the entire world. Chapter 11 discusses the relationship between globalization and consumer culture in more detail.

Warde (2000) describes four processes that characterize the cultural diffusion of ethnic food: preservation, naturalization, improvisation, and authentication. On one hand, ethnic food can be used to preserve and maintain traditional identities and lifestyles, such as **gastronationalism** or the "use of food production, distribution, and consumption to demarcate and sustain the emotive power of national attachment, as well as the use of national sentiments to produce and market food" (DeSoucey 2010:433). In an effort to confront globalization and regional integration, some nations have become quite protective of their distinctive cuisines and ingredients, like the French with foie gras. Several countries have been granted Protected Designation of Origin and Protected Geographic Indication labels endorsed by the European Union to preserve their unique food, including Kalamata olives from Greece and Clare Island salmon from Ireland (DeSoucey 2010:437–38). One the other hand, ethnic food can be naturalized and adjusted to match local taste, such as making a dish less spicy. Adding foreign ingredients to ethnic food or improvising makes it increasingly hybrid, but it can also remain authentic without catering to local taste. The latter process may attract foodies looking for exotic eating experiences and immigrants looking for traditional dishes prepared with ingredients from their homelands.

Food and the Places of Consumption

Eating In

Mennell and Elias describe how eating at home has evolved over time, including the utensils that we use to eat food, the portions of food served, and the sequence in which dishes are served (Wood 1995). Traditionally, eating food at home was situated within the family. In her studies, Douglas found that hot meals represented closeness and provided familial stability, while Murcott learned that a "cooked meal" was "central to the well-being of the family" in his study of families in South Wales (Wood 1995:52–53). In general a "home-cooked" meal is more likely to evoke feelings of warmth and comfort than industrialized food; processed and prepared foods lack the nutrition and care that are part of a "proper" home-cooked meal (Ashley et al. 2005:124–25). According to Charles and Kerr, four components comprise a "proper meal": a "structured menu, mannered rituals, nuclear family companionship, and housewifely provision" (Warde and Martens 2000:106). DeVault (1991) reminds us that a meal is not simply about cooking food but all the other unpaid labor that goes into the provisioning of food, from making shopping lists and planning daily meals to setting the table and washing dishes.

Gendered relations in particular are accomplished and negotiated through provisioning, preparing, serving, and eating meals at home. Women are overwhelmingly responsible for **social reproduction** or those activities that are concerned with "procreation, socialization, sexuality, nurturance, and family maintenance" (Abramovitz 2010:15). According to the U.S. Department of Labor, 65% of women do all the grocery shopping, and 68% prepare meals for households (Koch 2012:14). However, "women frequently use food to offer family members pleasure yet have difficulty experiencing food as pleasurable themselves, particularly in a domestic context" (Ashley et al. 2005:129). The fact the women typically select what food is to be served for meals does not necessarily give them authority, especially if they have to balance the preferences of their children and husband with the cost of food. Furthermore, women are often blamed if they do not cook meals, which others interpret as a sign that they are neglecting their duty of care. If their children are obese, then it is because their mothers did not cook nutritious meals for them or cultivate their taste for healthy food preferences (Ashley et al. 2005). Thus, as Wood (1995:55) points out, choosing food for the family may be more of a burden than an act of power. Additional gender inequalities at a meal may be reflected by a woman serving the males of the household first and herself last or giving herself and other females at the table smaller portions than the males (Wood 1995).

Several new trends are being witnessed in regards to dining in. The meaning of a "proper meal" is changing to include meals that use partially processed and manufactured ingredients instead of just those that are made from scratch. Delivery food has even been found to be suitable for a family meal as long as the meal itself is ritualized. Some families do not even think that sitting down together defines a proper meal anymore—as long as prepared food is consumed in the home, it is okay if individual family members eat separately. The younger generation is not very concerned about maintaining the tradition of homemade meals, with some preferring food cooked outside the home, like hamburgers and pizzas, to the same items made at home (Moisio, Arnould, and Price 2004; Rawlins and Livert 2014). Even though women remain the ones who most frequently cook and shop for food in their households, these new "eating in" trends reflect the changing role of women in the public sphere. As more women are working full-time outside of the home, the expectations of the duties they perform in the private sphere are starting to change.

Dining Out

Americans spend half of their food money eating out, and 25% of them purchase fast food daily, amounting to $100 billion in 2000, which is more than they spent on higher education, automobiles, and personal computers (Schlosser 2001:3). More specifically, one in three children in the United States eats fast food daily (Pollan 2006:109). The fast-food industry is organized by the principles of formal rationality, or what Ritzer (2013) calls **McDonaldization.** These principles include efficiency, calculability, predictability, and technological control. Consumers want to get their food as quickly and conveniently as possible, making fast food the most efficient way from being hungry to being full. They also want to get as much food for as little money as possible, and fast food is the most calculating way to accomplish this. Many consumers find comfort in the fact that fast food is predictable or the same across time and space—the hamburger that they ate as a child in Chicago is the same as the one they can eat as an adult in London. Controlling fast-food workers and consumers with technology is the most formally rational way to achieve efficiency, calculability, and predictability. Workers are deskilled and almost robotic as they just push a button to take orders, and consumers hardly need to think as they order their food using meal numbers ("I'll take the number 1 with a Coke") and pay for it with a swipe of their credit card. But, as Ritzer highlights, these formally rational principles of the fast-food industry have unintended, irrational consequences. Fast food makes us unhealthy, its production is environmentally unsustainable as rainforests are turned into cattle ranches, and fast-food restaurants are dehumanizing, stifling human sociability and worker creativity.

Many scholars have commented on the social performances of customers, servers, and even chefs that take place when dining out and how the **meal experience** of eating out is not just about food but décor, ambience, and lightning (Campbell-Smith 1967; Fine 2008; Finkelstein 1989; Wood 1995). According to Finkelstein, dining out is a form of uncivilized sociality because restaurants "encourage certain styles of interaction that render dining out a mannered act" (1989:106). Servers and customers follow predictable scripts that make their social interactions insincere, yet customers want restaurants to "satisfy deeper emotional desires for status and belonging" (Finkelstein 1989:105). Indeed, these desires are turned into impersonal commodities, leaving the customer with a feeling of detachment and the server with a sense of alienation as he or she is forced to engage in emotional labor to earn a living (Fine 2008; Hochschild 1983). According to Ehrenreich (2001:35), "Customers are in fact the major obstacle to the smooth transformation of information [i.e., orders] into food and food into money." Servers, of course, must at least act like they are enjoying their jobs and their interactions with customers if they want to receive tips. Not only do servers have to engage in emotional labor when dealing with customers, but they also have to mediate disputes between customers and chefs. For example, chefs get annoyed when customers return their food or do not eat it, while customers get irritated if the chef refuses to take into account their food preferences (Fine 2008). Undoubtedly, the relationship between customers and servers is a complicated series of acts.

Yet, even though the behaviors of diners and servers can be complicated, it would be a mistake to forget that most people eat out because they find it pleasurable. The restaurant can be thought of as a **diorama** and "provides a context in which a controlled mutual scrutiny between individuals can be enjoyed" (Finkelstein 1989:17). It also offers a place of "sheltered anonymity" where people can be whomever they want to be, experimenting with different roles and wearing extravagant clothing (Finkelstein 1989:14). Dining out also provides an opportunity for people, especially mothers, to enjoy freedom from the domestic responsibility of meal preparation, service, and cleanup. In addition, it gives every member of the household an individual choice of exactly what he or she wants to eat (Warde and Martens 2000). Probyn (1998:169) even suggests that eating at McDonald's has played "an essential role in the spaced cleared by the dispersal of women" from the household, liberating them from the traditional gender roles. Some worry that the trend of eating out will threaten the "proper meal" prepared and consumed at home, but empirical research has not found this to be true.

Dining out has neither "de-skilled" home cooks nor changed traditional gender roles in regard to food planning, shopping, preparing, and serving significantly (Rawlins and Livert 2014; Warde and Martens 2000).

Supermarkets

Approximately 60% of the food consumed in U.S. households is purchased at **supermarkets,** retail stores that have a variety of departments designated for specific food products and make at least $2 million in annual sales (Koch 2012:20–21). Before the invention of the supermarket, consumers first purchased their food from street peddlers and subsequently at local markets or grocers. The corner grocery store became a common feature in most American urban areas by the 1920s. These were small spaces where customers ordered their food from a clerk who stood behind a counter and retrieved the items that were requested, usually from bulk goods stored in barrels or other large containers (Mayo 1993). These items were typically put in a box and delivered to the customer's house (Koch 2012). Prices were not posted, so customers were expected to haggle and bargain for the cost of their orders, which were often purchased through store credit. The relationship between customers, who were overwhelming women, and clerks, who were mostly men, had to be carefully negotiated. Female customers were expected to bargain for the lowest prices and highest quality of goods, but they could not always determine if they were successful at the point of purchase. Clerks could give their favorite customers the freshest produce or cut off credit to those who were not being loyal. Since both shoppers and clerks most often lived in the same neighborhood, they could share gossip, including family celebrations and tragedies. The personal nature of local, independent grocery stores could be both empowering and controlling for female shoppers (Deutsch 2010:32–36).

The local grocery store gave rise to chain grocery stores in the 1920s and 1930s, which introduced the practice of self-service. Piggly Wiggly opened the first self-service chain grocery store in 1916 as a way to increase profits by hiring fewer clerks and eliminating delivery and credit (Tolbert 2009:180). Instead of clerks, self-service stores required consumers to select their own items from shelves that had posted prices, which obliged consumers to make their own choices in regards to quality and price. Now the "product and the consumer" were "in immediate contact with each other" (Koch 2012:25). This eliminated the practice of haggling but also made grocery shopping more impersonal. Self-service stores were designed as "one-way streets" to encourage "movement rather than conversation" (Tolbert 2009:185). Piggly Wiggly used swinging doors and then turnstiles to keep shoppers moving efficiently (Tolbert 2009:187). The invention of the shopping cart made these new spaces of consumption even more orderly and efficient (Grandclément 2009). The packaging of standardized foods in cans and boxes became "building blocks used to design the store interiors" (Mayo 1993:85). Compared to the dark smelly corner grocery stores of the past, new self-service chain stores were bright and clean, offering full lines of national brands, and viewed as an acceptable place for women to go by themselves (Deutsch 2010; Koch 2012; Tolbert 2009).

Over time, chain grocery stores overpowered the small independent ones, even though an **anti-chain store movement** was organized to try to prevent the unfair price advantages of the larger chain stores. Eventually, it was not just price competition but the implementation of the sales tax that hastened the demise of many small independent stores. Small retailers had a difficult time absorbing the sales tax into their sales practices and calculating it into their bookkeeping systems (Deutsch 2010; Mayo 1993). But the number of chain grocery stores themselves began to decrease as they consolidated into national supermarket chains starting after World War II and especially in the 1980s as the deregulation allowed them to expand beyond their regional bases. The popularity of processed food resulted in food manufacturers having more control over the interior spaces of supermarkets. In fact, these manufacturers manage the food delivered to many stores and have the power to stock shelves in them, ensuring key product placement spots for their products at the end of aisles or on shelves that are at eye level with the average customer (Koch 2012). Supermarkets added more nonfood items, including cosmetics, magazines, toys, and hardware, over time as well (Mayo 1993:177). Nonetheless, the largest profit margins continue to be realized from "real" food, especially produce, bakery, meat, and deli, which is typically placed in the perimeter of most supermarkets to force consumers to navigate the entire space of the store and hopefully make more impulse purchases (Koch 2012:90).

Even though people are shopping more often at large, chain supermarkets that are open 24 hours a day, seven days a week, this does not mean they have completely forsaken some of the practices that characterized food shopping in the past, including weekly routines and interacting with others (Ashley et al. 2005:106). Participants in Koch's (2012) study of grocery shopping expressed pleasure in going to the supermarket as a way to get out of the house and interact with other people. Daniel Miller argues that love is "a powerful taken-for-granted foundation for acts of shopping"

(Miller 1998:20). Some grocery shoppers in his study viewed purchasing food as an act of care for their families that they take pride in, such as selecting a choice cut of beef that they know will make their husband happy or a piece of candy that will bring joy to their child. He also found that some grocery shoppers will express love for themselves at the supermarket, treating themselves with chocolate or other items to reward themselves for their domestic labor. Interestingly, "many of these treats are eaten before they even reach the check-out, so that they are paid for using the empty wrappers" (Miller 1998:42). In some grocery stores, a shopper can even treat herself to a pint of beer or a glass of wine as compensation for the labor of provisioning.

Conclusion

In sum, the production, distribution, and consumption of food are more complicated than typically assumed, and our choice of what to eat involves a variety of contradictions. Modern consumers confront on a daily basis what Claude Fischler (1988) calls the **omnivore's paradox:** the increasing variety of food has left us anxious and uncertain about what is safe and healthy to eat (Warde 1997:30). Alan Warde cleverly captures the most significant contradictions in his study of food in the United Kingdom, finding that the antinomies of novelty and tradition, health and indulgence, economy and extravagance, and convenience and care typify most of our food choices. We find ourselves torn between wanting to experience difference but also the comfort that accompanies routine. Sometimes we want to treat ourselves to flavorful, fattening food, while other times we discipline our food choices according to the advice of dietary experts. Depending on our income, the cost of food may restrict what we eat, with expensive meals budgeted for special occasions. Finally, we may opt to eat food that is quick and easy to prepare even though we know it is at odds with our desire for quality. Homemade food is a contradiction that is becoming harder to resolve with the time constraints found in households with dual earners and single parents. Consumers must negotiate these contradictions when deciding which food chain to support, what to cook if they eat in, what type of restaurant to select if they eat out, and what food to place in their grocery carts.

6

Tourism

Tourism is the world's largest industry, with just over 1 billion travelers generating $1.4 trillion (U.S.) export earnings in 2013. The majority of tourists (52%) travel to enjoy leisure time, but others (27%) travel to visit family and friends, make a religious pilgrimage, or receive health treatments (The World Tourism Organization 2014). Even though tourism is often thought of as a pleasurable way to escape the routines of our everyday lives, it would be remiss to ignore all of the work that goes into taking a vacation. In the words of Zygmunt Bauman, "There are many hardships one needs to suffer for the sake of tourist freedoms" (1989:98). Planning where to visit, waiting at the airport for a delayed plane, walking for hours in the hot sun or freezing rain to see all the local attractions, and trying to relax in a noisy hotel room can make traveling more work than play. Given the stress involved, why do so many of us voluntary choose to become tourists at all?

This chapter will examine some of the reasons why we endure the uncontrollable perils of contemporary tourism. From searching out authentic cultural experiences to transforming our bodies, most of us travel to find "pleasurable experiences which are different from those typically encountered in everyday life" (Urry 2002:1). The first section of this chapter on the objects of consumption will explain the economic development of the international tourism industry and how encounters with local people and their culture have become commodified and objectified in the form of souvenirs and sex. The next section of this chapter on the subjects of consumption will explore whether tourists should be understood as passive gazers or embodied actors and discern if it matters if they are searching for authentic experiences or simply want to have fun on their vacations. The final section of the chapter on the places of consumption will describe two popular yet seemingly disparate tourist attractions, Disney World in Orlando, Florida, and the U.S. national parks, suggesting that tourist experiences at them might be more similar than one might suspect.

Tourism and the Objects of Consumption

Economic Development and the Tourism Industry

One of the main reasons why there are now over 1 billion tourist today compared to 25 million tourists in 1950 is the establishment of a more affordable and democratic global tourist industry, particularly in terms of transportation and accommodations (United Nations World Tourism Organization [UNWTO] 2016a). With just over 1 trillion dollars (U.S.) in international tourist receipts in 2015, businesses that provide tourist goods and services and governments of tourist destinations have a considerable interest in ensuring that tourism growth remains strong (UNWTO 2013). Developing an infrastructure that attracts tourists has proven to be a catalyst for economic development, especially employment. In 2012, 1 in 11 jobs worldwide were connected to the tourist industry (UNWTO 2016b). In addition to employment, other benefits of tourism include increasing incomes and standards of living for local residents; the construction of roads, electric grids, and sewer systems; and the preservation of heritage sites. However, these benefits may be outweighed by negative costs, like congestion, inflation, crime, and low-wage, unskilled jobs (Goeldner and Ritchie 2009). In fact, the short-term economic benefits of developing a tourist infrastructure may prove contradictory in the long term. Destinations that are luring tourists by marketing themselves as unique places to discover or boast pristine natural environments can become quickly overcrowded and their environments degraded if they become too popular.

According to R. W. Butler (1980), tourist destinations tend to experience cyclical success that is connected to the economic development of the tourist industry. At first, locals are involved in catering to adventure tourists who desire to discover a new locale. This is followed by more

intense development of the tourist infrastructure as formal organizations take over control from locals. Franchises and international chains
become increasingly involved in the third cycle, which results in a period
of stagnation as the location becomes homogenized and unfashionable.
Over time, the final cycle of rejuvenation occurs as new activities are
introduced that emphasize an innovative quality to the location. For
example, if a location is known for its summer boating, it may introduce
other activities, like zip lines, or it may create an infrastructure to enjoy
activities to do in another season, like groomed trails for snowmobiling
in the winter (Sack 1992:157–58). Perhaps the most critical element in
Butler's **tourist-cycle model** is the gradual loss that locals experience
as the tourist infrastructure develops. Although they may benefit from
the development of tourism such as access to new technologies, like
wireless Internet service, many may not have the economic means to
afford what is being established for the comfort of tourists, especially
if locals are working in the low-wage service jobs offered by the tourist
industry. Cohen suggests that as the tourist infrastructure grows, locals
often become dislocated when international organizations and corporations become more involved. Indeed, Cohen states that "tourism is not
a particularly effective mechanism of social mobility" (Cohen 1984:386).
In their study of the tourism in Quintana Roo, Mexico, Pi-Sunyer and
Thomas (1997:49) found that tourism has resulted in an increasing division of wealth as locals who work for the tourist industry are "assigned
very subordinate roles in the development process sometimes to the point
of invisibility." These are the unskilled, poorly paid locals that tourists are
most likely to encounter as maids, bartenders, restaurant servers, and taxi
drivers during their travels.

Cultural Commodification and Objectification: Souvenirs and Sex Tourism

Locals may lose not only economic control over the tourist industry but
also their culture as they confront "a constant struggle to reinterpret their
culture as Western values and beliefs, most notable individualism and
consumerism, become more pervasive" (Wearing, Stevenson, and Young
2010:56). This is particularly problematic if Western cultural standards
become the norm and "pieces of the First World" become "ensconced in
the Third World" (Pi-Sunyer and Thomas 1997:49). For example, if tourists
expect stores to be open in the afternoon, then cultures may abandon the
tradition of the siesta, a short nap, and the leisurely lunch that generally

precedes it. Even more troublesome is when tourists insist locals speak English, which threatens to destroy indigenous languages and dialects. MacCannell argues that the commodification of culture can produce **cultural cannibalism.** This occurs when local culture literally "eats itself up" as attractions of otherness become the dominant culture (Wearing, Stevenson, and Young 2010:57). Of course, not too much local culture can be destroyed or altered because then it would prove difficult for the tourist industry to attract tourists to these marketed "exotic" destinations.

Locals may begin to resent tourists for changing their traditional life-styles and discover ways to try to take advantage of them through staging cultural events. "Dances and rituals have been shortened or embellished, folk customs or arts altered, faked, and occasionally invented" to profit off of ignorant but curious tourists (Cohen 1984:387). Some fear that commodifying crafts and customs by turning them into tourist souve-nirs and spectacles makes local culture "meaningless to the people who once believed in it" (Greenwood 1989:173). When parades or reenact-ments become public shows to be performed for the benefit of outsiders, locals may no longer want to participate in them anymore and come to interpret them as "an obligation to be avoided" (Greenwood 1989:178). Others argue that tourism gives a boost to indigenous arts and crafts and that their commodification has not resulted in **trinketization,** or cheap, mass-produced objects manufactured for the tourist trade. For example, Deitch (1989) found that the growth of Southwest Native American arts and crafts market has encouraged cultural self-awareness and pride in many Native American communities. These arts and crafts, including jewelry, beads, pottery, rugs, and baskets, have increased in economic value over the years but have also changed over time. Silver is now used more often than gold in jewelry making, and new arts, like sand paint-ing, have emerged. As Hawken (2007) reminds us, culture is not static but dynamic, and to assume that locals would not adapt their cultural traditions and ways of life evokes Western conceit—that we can develop culturally, but they cannot. For tourists seeking authenticity, this under-standing of cultural dynamism might provoke them to question what precisely authenticity is.

Whether mass-produced trinkets or handmade arts and crafts, souvenirs as objects of consumption are important because they allow tourists to bring something tangible back home, signifying the places that they have been and representing the memories that they made there. Celia Lury (1997) identifies several types of tourist objects, including what she calls traveler-objects and tripper-objects. Traveler-objects are souvenirs that "travel well" because they "retain their meaning across contexts and retain an authenticated relation to an original dwelling," like artwork and handmade crafts. Tripper-objects also travel well, but they derive their meaning from "their final resting place." Tripper-objects are meant to "be brought home," like a mass-produced souvenir that can be found across different locales or even a common rock that one might have found on a beach she was visiting. Some tourist objects fall between these two broad categories, like a T-shirt with the name of a tourist destination on it, which clearly is mass-produced, so not necessarily authentic, but signifies a direct relationship to the place itself (Lury 1997:78). Both trinkets and handmade crafts can evoke meaningful memories for their owners—and, like other objects of consumption, have their particular biographies.

A more controversial object of consumption is sex and the commodification of the body. **Sex tourism** is "travel for which the main motivation is to engage in commercial sexual relations" (Clift and Carter 2000:6) and has its origins in the 1940s, when it became a popular recreational activity for military personnel. While sexual encounters between tourists and locals certainly existed before the 1940s, they were not coordinated and marketed by the tourist industry. The sexual and racial **objectification** of the "exotic other" by Western tourists that characterizes contemporary sex tourism has a long history, especially prominent during the days of colonial imperialism. Indeed, many of the popular sex tourist destinations today with the exception of Thailand are located in former European colonies, particularly Indonesia, Vietnam, the Philippines, and the Caribbean (Mullings 2000; Seabrook 2001; Taylor 2000; Truong 1990). Not surprisingly, sex tourism has changed local cultural norms. Kousis (1996) found that before tourism, the sexual behavior of men and women in rural Cretan was quite restricted; however, these restrictions were relaxed for local men once female tourists started to arrive and engage in sexual relations with them (Clift and Carter 2000:13).

Interestingly, the manner in which the tourist industry markets sex tourism in developing countries as "different" and "exotic" has persuaded many sex tourists to believe that they are not just "johns" purchasing the services of prostitutes (Taylor 2000:48). Some sex tourists develop relationships with sex workers, being monogamous to them for the duration of their trips and even referring to them as their "girlfriend" or "boyfriend" (Mullings 2000:244). In her ethnography of sex work in Ho

Chi Minh City, Hoang studied one sex bar that was established to promote long-term relationships instead of direct, sex-for-money exchanges. The madam, or "mommie," who ran this bar told Hoang that this arrangement "allowed women to relax and not feel as though they needed to hustle to get money from their clients" in addition to being a clever tactic that allowed them to make larger sums of money over time (2015:122–23). Seabrook (2001:35) found in his study of sex tourism in Thailand that some Western male tourists even felt like they were victimized by their so-called girlfriends, who claimed that they loved them but demanded that they pay for their services at the end of their vacation. Taylor found that some sex workers also fantasize that they are more than just prostitutes, especially if they develop long-term relationships with a tourist who visits them annually or sends them gifts. Western female sex tourists, in particular, have been described as "romance tourists," searching for love (Pruitt and Lafont 1995). However, these women, like male sex tourists, have the power to objectify the other. Indeed, different markets have been developed in the Caribbean to cater to the different desires of female sex tourists from "Rent a Dread," black men with Rastafarian dreadlocks in Jamaica, to "Beach Boys," black men with well-toned bodies, in Barbados and Trinidad (Mullings 2000).

Sex tourism is more complicated than voluntary, commercial sexual transactions between a tourist and a sex worker. The recognition of sex work as a job means that sex workers are "no longer working at the margins of society," and it may even be a job that sex workers take "pride" in (Ryan and Hall 2001:55). Hoang discovered that women who voluntarily chose to engage in sex work found it less abusive and more autonomous than laboring for long hours in a factory or as domestic maids (2015:109). One could even argue that sex workers objectify their clients by fantasying that they can satisfy their economic and emotional needs or establishing long-term relationships with them (Mullings 2000:239). In sex bars that cater to Western budget tourists, Hoang found that female sex workers indulged their clients' desire to fulfill traditional masculine gender roles, encouraging these men to "save" them from "global poverty" by sending gifts and large remittances (2015:124). However, these examples do not necessarily change the inherently unequal relationship between sex workers and sex tourists due especially to the fact that sex workers do not "have the power to commodify" (Hall 1996; Mullings 2000:239). Furthermore, there is a growing concern within the sex tourist industry of sex trafficking and sex slavery, especially when it involves children (Davidson 2000; Hoose, Clift, and Carter 2000). Sex trafficking has moved from the cities to the countrysides and is not confined within developing countries but has become a global problem that needs to be addressed as a violation of human rights (Seabrook 2001). In addition, the transmission and spread of HIV/AIDS has become a global public health issue that sex tourists and sex workers need to take precautions to protect themselves against.

Tourism and the Subjects of Consumption

Passive Gazers or Embodied Actors

From scenes to views to landscapes, there is little doubt that "tourism relies on the visual" (Sack 1992:157). Anyone who has been ensnared by friends or family members to look through vacation photos or watch vacation videos can attest that tourists spend a lot of their time trying to capture and preserve what they have gazed upon during their travels. However, the direction of their gaze is not accidental; "modern international sightseeing possesses its own moral structure, a collective sense that certain sights must be seen" (MacCannell 1999:42). Indeed, the tourist industry highlights certain attractions with routing and signposting that "tell tourists where and when they may gaze" (Smith and Duffy 2003:118). **Sight sacralization** is a process that attempts to direct tourists to objects and landscapes that the tourist industry deems significant. According to MacCannell, five stages characterize sight sacralization. In the first stage, or the naming phase, a "sight is marked off from similar objects worthy of preservation" (1999:44). Framing, or "the placement of an official boundary around the object," and elevation, which involves putting the object on display in a case or on a pedestal, occur in stage 2. Glass might be used as protective framing, while spotlights might be used as enhancement framing. Enshrinement of the object of the tourist gaze happens in stage 3, while stage 4 is characterized by mechanical reproduction when copies of the tourist object are created. The last stage of social reproduction is reached when places name themselves after a sacralized sight. In sum, the tourist gaze is carefully choreographed and therefore not as random or spontaneous as many tourists might be inclined to believe.

But even though the gaze of tourists is almost always guided, not all tourist gazes are the same. According to Urry (2002:41), some tourists are more attracted to what he calls the **romantic gaze,** with its "emphasis on solitude, privacy, and a personal, semi-spiritual relationship with the object of the gaze." Other tourists feel more comfortable around other people and prefer the **collective gaze** found in public places that "would look strange if they were empty," like a shopping mall or amusement park. He suggests that there is a socioeconomic class dimension to the tourist gaze, with upper- and middle-class tourists preferring the seclusion of the romantic gaze, while working-class tourists enjoy being in crowds so seek out the collective gaze. The challenge is for the tourist gaze to escape being turned into what Holloway calls the tourist daze, which results when tourists are "dragooned into beholding sites and sights with which they enjoy no rapport, have little or no idea where they are or why they are there" (Voase 2006:28).

Franklin argues that theories of the tourist gaze present the tourist as too passive and detached, neglecting that many tourists engage in **rituals of transformation** that deliver them "from one state or condition of the life course into the next" similar to pilgrimages of the past (2003:11). Franklin situates tourism as a ritualized experience because (1) it involves a period of time spent away from the mundane, (2) it creates a liminal space unique from home and work, (3) people behave differently in tourist spaces than they do in everyday life, and (4) tourists usually feel a sense of conversion when they return to their everyday lives (Franklin 2003:113). Given the ritualistic qualities of tourism, tourists should be understood as **embodied** as they are continuously modifying their physical behavior and psychological or spiritual state of mind (Franklin 2003). In other words, instead of just gazing, tourists are doing stuff—eating, conversing, walking, reading, sunning, and surfing. And by doing stuff, tourists do not simply transform themselves, but they also change the places that they visit. Thus, tourists can be viewed as having a more interactive and flexible relationship with the places they visit, the host community, and one another (Wearing, Stevenson, and Young 2010). One way this interactive relationship transpires is when the host community returns the tourist gaze. For example, locals might use tourists to try to popularize a political message or tell a narrative of their history that gets acknowledged from outsiders (Smith and Duffy 2003:134).

Dark Tourism

One growing niche in the tourist industry is dark tourism, which involves tourists visiting places where wars, conflicts, disasters, and accidents have occurred (Lennon and Foley 2000; Tarlow 2005). Popular sites include the Chernobyl nuclear power plant in the Ukraine that caught fire and exploded in 1986, releasing a massive amount of radioactive material into the air. Considered the worst nuclear accident in the world, 56 people were killed and over 300,000 were forced to permanently evacuate the area ("Chernobyl" 2010). Today, tourists can take day excursions in the formerly demarcated "Exclusion Zone," a 30-kilometer radius of radioactive land surrounding the nuclear power plant. Tourists can explore abandoned towns, like Pripyat, where they can observe empty school classrooms, a derelict amusement park, and even Soviet propaganda posters left behind by the former regime. Tourists are not allowed to touch anything, including vegetation and the soil, to limit their exposure to the radiation that remains. Before leaving, their radiation levels are tested by body scanners to ensure they are safe (Isalska 2015).

Another popular dark tourism destination is Belfast, Northern Ireland, where tourists can visit sites of violence associated with the Troubles—the popular term used to refer to the civil war between Protestant British unionists and Catholic Irish nationalists. Tourists can board red, double-decker busses in the city center and gaze upon the "most bombed hotel Europe," popular murals of paramilitary groups, and sections of the so-called Peace Wall that divides Protestant and Catholic neighborhoods. For a personalized tour of how the Troubles affected local communities, tourists can hire a black taxi. Black taxis are often driven and narrated by individuals who witnessed or participated in the Troubles and provide access to places where the mass tourist-operated double-decker busses are not welcome. Like many other things in Belfast, these taxi operators are either Protestant or Catholic and therefore not only defend their side of the conflict but can only drive tourists into either Protestant or Catholic neighborhoods. As black taxis shuttle tourists between local commemorations that memorialize the victims of the Troubles, they may provide them the opportunity to engage in conversations with local residents. These encounters may challenge tourists' understandings of perpetrators and victims of violence in addition to providing local residents the chance to tell their version of history (Dépret 2007; Wiedenhoft Murphy 2010).

(Continued)

(Continued)

Questions

1. Why do you think that some tourists are attracted to places where wars, conflicts, and disasters have occurred? Do you find yourself fascinated or appalled by dark tourism? Why?

2. Do you think that dark tourism exploits or empowers the victims of wars, conflicts, or disasters? Why? How?

3. Select a dark tourism destination and research this site online, such as the genocides in Rwanda or the Balkans, the 9/11 terrorist attack in New York City, the disaster of Hurricane Katrina in New Orleans, or conflict in Beirut, Lebanon. Provide a brief synopsis of this site, including an itinerary of what specific attractions tourists can expect to observe and experience. Would you recommend this tourist destination based on your findings? Why or why not?

Searching for Authenticity or Fun

Immersion or experiential travelers are embodied tourists searching for authentic experiences with local cultures, attempting to make their vacations into anthropological excursions (Bellafante 2012). The search for authenticity is one of the key tropes in the study of tourism, popularized by MacCannell (1999), who argued that authenticity was impossible for tourists to discover and if they think that they have done so, they can never be confident that they are experiencing it. According to MacCannell, tourists commonly encounter **staged authenticity,** cultural customs, rituals, and sights that are constructed for them and not the locals. Even when locals claim to provide tourists access to genuine "backstage" areas, "it is always possible that what is taken to be entry into a back region is really entry into a front region that has been totally set up in advance for touristic visitation" (MacCannell 1999:101). Some tourists hope to find values that they think are missing from their everyday lives, like community or spirituality, when they visit what they consider authentic places. These so-called **new moral tourists** are cautious not to degrade local culture and desire to educate and enlighten themselves by visiting premodern, typically non-Western places. They want to learn different customs and languages and not be surrounded by McDonald's, Wal-Mart, and Holiday Inn. But their "self-conscious search" for these "backstage regions" may be a bit disingenuous (Butcher 2003:3, 5, 25). Not only might these new moral tourists end up romanticizing locals as timeless, unchanging objects, but they could forget they are not in a traditional guest-host relationship. By definition, tourism is the commodification of hospitality, and tourist-local relationships are not based on an enduring mutual trust because they are mostly "transitory, nonrepetitive, and asymmetrical" (Cohen 1984:379). But this is not to claim that tourists never develop long-term friendships with locals who they meet during their travels or return to visit them as invited guests.

Other tourists are not so concerned with discovering an authentic site or undergoing a transcendental experience; rather, they are simply looking to relax and have some fun. According to Rojek (1993:177), these **posttourists** are aware of, but do not care, if their experiences are commodified, nor do they find it particularly desirable to experience different cultures. All-inclusive resorts are perhaps the perfect destination for posttourists, who want little more than to escape the monotony of their everyday lives, relax, and have some fun. Posttourists find pleasure in the "accessories" that accompany popular tourist sites, like gift shops, theme restaurants, motor coach excursions, and even other tourists. Indeed, some tourists find these accessories more exciting than the actual tourist site itself. Tourist apps for mobile devices are the most recent accessories that posttourists can use to enhance their travels. Tourist can play trivia or geocaching games and win prizes when they visit programmed locations on these apps, encouraging the idea that playing the game might be more fun than experiencing the actual location (Rosenbloom 2013).

Given the fun and freedom experienced by many tourists, some develop **communitas,** a unique social bond between strangers who are traveling or on vacation together (Franklin 2003:48). A sense of comradery can develop among tourists in the process of sharing their impressions of the sights they are observing or the food that they are eating. This may be especially pronounced with prearranged group tour packages when the same people do everything together for days or weeks at a time. The **liminality** or suspension of daily reality associated with tourism weakens barriers, like socioeconomic class or religious affiliation, which might limit social interactions between tourists at home (Turner 1969). Tourists can escape their own identities, especially those associated with work, and avoid at least some of the "real"-world restraints on their behavior. Drinking before noon, wearing a bathing suit all day long, having a one-night stand, or singing karaoke in front of a crowd of strangers are some of the liminal "rites" that tourists enjoy during their travels. Those familiar with the "What Happens in Vegas, Stays in Vegas" marketing campaign can readily recognize the notion of liminality it implies.

Tourism and the Places of Consumption

Disney World: Authentic or Imagined Fun?

Tourism is most commonly associated with places of consumption and no place exemplifies a contemporary tourist destination more than Disney World. King and O'Boyle (2011:7) argue that Disney is not really an amusement park at all but a theme park that a "visitor can fully engage . . . without ever stepping foot on a ride" by observing the architecture or watching a live performance. Disney World in Orlando, Florida, has taken the theme park to the extreme with the Magic Kingdom (opened in 1971), EPCOT (opened in 1982), and Disney Hollywood Studios (opened in 1989), attracting almost 60 million tourists annually. According to Bryman (2004), the key principles of the Disney amusement park model are theming, hybrid consumption, merchandising, and performative labor, or what he calls **Disneyfication.** The "application of a narrative to institutions or locations" (Bryman 2004:15), or **theming,** is the key to navigating the world of Disney because it "eases the mental chaos of the interpretive processes" (King and O'Boyle 2011:15). Disney's narrative begins in the Magic Kingdom on Main Street, where visitors walk through a quaint representation of a small town in turn-of-the-century America. From here, tourists can choose what themed "land" they want to visit next, including Adventureland with its jungle theme, Frontierland with its old West theme, Fantasyland with its princess theme, and Tomorrowland with its space theme. At EPCOT, visitors are exposed to the theme of technological innovation at Future World and the theme of international culture at World Showcase, where the customs and cuisines of 11 countries can be encountered. Those more interested in the themes of nostalgia and glamour can visit Disney Hollywood Studies, where attractions are based on popular movies and television shows (https://disneyworld .disney.go.com/).

All of these themed lands integrate various forms of consumption, like eating, shopping, and live music, encouraging tourists to participate in **hybrid consumption.** Indeed, Disney as a totality is a hybrid amusement park, theme park, and vacation resort that contains hotels so visitors do not have to return to reality by staying outside the park only to return the next day if they purchase the popular Disney four-day theme park ticket. According to Sack, the "power of Disney World is enhanced by the fact that it contains other places of consumption" like golf resorts, water parks, and gift stores. It also includes a plethora of objects of consumption to purchase. Merchandising or "the promotion of goods in the form of or bearing copyright images and logos" is prevalent throughout all the different themed lands (Bryman 2004:79). Visitors who purchase and wear Mickey Mouse ears and Cinderella slippers become walking advertisements for the Disney brand. Vinylmation, miniature plastic collectible figures of Disney movie and cartoon characters, are popular tripper-objects that can be displayed by tourists when they return back home.

Disney offers tourists **hyperreality** or "a tightly edited, stylized, and focused version of reality, shaped to advance a specific narrative" (King and O'Boyle 2011:12). Even though Disney is a collection of different theme parks based on fantasy, concealed behind these themes is the broader narrative of bourgeois ideology (Gottdiener 1982), particularly the ideal family and corporate power. According to Giroux (1993:98), "The pervasive symbol of ideological unification through which Disney defines its view of capitalism, gender, and national identity is the family." A critical analysis of Disney's narrative of the ideal family centers on socioeconomic class. Admission prices are high at Disney, currently $99 for a one-day ticket, which makes it a pricey if not impossible option for lower-class families. Furthermore, one needs a car to get to Disney World, which excludes those who rely exclusively on public transportation or cannot afford—or do not qualify—to rent a car. Privileging white, middle-class families is not accidental because when Walt Disney constructed his theme park, he wanted to differentiate it from working-class amusement parks like Coney Island and carnivals (Bryman 1995:92–94). Hyperreality even encroaches upon the behavior of employees at Disney World, who are compelled to engage in **performative labor** as they manage their feelings to maintain their jobs, like smiling in public when privately unhappy or acting like one is playing when one is really working. Disney carefully controls the appearance of its employees to conform to middle-class family ideals—no long hair for men or bra straps showing for women. Disney also requires that its employees follow predetermined scripts that use distinct encoded words when interacting with tourists.

For example, visitors to Disney must be called "guests," employees must call themselves "cast members," and their uniforms are "costumes"; lines guests wait in are referred to as "preentertainment areas" and hiring as "casting" (Bryman 1995:108–9).

Corporate power is celebrated at Disney, most openly at EPCOT, where over the years, international corporations have sponsored specific exhibits at Future World. Once sponsored by Bell/AT&T, the golf ball–looking Spaceship Earth is currently sponsored by Siemans. The former Universe of Energy (renamed Ellen's Energy Adventure) was sponsored by Exxon until 2004. The World of Motion (remodeled into the Test Track ride through an automobile design lab in 1999) is supported by Chevrolet and The Land, a pavilion originally sponsored by Kraft and then Nestle, used to showcase agriculture and food technology (http://www .themeparkinsider.com/flume/201308/3591/). Bryman describes the pro-corporate ideology of EPCOT as encouraging disempowerment— "we are all supposed to sit back and let corporations do the planning of the future on our behalf" (1995:147). Corporations are lauded as heroes and the harmful products that they make or the environmental disasters that they have caused are conveniently omitted (Bryman 1995:148, 129). But this is hardly surprising because Disney is selling us fantasy, so it makes sense that corporate capitalism is presented as "fun times, excellent quality and service and [a] bright future with exciting new products that . . . bring a life of leisure to all" (Scibelli 2011:220). Furthermore, the ideal bourgeois family that Disney attracts is unlikely to find Disney's endorsement of corporate power and capitalism in general problematic because it simply "confirms and reaffirms the conventional and the normal" (Bryman 1995:98).

In addition to bourgeois ideology, faith and reliance on technology is a key component of the hyperreal fantasy world manufactured by Disney. Like McDonald's, Disney is based on the principles of formal rationality, efficiency, calculation, predictability, and dehumanization, which inevitably result in irrational consequences (Ritzer 2013). Before their trip, tourists are encouraged to purchase four-day passes and plan their daily itinerary using interactive guides offered on Disney's website so that they use their time at Disney most efficiently. Disney now offers a "magic band" that visitors wear around their wrists and use to gain access to the theme parks that they have prepaid for, charge food and drinks with, and use as a key for their hotel rooms. Of course, each theme park itself is organized around a particular narrative that helps tourists both physically and mentally navigate space in a predictable and orderly fashion. Like fast-food workers, Disney "cast members" are dehumanized by the costumes they must wear and the scripts they must follow. Nature, in particular, is presented as something that should be "subsumed by the doctrine of progress" and "beaten into submission" (Fjellman 1992:270 and Wilson 1992:180, both quoted in Bryman 1995:105–6). Yet, ironically, Disney World has yet to conquer the natural environment of Florida, which is a "physically abusive environment—glaring sun, hot temperatures . . . punctuated by sudden thundershowers" (King and O'Boyle 2011:15). The irrational consequences—the crowds, the lines, the blisters, and the sunburns—lead one to question whether the tourist experience at Disney is authentic fun or just imagined fun.

National Parks: Staged or Natural Authenticity?

On the surface, national parks and nature in general present a seemingly stark contrast to the manufactured, fantasy world of Disney; therefore, one would expect tourist expectations and experiences to be quite different. Yet, the national parks were established as places to escape reality too—of the city. Whether they be "tender-minded Romantics" who view nature as holy and pure, uncontaminated by modern civilization, or "tough-minded Darwinians" who seek vitality and health by hiking and hunting in the wilderness, the national parks hope to entice a wide variety of tourists (Cartmill 1993, quoted in Franklin 2003:219). Over time, these natural settings became institutionalized in the United States by the federal government through the National Parks Service. According to MacCannell (1999:81), modern tourism reorganized nature by treating it "not as a force opposing man" but "something we must try to preserve." A significant aspect of this preservation was taming nature to make it more observable and manageable for tourists. Roads were built to guide the cars that tourists were expected to drive to access the parks, permanent trails were paved to direct the movement of walkers and hikers, campsites were established that offered public showers and coin-operated Laundromats, and for those who wanted to enjoy all of the modern conveniences of home, hotel-inspired lodges were built (MacCannell 1999; Ross-Bryant 2013).

The United States was the first country to establish national parks with the opening of Yellowstone in 1872, followed by Glacier National Park in 1910 and the Grand Canyon in 1919. The express purpose of the parks was **recreational tourism** in the midst of "scenery of supreme and distinctive quality" to be enjoyed by as many Americans as possible (Ross-Bryant 2013:15). In the words of filmmaker Ken Burns, this was land that was designated not for kings or nobility but for everyone; thus, the parks were linked to the ideals of democracy and promoted as a way to encourage good citizenship (Ross-Bryant 2013:17, 12). Supporting this inclusive objective, the admission to national parks is nominal and in some cases free, which is one reason attendance at the parks is particularly pronounced during times of economic recession. A year after the 2008 recession, 285 million people spent 1.25 billon hours inside the parks, the most since 2000 (Briggs 2010).

While preserving nature in the parks for the sake of tourists is important—and marketing it as pristine, untouched, pure, and wild is a strategic way to attract them—preserving nature for its own sake is secondary and clearly at odds with the increasing presence of humans in these spaces. Indeed, the ecological footprint of tourists to the national parks is quite large and has been since the first tourists arrived from Eastern cities on the railroads to Yellowstone, Glacier, and the Grand Canyon. But the automobile came to replace the railroads as the primary way tourists arrived at the parks by 1915 (Ross-Bryant 2013:131). Today, the massive number of cars in the parks causes traffic congestion that clogs roads, emits greenhouse gases, and contributes to an intensifying air pollution problem. According to the U.S. Environmental Protection Agency, the human impact on the national parks has become so dire that in 2004, eight of them violated federal air-quality standards. The extreme levels of carbon pollutants released by snowmobiles at Yellowstone have exposed park workers to emissions that are 10 times higher than levels found on Los Angeles freeways, requiring that they be given respirators in addition to hearing protection due to the loud noise (Gibson 2009:148, 152). From discarded water bottles carelessly thrown on the side of the road to the noise from hovering sightseeing helicopters, one may question what exactly is so different in these "pristine" spaces than in their suburban environment back home—or Disney World.

The reliance on the automobile in the parks prompted a particular form of **landscape management** that relies on controlling "virtually everything within the field of vision" (Wilson 1992:36). When the Blue Ridge Parkway was built to connect the Shenandoah and Great Smoky Mountain national parks, mileposts were erected to make drivers feel like they were making "progress," local "hillbillies" were resettled and their dilapidated shacks removed, and weeds and unattractive plants and trees were replaced with those that flowered in the spring and had colorful foliage in the fall. To further organize the gaze of tourists, curves were strategically placed to force drivers to slow down and observe fields of sheep and other landscape produced for their benefit (Wilson 1992:35–37). The car—and its modern conveniences like heat and air-conditioning—make it possible to "experience" nature through a window of safety glass, encouraging a visual objectification of nature that is external to us and consumable by us (Macnaghten and Urry 1998:113).

The national parks also encouraged the visual objectification of Native Americans. When the Grand Canyon opened, Native Americans became "living ruins" and were "treated as if they were scenery, part of the landscape, which could be observed and admired by the tourist." The Hopi House was established where tourists could see "real, live Indians" weaving baskets and making pottery, an excessive exhibition of staged authenticity (Ross-Bryant 2013:81–88). Likewise the Blackfeet Indians at Glacier National Park were removed from the land and used as tourist accessories. According to Ross-Bryant (2013:107), when tourists stepped off the train, they were greeted by Blackfeet Indians, donning warrior dress or wrapped in blankets, who carried their luggage to the Glacier Park Hotel. Inside the hotel, visitors could gaze upon Native American arts, crafts, and even tepees but "would not see the Blackfeet in the wilderness engaged in their traditional riding, fishing, or hunting" (Ross-Bryant 2013:109). Ironically, the hides, horns, and mounted heads of the very animals that the Blackfeet should have been hunting on the land became the décor of the hotel lobby. Thus, wilderness itself was safely brought indoors to be appreciated by tourists. The Old Faithful Inn at Yellowstone managed to bring the actual campfire indoors by constructing an enormous, centralized stone chimney with four adjoining fireplaces that tourists could enjoy while relaxing on rocking chairs (Ross-Bryant 2013:107, 63). Like the crowds, there is a surprising similarity between how the national parks and the Disney theme park package nature and the conquest of Native Americans.

Demarcating certain bounded spaces as natural and recreational constructed the assumption that both were special and distinctly separate from humans and our everyday activities. As our modern lives become increasingly McDonaldized, we feel a sense of disenchantment, looking to nature to reenchant us with magical experiences (Gibson 2009). However, the commonality of this sentiment has resulted in the very places we look for enchantment to become disenchanted by crowds, air and noise pollution, and litter. Situating the national parks as environments that are separate from the ones we inhabit daily might cause us to ignore the fact that our behavior at home influences them. The effects of climate change in parks, for example, are caused by human activities that happened not just inside them but outside them as well. We should recognize, according to one former Park Service employee, that the parks are not timeless but ever-changing (Ross-Bryant 2013:227). A backpacking guide echoes this opinion, stating that we need to stop thinking of the national parks as "static museum exhibits" but as "dynamic landscapes subject to the same forces that the rest of the world experiences" (Briggs 2010). Wilson (1992:17) suggests that people should be living on the land and caring for it, which would nurture an ethic of **restoration,** a recognition that once land has been "disturbed" by humans, its future relies on human intervention. This logic was adopted by the National Park Service when it began to establish parks in the Alaskan wilderness during the 1960s, allowing subsistence hunting and habitation to occur within park borders (Ross-Bryant 2013:213).

It would be a mistake to ignore the potential benefits of attracting large numbers of visitors to the national parks. Franklin argues that "tourism contributes to environmentalism and nature conservation by building strong bonds between (typically urban) visitors and natural spaces" (2003:60). For example, tourists who return annually to a particular spot on a river to fish may become actively involved in protesting a proposed dam that would alter the river and obstruct the passage of fish. Visiting a national park for a family vacation can encourage the idea of **sustainability,** or minimizing our ecological footprints to preserve nature for future generations to enjoy, especially if grandparents and parents teach their children this lesson. Tourists can help protect and preserve additional public land by joining conservation organizations, writing letters to their congressional representatives, or joining an active protest movement against mining on private land that adjoins national parks. Also, tourists can avoid the crowds and staged authenticity of nature displayed in the hotels or gazed upon through a car window by walking or hiking and taking advantage of the primitive camping options that are offered in the parks. Furthermore, it would also be foolish to frame technology as an absolute enemy of nature. Nature apps can help hikers identify birds by sound, animals by their scat and paw prints, and whether or not a berry they find is edible or poisonous. Webcams that stream live video of eagles nesting or deer on game trails can raise environmental awareness and help people feel connected to nature, imploding the boundary between the indoors and the outdoors.

Conclusion

In addition to the indoors and the outdoors, the boundary between "home" and "away" also seems to be breaking down for a variety of reasons. First, "tourism is *infused* into everyday life" (Franklin 2003:2). Many of us live in places—whether urban or rural—that are tourist destinations and spend our leisure time doing what tourists generally do like eating out, visiting zoos, and attending cultural or sporting events. Second, tourist destinations and our homes are becoming more analogous. The restaurants and stores we eat in and shop at in our hometowns are often the same ones we patronize on vacation. Even souvenirs, like Mickey Mouse ears or hand-carved Irish crosses, can be purchased at the local shopping mall—no trip to Disney World or Ireland required. MacCannell questions if "real mobility is . . . technically possible once every move takes the traveler to a place no different from the place he just left" (2001:398). Like the implosion between being at home and being on vacation, the dichotomy between "work" and "leisure" is becoming more complicated. On one hand, leisure-time involves work as many tourists have become their own travel agents, booking flights and hotel rooms and planning their itineraries. Mobile technologies allow tourists to work while on vacation, using emails to correspond with employers or Skype to virtually attend an office meeting. On the other hand, work has become more flexible. Some employees can work from home or take personal time off, which does not distinguish between sick days and vacation days. Many workers travel for their jobs, using the same tourist infrastructure and amenities as holiday travelers. The hours when one is an employee working "on the clock" or a tourist relaxing "on downtime" are harder to differentiate.

7

Higher Education

Just as mass production and consumption originated in the United States, so too did mass higher education. The United States was the "first country in the world in which the children of the middle classes went to college" and where "college became a passport for prosperity" ("Special Report" 2015). According to the U.S. Census, more than 20 million people were enrolled in some institute of higher education, including for-profits, in 2012 compared to 2.3 million in 1950 (Stich 2012:5). However, the ability of higher education to provide social mobility is no longer a guarantee. The preposterously high cost of tuition has turned a university degree into an object of consumption that few can afford to purchase without assuming some level of debt. Higher education in the United States has become commodified increasingly since the 1970s as a result of changes in public policy and the labor market. The passage of the Higher Education Act of 1972 identified students as consumers, who became direct recipients of federal student aid instead of institutions of higher education. State legislatures started to decrease public subsidies to colleges and universities during the 1970s, compelling institutions of higher education to adopt corporate marketing strategies in an attempt to lure students to their campuses. Flashy advertising campaigns, the construction of luxury accommodations and amenities, and sponsorship by corporations for athletic programs signaled that colleges and universities had more of a "product" to offer than just learning.

At the same time as these public policy changes occurred, the labor market shifted from a foundation of industrial manufacturing to service and knowledge. Unlike industrial jobs, most of the better paying occupations in the postindustrial economy require college and university degrees, driving the student demand for higher education credentials. This surge of demand has resulted in the rising selectivity of student admissions to nonprofit private and public colleges and universities, increasing enrollment in community colleges, and the sharp growth of for-profit universities. Of course, these various places of consumption in higher education are quite stratified in terms of the socioeconomic composition of their student bodies, particularly income and age, academic rigor and expectations, curriculum and vocational training, student life, physical facilities, and the status of the credentials they confer.

Similar to the previous two chapters in this section of the book, this chapter will apply the conceptual framework of the objects, subjects, and spaces of consumption, but it will begin with explaining the places of higher education to provide a historical narrative of the creation of their development from the origins of elite private schools to massive open online courses (MOOCs) that can be virtually attended today. Pierre Bourdieu's concepts of field and position are used to describe the hierarchical relationships between the different places of higher education, and the scope of corporate influence on them is explored. Next, the idea of higher education as an object of consumption is analyzed, including the debate over exactly what product students should be purchasing with their tuition dollars. Are students consuming human capital or credentials that can be traded in for a future job in the labor force or time to engage in critical learning and self-discovery? Is higher education a product that can or should be equivalent to other commodities in the marketplace, or is it something more profound, associated with democratic principles of inclusion and other moral values? If higher education is a commodity, how can we evaluate it? Finally, the emergence of the student as a consumer will be discussed, particularly how the expense and experience of higher education are correlated with the reproduction of inequality through economic, cultural, and social capital. The fact that most students are forced to take out loans to pay for higher education has resulted in record-high debt, which is making it difficult for young adults to grow up today and achieve the American Dream. Furthermore, treating students as consumers is changing their expectations of higher education, including how engaged they are in learning. The mentality of "pay the fee, get the C or B" captures the student-as-consumer attitude quite well. This chapter will conclude with a brief exploration of some ideas on how to help solve some of the problems associated with higher education today, especially its costly price tag.

Higher Education as a Place of Consumption

A Field of Struggle

Pierre Bourdieu's concept of a **field** as "a network, or configuration, of objective relations between positions" is useful toward understanding the hierarchical power dynamics between the various places in higher education (Bourdieu and Wacquant 1992:97). The different universities and colleges or positions that constitute the field of higher education in the United States today include four-year private colleges and universities, four-year public colleges and universities, community colleges, for-profit or proprietary universities, and MOOCs. Struggles ensue between these different spaces of consumption as they compete to circumscribe the rules of the field, such as what knowledge is recognized as legitimate, in addition to who has access to the various positions within it. Those institutions of higher education that accumulate the most capital will be able to dominate the field and in turn acquire more prestige. But given their objective relationship to other positions, they must contend with challenges from other institutions within the field to remain on top of the hierarchy and retain their status. According to Bourdieu, "Those who dominate in a given field are in a position to make it function to their advantage, but they must always contend with the resistance, the claims . . . of the dominated" (1992:102).

The objective relation between institutions of higher education is one of the reasons why "*where* one goes to college matters as much as, if not more than, *if* one goes to college" (Bowen, Chingos, and McPherson 2009:17, cited in Stich 2012:7). Historically, consumer demand has shaped how higher education expands in the United States, with new types of positions within the field being created to accommodate "each new wave of college enrollment" (Labaree 1997:209). Of course, each of these positions varies by status, and newer types of institutions are generally ranked lower compared to older ones—even if the latter might have the potential to resist or challenge the dominance of the former (Labaree 1997:212). Private universities and colleges have dominated the field of higher education in the

United States since their inception—some dating back before the American Revolution, like Harvard (1636), Yale (1701), The College of New Jersey (1746) that became Princeton in 1896, and King's College (1754) that became Columbia in 1784 (Delbanco 2012:67). Religious instruction and study were primary during the early years that these institutions opened, but philosophy, history, and math were also emphasized as a way to connect different types of knowledge together and help students develop their character (Delbanco 2012:39–41). State universities and secondary, public land-grant universities were established to meet growing demand in the nineteenth century. The Morrill Land-Grant Act of 1862 provided up to 30,000 acres of federal land for states to establish public institutions of higher education that stressed a vocational curriculum to help students develop human capital or practical skills, particularly agricultural and mechanical skills that were deemed important by the government for future economic growth. In the late nineteenth century, a profound and enduring shift occurred when the German model of higher education was adopted by the United States, which stratified the land-grant institutions into those that would continue to provide vocational training and remain "A&Ms" and those that would become academic universities, with specialized departments and disciplines that stressed research and professional education in addition to providing master and doctoral graduate programs (Labaree 1997:210–11). During the twentieth century, the number of higher education institutes grew from 1,000 to 4,000, and the number of students enrolled in them increased from 250,000 to 14 million. The rise of big science and public bureaucratic organizations after World War II helped to boost support of federal funding for both public and private research universities, and the 1944 GI Bill provided the demand in the form of veterans (Loss 2012:1–3).

As more land grants turned into universities and elevated their status in the process, two-year junior or community colleges became the places where most vocational training became located (Labaree 1997:212). The growth in community colleges also expanded greatly after World War II. Enrollment in these types of institutions is frequently described as democratic because access is universal via open admission policies (Delbanco 2012:110). Furthermore, community colleges have the potential to function as an inexpensive way to accumulate two years of course credit that can be transferred to a four-year public or private university where a student can finish the last two years of an undergraduate degree. But, as Labaree (1997:193, 196, 198) points out, in practice, community colleges have been used to "guard the gates" of more prestigious four-year universities by "draining off excess demand" for higher educational opportunities.

Furthermore, they often fail to be a vehicle for social mobility. Many students enrolled in community colleges do not transfer to four-year schools—and those who do often find that many if not all of their credits are not transferrable, so they have to spend the time and money to repeat course work (Bidwell 2014).

Students who attend for-profit institutes of higher learning face a similar problem. For-profit schools are the most recent places of consumption established to meet the current demand for higher education. Most for-profit universities offer short-term programs that focus on specific job training skills and award certificates instead of traditional degrees; few if any courses taken at them transfer for credit at four-year colleges and universities. However, not many of the nontraditional students who overwhelmingly enroll in for-profit schools have any intention of continuing their education (Breneman, Pusser, and Turner 2006). While the for-profit sector has experienced the largest growth within the field of higher education in the past few decades—enrolling .2% of students in the 1970s to 9.6% of students in 2010—Mettler (2014:34) argues this growth is often at the expense of their students' future success because some for-profits are more interested in recruiting students than actually graduating them. Many classes offered at for-profits are strictly online, which provides convenience and efficiency but limited—if any—personal interaction between faculty and other students. For example, at Kaplan University, 94% of its 42,000 students are enrolled in online courses ("Special Report" 2015).

MOOCs

Some view MOOCs as a way to overcome the problem of the cost and limited access of the places of higher education. Most MOOCs are free, open-access, online courses, many delivered by professors at elite institutions that can enroll hundreds of thousands of students at the same time from around the world. The three most popular MOOCs are Coursera, a for-profit company with partnerships to 30 elite universities; Udacity, a for-profit company that is partnered with Stanford University; and edX, a nonprofit organization created by Harvard and MIT. Coursera is the largest of the MOOCs, which launched faster than Facebook with over 70,000 new students enrolling in courses per week in 2012 (Lewin 2013). The typical MOOC course consists of video lectures and interactive forums that

(Continued)

(Continued)

connect faculty and students to one another; exams and assignments are required to complete most courses, with grading primarily done electronically with computer programs.

Students who want credit often pay a small fee, usually around $40 per exam. However, most students who enroll in these courses never finish them—nor do many intend to; the average MOOC student already has a bachelor's degree and a full-time job and enrolls in a course to watch or listen to a few lectures that suit his or her interest (Selingo 2014). Students who do complete these courses tend to be "self-motivated, bright students," similar to ones found at Harvard and MIT that the typical MOOC faculty teach on their physical campuses (Selingo 2014). Because of their partnerships with elite institutions, Selingo (2014) argues that MOOCs act "as gatekeepers for American higher education online, replicating in their virtual world the pecking order in the physical world" (Selingo 2014). Although they are certainly less expensive than the cost of traditional courses, MOOCs need to be partnered with an accredited university to legitimize their credits and degrees. An additional potential problem is that for-profit MOOCs partnered with corporations, like AT&T and Google, could promote knowledge skewed toward science and technology over the humanities.

Questions

1. Have you ever taken a MOOC or a traditional online course? If yes, what are some of the benefits and challenges you experienced with online learning? If no, would you be willing to take a course online? Why or why not?

2. Do you think that online learning will replace learning in a physical classroom for the majority of university and college students in the future? Why or why not?

3. If you were an employer, how would you evaluate a job candidate with only online learning credentials? What are some specific strengths and weakness this candidate might possess?

Corporate Colonization

Corporate influence on higher education is not simply a problem with for-profit schools; many private and public colleges and universities look to businesses for funding opportunities and sponsorships that some view as a threat to the autonomy and supposed democratic character of higher education (Bok 2005; Giroux 2014; Gould 2003). Regardless of the hierarchical positions of institutions within it, ideally the field of higher education should embody the **public sphere,** "a space beyond the control of either the State or private interests where public conversation, deliberation, and innovation can take place" (Habermas 1991; Pusser 2006:38). Unfortunately, this public sphere is being colonized by corporations. According to Bok (2004:43), "Commercialization threatens to impair the university's reputation for objective, disinterested teaching and research." As places of higher education adopt a corporate ethos, they inevitable turn knowledge into an object of consumption and their students into subjects of consumption. Buying and selling knowledge can encourage unethical conduct, such as enrolling student athletes who fail to meet academic standards and hiring faculty who are more interested in pursuing private funding than teaching students or conducting research for the public good. Setting a precedent that knowledge is a commodity might even encourage students to think that it is acceptable to buy and sell lecture notes and papers (Bok 2004; Giroux 2014; Williams 2001). Equally problematic, corporate influence can prevent a serious critique of corporate power and neoliberal policies at places of higher education. This is especially worrisome as institutes of higher learning engage in corporate cost-cutting labor strategies, like outsourcing faculty to part-time, adjunct faculty and charging user fees to students for things that were once free, like parking and printing, or upgrades to luxury dormitories or meal plans (Gould 2003; Slaughter and Rhoades 2004).

The two most evident influences of corporations in higher education involve sports and scientific research. Corporate funding and sponsorship of university sports dates back over 100 years ago, when tobacco companies advertised at sporting events and in game programs. But corporate influence truly came to dominance in the 1990s "when schools began to allow faculty and staff members to endorse products so long as the institutions received a cut of the corporate remuneration" (Sperber 2004:23). Previously, coaches signed independent contracts and received money directly from corporations to endorse their products for a particular sport. Now corporations negotiate with the institution as a whole to endorse their products for the entire school. Places of higher education have become Nike or Adidas schools, some receiving tens of millions of dollars as compensation for prominently displaying corporate logos on all athletic gear and at the stadiums for all sporting events. The singular "branding" of these schools is so circumscribed that some contracts prohibit athletes from spatting—taping over corporate logos on their uniforms and shoes—and give corporate representatives the right to inspect locker rooms to make sure their logos are being used properly (Slaughter and Rhoades 2004). Many contracts also contain a disparagement clause that "bans criticism of corporate partners by members of the university community" (Slaughter and Rhoades 2004:264). This is an especially problematic aspect of the colonization of the public sphere by corporations as it essentially bans protest on campuses against unethical corporate practices, like child or sweatshop labor—two human rights abuses that are strongly associated with the production of athletic apparel and shoes (King and Slaughter 2004:264). Interestingly, with all the corporate money involved in funding and sponsoring university sports, it usually fails to generate any revenue. Indeed, it might actually take money away from academic programs if the public believes otherwise, using corporate sponsorship as a reason why they should not have to pay higher taxes to fund higher education (Sperber 2004:29). With all the corporate sponsorship and fanfare of college sports such as football bowl games (most now renamed by corporations like the Capital One Orange Bowl) and basketball's bracketed "big dance," the public might also be ignorant of the fact that the United States is "the only nation where universities use their students to present athletic spectacles for profit at the cost of compromising academic standards" (Bok 2004:35).

The relationship between places of higher education and corporations in regards to research may compromise academic integrity even more than athletics. Corporate funding of academic research has grown stronger since the Bayh-Dole Act was passed by Congress in 1980. This act allows universities "to own and profit from federally funded research performed by faculty" and corporations "to claim ownership of patents taken out on products and processes discovered during the course of federally funded research" (Slaughter and Rhoades 2004:2). Since this act was passed, universities have increased their volume of patents significantly; prior to 1981, fewer than 250 patents were issued to universities annually, but by 2000, over 5,500 were granted to universities earning more than $1 billion in royalties and fees (Bok 2005:12; Slaughter and Rhoades 2004:17). Viewing knowledge as a commodity that can be owned and patented has been correlated with the triumph of science and research—and subsequent devaluation of the humanities—at places of higher education (Slaughter and Rhoades 2004; Delbanco 2012). Knowledge that is associated with a profitable exchange value is stressed, and faculty members who can produce this kind of knowledge are compensated handsomely. But, as Bok (2004:40) reminds us, this undermines the purpose of scientific research in academia as a shared resource for the common good and "disrupts collegial relationships." According to Delbanco (2012), we should be wary of equating scientific discoveries with progress because they often fail to help us with morals and ethics. As corporations funnel more money into scientific research and development in addition to other programs of study they find useful, like business, places of higher education may lose their autonomy over their curriculum and even hires. For example, according to Giroux (2014:119), the well-known conservative Koch brothers agreed to give $1.5 million to Florida State University if their representatives were allowed to screen and sign off on faculty hires in the economic department. Funding endowed chairs and professors, often with corporate brands in their professional titles, gives corporations further power over what academic departments, and therefore forms of knowledge, will thrive or perish (Bok 2005). This, in turn, shapes the object of consumption that places of higher education can sell successfully.

Higher Education as an Object of Consumption

Even though the United States was the pioneer in establishing institutions of mass higher education, today it is facing something of a crisis in terms of affordability, accessibility, and attainment. Compared to other developed countries, the percentage of young adults with at least some post–high school education is falling in the United States and, "for the first time in our history, we face the prospect that the coming generation of adults will be less educated than their elders" (Delbanco 2012:26). While 75% of young adults between the ages of 18 and 24 years attended an institution of higher education in 2010, only 47% of them completed their degrees by age 24, and only 33% of people between the ages of 25 and 34 years held four-year degrees in 2010 (Mettler 2014:22). At most four-year public, nonprofit universities, only 19% of full-time students graduate in four years (Lewin 2014). From an economic perspective, these numbers are troublesome because over one's lifetime, a person who completes a college degree earns 60% more than a person who does not (Delbanco 2012:25). College graduates receive a wage premium compared to those who only earn a high school diploma, making an average of $40,000 per year compared to $25,000; furthermore, only

6.8% of college graduates are unemployed compared to 24% of individuals who only graduate from high school (Mettler 2014:21–22). Besides economic capital, places of higher education also sell social and cultural capital in the form of their respective student bodies, reputations, and credentials. Each of these forms of capital has been fashioned into an object of consumption that is being marketed and sold to future students and their parents, and they tend to be mutually reinforcing. Colleges and universities that can deliver high future earnings also tend to have good reputations and student bodies with strong social and cultural capital.

Human Capital and Credentials

Human capital, or concrete work skills, is one object of consumption that institutes of higher education sell, particularly those that offer vocational courses and more technical programs of study. The premise of human capital theory is that each individual has exogenous preferences that schools can help them develop into marketable skills needed by potential employers (Bowles and Gintis 2002). Viewed from this perspective, higher education provides social efficiency by matching training opportunities to current job positions for students; enhancing an individual's potential for economic productivity at the micro-level is viewed in turn as helping to fuel economic growth at the macro-level (Labaree 1997). While individual preferences are probably more endogenous than exogenous—influenced by external conditions instead of internal ones—critics of human capital theory further challenge its premise that the goal of education should be primarily about producing workers (Bowles and Gintis 2002). Even though when asked, most people say that they are attending or want to attend college for economic reasons, political goals, such as an informed citizenry, and liberal educational goals, such as self-discovery and critical thinking, are important too (Delbanco 2012:25). Ironically, technical work skills may not actually produce good workers (Bowles and Gintis 2002:77). An individual might be a highly skilled electrician, but if he does not show up for appointments on time, organizes his billing and other paperwork inefficiently, and does not know how to communicate effectively with clients, then he is probably not a very productive worker.

Credential theory proposes that it is not human capital but the degree or credential itself that is the object of consumption in higher education (Collins 1979). In contrast to human capital, which indicates an individual was trained to possess a specific skill at a specific time, degrees are a "permanent, status identity that transcends time and place limitations of ordinary competence" (Brown 2011:27). Max Weber argued that competition over educational credentials was the defining feature of inequality in a modern society as they are exclusionary and act as "cultural entry barriers to positions" within the labor market (Brown 2011:19). A university degree signals to potential employers that a job applicant possesses certain cultural dispositions that will make him or her a competent worker within a formal organization, including language and communication skills, loyalty, and trustworthiness (Brown 2011:25). Lower-status credentials, like a community college degree, signal that a potential employee not only possesses certain technical skills but is comfortable with following a routine and taking instruction from those above him or her, while higher-status credentials suggest that a person can be trusted to work autonomously without constant supervision (Brown 2011:27–28). Credentials may signify that a potential hire is a strong "cultural fit" with his or her future boss and coworkers. One recent survey found that employers prefer to hire workers who are "like-minded" and share their own tastes and hobbies (Rivera 2015). Not surprisingly, both organizational and personal preferences reproduce class inequality in higher education and the workplace.

Bowles and Gintis (2002, 2010) use the concept of the **correspondence principle** to describe how the social relations in schools replicate those in the workplace, such as receiving rewards in the form of grades or wages for producing good work and the hierarchical organization and authority positions that each possess. Educational institutions, like workplaces, reinforce a belief in the value of **meritocracy**—that if an individual works hard, he or she will be successful (McNamee and Miller 2009). This understanding of social mobility hides the structural conditions that create inequality, positioning personal attributes as the source of achievement and failure (Khan 2012). According to Labaree (1997:258), "A credential-driven system of education can provide meritocratic cover for socially reproductive outcome" and produce a "spiral of credential inflation" where individuals need higher levels of credentials for social mobility. Like more money, the more credentials that one accumulates is associated with success, which has resulted in a systemic problem of **credential inflation.** Occupations that did not require four-year college degrees in the past now do, like administrative assistants, police officers, and nurses, and those that used to require four-year degrees often require advanced degrees, like an MBA (McNamee and Miller 2009:111).

The demand for credentials coupled with a tight labor market has resulted in underemployment too, with college graduates settling for jobs as coffee baristas, food servers, and retail sales clerks that do not require any level of higher education.

Social and Cultural Capital

In addition to economic capital, students can increase their social and cultural capital at select colleges and universities. The idea that places of higher education should foster a "collegiate way of life," requiring students from different places to live together, eat meals together, share social experiences, and engage in **lateral learning**, the belief that students can actually learn things from each other, has become a valuable object of consumption (Delbanco 2012:54). The collegiate way of life is an **associative good,** implying that students care about the sociability, intellectual aptitude, and family connections of other students perhaps even more than the other products that colleges and universities are trying to sell them like curriculum or campus facilities (Hansmann 1999). "In short," states Henry Hansmann (1999:1), "the thing that a college or university is selling to its students is, in large part, its other students." Elite private colleges and universities, in particular, emphasize the quality of their students—both past and present—and how their usually small cohort numbers facilitate social networking and personal interactions between students, faculty, and staff. Their selectivity works to simply strengthen their reputations, which in turn helps them recruit quality students from across the nation and even world. It is important to note that the collegiate way of life does vary between places of higher education, with some stressing sociability like sports and Greek life, some emphasizing rigorous academic programs, and others accentuating religious values (Hansmann 1999:4–5).

Over the past few years, the idea of higher education as an associative good is something that has shaped the student body not only at elite private schools but also at public colleges and universities, which are relying more and more on out-of-state tuition to compensate for the loss of state funding. This practice has created a situation where public state universities have become divided between elite ones that recruit from a national pool and those that focus on regional and local in-state students (Carey 2015a). The number of applicants from "good" students has increased at elite public universities, which in turn has elevated their status as they have become more selective because out-of-state students tend to have higher standardized test scores and grade point averages compared to in-state students. Out-of-state students, who pay tuition and fees at public universities that approximate the cost at private schools, also tend to have higher levels of economic, social, and cultural capital than in-state students; they are more likely to depend on the financial and social support of their parents, have experience with living away from home, and know at least one other student on campus (Armstrong and Hamilton 2013:30, 37). According to one study of a Midwestern university between 2004 and 2009, the number of applicants increased from 21,000 to 30,000, the average grade point average increased from 3.4 to 3.7, and the acceptance rate dropped from 83% to 69% (Armstrong and Hamilton 2013:30). As more out-of-state and even international students are accepted at elite public universities, in-state students face increasing competition among each other, with the losers settling for slots at less prestigious regional public universities or community colleges (Carey 2015b). Those who are accepted at elite public universities, especially those from working-class or lower-income backgrounds, tend to be "motivated for mobility," but their attempts to escape from their hometowns are difficult as that is where their social networks remain; they generally receive little financial or academic support from their parents, so usually must work at least a part-time job while at school. Their lack of financial and cultural capital tends to isolate them from the more wealthy out-of-state students who are "primed to party" and view college as a place to socialize through sports and Greek life and those who are academically motivated and have parental guidance to help them (Armstrong and Hamilton 2013).

Evaluating the Product of Higher Education

Many people wonder whether higher education is worth the cost and, if it is, how future students and their families can make well-informed decisions about the value of a degree from a specific school. Similar to other goods that are difficult to quantify and resemble services more than tangible objects, such as health care, the administrators of higher education possess more information on their products than students who consume them. According to Pusser (2006:32), "Higher education is a difficult commodity to assess in advance and often takes considerable time to consume and evaluate" (Pusser 2006:32). Independent sources, like *U.S. News & World Report* and *The Princeton Review*, which rank different types of universities and colleges according to a variety of criteria—from selection rates to student-to-faculty ratios to how "hard" students party—have become one source of information. In light of the fact that student loan debt in the United States has reached $1.2 trillion, President Obama recently announced an assessment plan to help future students and their families better understand the value of degrees from different schools and make institutions of higher education more accountable for the products that they are selling by linking the availability of federal financial aid to college performance in three key areas: access, affordability, and outcomes. Information will be made available on the percentage of students who receive Pell grants, net price, loan debt, graduation rates, and the earnings of graduates (Dynarski 2014; U.S. Department of Education n.d.). Whether this information will help students become better consumers of higher education is debatable, especially since not all students have the freedom of choice of where they can apply or if they get accepted to where they want to go. Furthermore, like the rankings from other sources, the president's assessment plan leaves out one key variable: student learning. Students might be completing degrees and translating these credentials into well-paying jobs, but this is not an accurate measure of whether students actually learn anything at college. Indeed, one recent study of 2,300 undergraduate found that 45% had not improved their critical thinking, analytical reasoning, or communication skills after two years, and 36% failed to do so after four years (Arum and Roksa 2010). Ironically, at the same time students are learning less at colleges and universities, their grades have been improving (Delbanco 2012:155). This so-called **grade inflation,** according to Gould (2003:32), "results in large part from the culture of consumerism" that "sees good grades as entitlements."

Higher Education and the Subjects of Consumption

Students as Consumers

One reason why students feel entitled to good grades is due to a "pay the fee, get the B" mentality, resulting in part from the high cost of tuition. Perhaps the most extreme way that higher education has turned students into consumers is by increasing tuition so much that student loans are needed by all but the wealthiest to pay for it and other related expenses, like room, board, and course materials. In 2012–2013, the average published tuition and fees for a bachelor's degree was $29,056 at private nonprofits and $8,655 at public nonprofits; for-profits charged an average of $15,172 in tuition and fees. Interestingly, the higher tuition at private institutions does not directly translate into higher burdens of student loan debt as the median among borrowers for 2007–2008 graduates who earned a BA was $17,700 at private nonprofits compared to $22,400 at public nonprofits and $32,700 at for-profits (Mettler 2014:29). The alleged sticker shock of published tuition, room, and board at private colleges and universities—often reaching over $50,000 per year—is rather deceptive as few students actually have to pay all of it. Most students receive **discount rates** from these types of institutions in the form of merit scholarships, grants, and tax benefits that reduced their average cost to $13,380 during the 2012–2103 school year (Mettler 2014:30). Unfortunately, the listed sticker price may deter academically qualified, low-income students from even considering to apply to private schools because they lack the knowledge about discount rate practices; thus, sticker shock acts as both an economic and cultural stratification mechanism that helps to socially reproduce the elite student body at nonprofit private institutions. This, in turn, limits the life chances of low-income students as graduates from elite private schools earn 45% more than graduates from other types of schools and represent a disproportionate share of corporate and government leaders (Mettler 2014:31).

Converse to the privileges of discount rates and the high return in value of degrees experienced by students who attend nonprofit private colleges and universities, students at for-profit schools usually pay full price on tuition for certificates and degrees that do not always translate into powerful or lucrative careers. The high tuition rates at for-profit schools, some topping over $46,000 per year for two-year programs that would cost at most $9,000 per year at a community college, necessitate that 96% of all students enrolled at nonprofit schools take out loans compared to only 13% who do at community colleges. Given that some fail to complete programs, while many of those who do graduate cannot find jobs with compensation comparable to the cost of their degrees, it is not surprising that about 25% of these students default on their loans within three years. Some for-profits, like Corinthian, service private loans for their students with interest rates as high as 18%—more than the average interest rate on credit cards (U.S. Senate 2011:1–4). Several for-profits have been accused, and a few proven legally guilty, of predatory recruiting practices that target vulnerable populations, such as low-income mothers who receive welfare; people who are recently divorced, fired, or laid off from their jobs; people in drug rehabilitation; and individuals who have experienced physical or mental abuse (U.S. Senate 2011:19). In need of steady income and self-worth from stable jobs, these individuals are susceptible to the false promises of guaranteed jobs and inflated earnings that some for-profits try to sell to them (Mettler 2014:35).

Obstacles to Future Consumption and Becoming an Adult

As mentioned earlier, student loan debt topped a record level of $1.2 trillion in 2013, which is jeopardizing debtors' ability to be future consumers, especially if they default. Currently, 14.7% of all borrowers default on federal student loans during their first three years of payment, which makes transitioning to adulthood more difficult (Lorin 2014). "Defaulting on a student loan has severe and long-lasting consequences. It can devastate a borrower's credit, making it difficult to rent an apartment or buy a car, and, increasingly get a job" (U.S. Senate 2011:31). Student loan debt cannot be erased by bankruptcy, and if a person defaults, then he or she cannot get another federal loan to return to school. The government can garnish wages, seize tax refunds, and even reduce Social Security payments to collect student loan debt (U.S. Senate 2011:31). Many young adults are denied home mortgages because of high student loan debt, blocking the primary way to accumulate wealth in the United States and affirm one's membership in the middle class (Matthew et al. 2015). The cost and structural need for higher education in the United States has made growing up harder to do. Combined with the 2008 recession and underemployment, student loan debt has made it difficult for many young adults to reach the traditional benchmarks of adulthood, like financial independence, working full-time, leaving their parents' home, getting married, and having children (Furstenberg et al. 2004). In 2014, one in five young adults lived with his or her parents, mostly due to debt, unemployment, or underemployment—and many of those who did not live at home were still financially dependent on their parents to pay their rent (A. Davidson 2014). Perhaps this is why 97% of respondents to a 2002 General Social Survey agreed that "completing education" was an important benchmark to becoming an adult (Furstenberg et al. 2004). This puts young adults who do not have the privilege of going to places of higher education in a dilemma because many are unable to achieve this benchmark to adulthood, as well as other ones, such as getting married and finding a job to support a family, leaving them "stuck in an extended adolescence" (Silva 2015:5).

Disengaged Consumers and Ignorant Citizens

One of the original purposes of higher education was to assist young people transition into adulthood by helping them mature through building their character and developing a sense of duty to the public good as informed citizens (Delbanco 2012; Gould 2003). Positioning students as consumers undermines this purpose by catering to their demands instead of challenging them to "engage in some serious self-examination" (Delbanco 2012:15–16). Rather than trying to help young adults build character, higher education has turned students into "shoppers at the store of education, buying a career-enhancing service" (Williams 2001:21). Imitating the marketplace by providing students with more choices in terms of courses, majors, and minors has left many of them "overwhelmed with all the possibilities" and little guidance to help them (Lewin 2014). This leaves many of them disillusioned, which contributes to their disengagement from higher education in general. According to Gould (2003:44–46), the typical consumer-student is more detached and uncivil, cares more about his or her grade point average than knowledge, and is typically less academically prepared for college than his or her predecessors. Compared to the past, students today spend less time studying, going to classes, and participating in campus groups as college occupies a smaller part of their daily lives. On one hand, more students are working jobs off-campus to pay for college and commuting from home to save money; the growing number of non-traditional students who have children, attend part-time, and transfer from community colleges are often excluded from the traditional collegiate way of life. On the other hand, technological distractions take time away from studying, paying attention in class to engage in lateral learning, and spending physical time socializing and interacting with peers on campus (Delbanco 2012:16). Of course, consumers want fun, and some places of higher education are offering a "playground of unregulated freedom" to them (Delbanco 2012:19). But the lack of regulation on this playground does not serve all students equally, with a growing number of them expecting and needing therapeutic services from campus counseling centers for learning disabilities, eating disorders, drug and alcohol abuse, depression, and anxiety (Gould 2003:44–46). In sum, higher education no longer offers "a safe space and concerted time for students to imagine any other perspective for their lives rather than being a consumer" (Williams 2001:23).

Conclusion

Clearly, there are many problems surrounding the commodification of higher education in the United States today, stemming from the "inability for market-based, consumer-driven systems to produce opportunities for universal access . . . or the redress of social inequalities" (Pusser 2006:24–25). Most Americans believe that something needs to be done to make higher education more affordable and equitable; 81% agreed in a 2012 poll that the "government needs to invest more in America's higher education system" (Mettler 2014:39). One solution might be to adopt the GI Bill model from the 1940s but extend it to all individuals, not just veterans, resituating education as a public entitlement (Williams 2001:25). Another solution involves reducing the time it takes to complete a bachelor's degree from four years to three years to help students save money. Andrew Ross (2014) proposes that student loan debt should be forgiven and has called for a jubilee to write off all current student debt. Others hold out hope for MOOCs to create a new type of credentialing system based on free or low-cost digital badges that will replace traditional degrees (Carey 2015b). Without some solutions to decrease cost and increase access, higher education will limit social mobility and reproduce class inequality.

Decreasing cost and increasing access, however, do not necessarily address the problems associated with the commodification of knowledge and treating students as consumers. While the former may be dealt with by limiting or prohibiting corporate funding, sharing scientific research, and valuing teaching as much as research, the latter involves efforts to engage students more meaningfully in the learning process and helping them build character. Recently, students have used their identities as consumers of higher education to make their concerns about racial discrimination and climate change heard by administrators. At the University of Missouri, student protests against racial discrimination on campus led to the resignations of the president and chancellor. Tellingly, the demands of these protesters were taken seriously when football players threatened to boycott their games until the president resigned (Eligon and Pérez-Peña 2015; Hartocollis and Bidgood 2015). Students alarmed by how the consumption of fossil fuels is contributing to climate change have organized at over 300 colleges and universities to demand that their schools divest endowments in fossil fuel companies. Stanford University, which has an endowment worth $18.7 billion, agreed to sell its coal stock in May 2014 as a result (Klein 2014:354). These cases of student activism are promising and will hopefully remind places of higher education, which were created to "serve the public interest," that they have "a moral responsibility to liberate" themselves from "odious profits" and should refuse to tolerate all instances of discrimination (Klein 2014:354). As the next section of this book will discuss, consumers have used their purchasing power to successfully achieve social change. Threats to withdraw financial support from places of consumption or corporations that produce the objects of consumption may be one of the only ways to force them to take notice of the social injustices that they create or support, especially in an age of neoliberalism when the market is so dominant.

PART III

Ethical Concerns and Consumer Activism

8

Political Consumerism and the Consumer Movement

The proposition of shopping for social change seems illogical because consumption itself is often identified as the primary culprit for social problems like inequality and environmental degradation. Accordingly, from a consumerist standpoint, the solution to solving these problems is simply to consume less. However, there is a growing perspective that the question driving this debate should be redirected from "to consume or not to consume?" to "how can we consume better?" Consuming better involves mobilizing the purchasing power of consumers toward goods that are produced under environmentally friendly conditions or by workers who earn a living wage. If such goods are unavailable, then consumers can exert pressure on corporations to change their production practices by withholding their purchasing power or patronizing companies that do produce such goods. Consumers can engage in **political consumerism,** "actions by people who make choices among producers and products with the goal of changing objectionable institutional or market practices" (Micheletti 2003:2), to make their concerns heard. A variety of tactics can be exercised by consumers in their efforts to politicize consumption, specifically boycotts and buycotts.

Political consumerism tends to position the interests of consumers secondary to other concerns, such as the welfare of workers or the environment. In contrast, the **consumer movement** is focused on trying to protect consumers from potentially harmful products and services. Product testing by scientific experts working within formal organizations, such as Consumers Union, best characterizes the tactics and actors within the consumer movements. Thus, unlike political consumerism, consumers are not typically active participants in the consumer movement per se. Furthermore, the consumer movement has tried to fight for social change through government regulations and legislation instead of through the marketplace like political consumerism. But, like political consumerism, the consumer movement endorses instead of challenges the ideology of consumerism. Rather than ask consumers to stop shopping, it aims to provide them with legitimate and reliable information about the safety and price of products and services so that they can make better choices.

This chapter begins by describing how consumers have politicized their purchasing power historically using boycotts and buycotts, starting with the American Revolution, labor unions, and the National Consumers League to the civil rights movement and more contemporary boycotts and buycotts. Next, it will explain the origins of the consumer movement in the United States during the late 1920s, including the establishment of Consumers' Research and Consumers Union. The fair trade movement and green consumerism will be analyzed as important cases of the new era of political consumerism we are witnessing today. This chapter will conclude with exploring some of the limits to political consumerism. Can—and, more important, should—consumers be conceived of as political actors with rights and obligations comparable to citizens? Is the marketplace a democratic space where all individuals can participate equally? These are just some of the questions up for debate in the politics of consumption.

Political Consumerism: A Brief History

Consumer Tactics: Boycotts and Buycotts

Consumer activism has a long and significant history in the United States, starting with the boycott of British goods by American colonists in the 1760s and 1770s, which eventually led to the American Revolution. **Boycotts** are attempts "by one or more parties to achieve certain objectives by urging individual consumers to refrain from making selected purchases in the marketplace" (Friedman 1999). According to historian T. H. Breen, American colonists interpreted their marketplace decisions as political acts and viewed consumer choices as a way to communicate their personal loyalties (2004:xv–xvi). Some of these boycotts focused on the nonimportation of British goods, which were directed at merchants to keep British goods out of their stores, while others, particularly the boycott of British tea, were focused on the nonconsumption of British goods by ordinary consumers. Voluntary associations were established to recruit supporters through signing subscription rolls that family, friends, and neighbors could see, which meant that enforcement of the colonial boycotts could take place face-to-face at the local level. Colonial consumer activism has been characterized as democratic because women could participate, even though they were not formal citizens with the right to vote (Breen 2004:20–24). Patriotic women, for example, not only signed subscription rolls but also joined the **homespun movement** when they began to weave and spin cloth for their family's clothes to boycott British fabric. The inclusiveness of women in consumer activism is important because it demonstrates that even before they had the rights of full citizenship, they could engage in some forms of political action.

Women continued to participate in consumer activism during the Antebellum era, particularly those who supported the abolition of slavery. By avoiding products made with slave labor, especially sugar and cotton, and supporting "free produce" stores that sold clothes and dry goods made with free labor, women and other consumers were able to use the marketplace to express their moral convictions (Glickman 2009). The idea of consumers using their purchasing power to try to help someone else was an important precedent established by abolitionist consumer activism. Encouraging "people to purchase goods following an established set of criteria" introduced the tactic of the **buycott** (Micheletti 2003:50). Also referred to as a positive boycott (Friedman 1999:11), buycotts recommend instead of prohibit consumer purchases and generally have been viewed as less controversial than traditional boycotts because they do not negatively threaten business and trade.

The buycott became a key tactic in the efforts of the National Consumers League (NCL) to try to help female workers during the Progressive era. Composed mainly of upper- and upper-middle-class housewives, the NCL was formed in 1899 with the goal of improving the working conditions of female laborers, eradicating sweatshop production, and abolishing child labor. In the words of Florence Kelley, the general secretary of the NCL from 1899 to 1932, "The power of the purchaser, which is potentially unlimited, becomes great, in practice, just in proportion as purchasers become organized and enlightened" (1899:303). The NCL created a **white label,** which was attached to goods that were produced in clean and healthy work environments, and a **white list** that included the names of stores that treated their employees fairly to mobilize and educate consumers. The white label and white list were buycott tactics that were intended to educate consumers and direct their purchasing power toward products that the NCL recommended. The NCL conducted its own investigative work to protect the integrity of its respective tactics, directly ensuring that manufacturers and retailers were abiding by its labor and health standards. Interestingly, NCL members used the scientific expertise they acquired from guaranteeing their buycott tactics to help win a Supreme Court case, *Muller v. Oregon* (1908), which established a maximum workday of 10 hours for women, proving that even though women could not vote in most states, they could use their power as consumers to fight for social change (Sklar 1998; Wiedenhoft 2008).

Organized labor also used boycotts and buycotts to politicize consumption during the Progressive era. The American Federation of Labor (AFL) started to publish its "We Don't Patronize" list in 1894, which listed manufacturers who refused to recognize AFL trade unions, neglected to meet union wage or workday hour standards, or were experiencing a strike by their workers. The AFL asked its members and their families to boycott products from these listed manufacturers; thus, the "We Don't Patronize" list operated as a **blacklist** instead of a white list because instead of recommending products, it prohibited them. Trade unions affiliated with the AFL also used the buycott tactic to politicize consumption by creating labels to be placed on union-made goods, including hats, cigars, ovens, shoes, paper, and overalls. These **union labels** were intended to enlist the support of consumers in the cause of organized labor through purchasing products made with union labor. Indeed, if enough consumers bought union-labeled goods, the AFL thought that the union label could potentially replace the strike as a way to achieve higher wages, shorter workdays, and safer working conditions. The union label was one of the only ways that women could participate in the labor movement at the time. Mobilizing the purchasing power of the wives, mothers, and daughters of union men was specifically identified by the AFL as the key to the future success of the union label (Glickman 1997; Wiedenhoft 2006). The AFL's union label still exists today—perhaps most commonly seen on beer cans and bottles produced by union beer manufacturers, like Miller and Anheuser-Busch.

Numerous boycotts and buycotts have been organized in the United States since the Progressive era. Arguably, the most famous boycott in U.S. history—the Montgomery bus boycott (1955–1956) to end racial segregation on public transportation—was the catalyst for the civil rights movement. Parallel boycotts were organized to end racial segregation at Woolworth lunch counters and other restaurants. The National Association for the Advancement of Colored People (NAACP) found the boycott tactic so successful that a lawsuit was brought against by white merchants in Port Gibson, Mississippi. These merchants claimed that a boycott against them was coercive because it made all black consumers fearful to patronize their businesses. The Supreme Court disagreed with these merchants in *National Association for the Advancement of Colored People v. Claibourne Hardware Co.* (1982), stating that boycotts should not be deemed illegal even if boycotters engaged in a "few violent acts" (Glickman 2009:300). More recently, the NAACP enacted a boycott on the state of South Carolina because it refused to remove the Confederate flag from the top of its statehouse; this boycott was subsequently ended after the governor removed the flag in July 2015.

Other groups and organizations fighting for social change have also launched boycotts and buycotts in the past few years. The lesbian, gay, bisexual, and transgender (LGBT) community organized a boycott of Chick-fil-A in 2014 after its CEO publicly opposed same-sex marriage. Human rights supporters started a global boycott in the mid-2000s against Coca-Cola because it is depleting ground water supplies in India to make its beverages—water that local farmers desperately need to grow crops. Some groups are using divestment strategies to boycott the policies of certain governments or corporations. 350.org is urging individuals, institutions such as universities, and municipal governments to divest their stocks and bonds in fossil fuels, while End the Occupation is urging divestment in Israeli companies to demonstrate support for Palestine. One of the most successful cases of a contemporary buycott is the fair trade movement, which will be discussed at length later in this chapter.

The Consumer Movement[1]

Unlike political consumerism, which tends to emphasize how consumers can use their purchasing power to help others or influence social change more broadly, the consumer movement positions the interests of consumers as its predominant concern. These consumer interests include objective information regarding the quality, standards, and price of products and services, most often supplied by scientific experts associated with an independent consumer organization. This information is intended to protect the safety of consumers from harmful products and services, such as toxic chemicals used in manufacturing or predatory lending practices. In addition, the consumer movement makes objective information available to help consumers make better financial decisions. Instead of boycotts and buycotts, the main tactics used by the consumer movement are product testing and lobbying for government regulation and legislation. Even though the interests of consumers are the central concern of the consumer movement, consumers themselves are rarely mobilized to directly participate in it except to pay membership dues if they join a particular consumer organization.

The consumer movement commenced in the late 1920s with the establishment of two consumer organizations, Consumers' Research (CR) and Consumers Union (CU) (Glickman 2009; Hilton 2009; Sorenson 1941). CR was founded in 1928 by Stuart Chase and Frederick Schlink after the success of their book *Your Money's Worth* (1936), which argued that American consumers were being manipulated by corporations and advertisers to buy inferior products because of a lack of information and product standardization. To education consumers, CR published *Consumers' Research Bulletin*, a magazine that provided subscribers with unbiased information on products the organization tested in its laboratories. By 1932, over 42,000 consumers subscribed to the *Bulletin*. Schlink and CR board member Arthur Kallet published the book *100,000,000 Guinea Pigs: Dangers in Everyday Foods, Drugs, and Cosmetics* in 1933, which inspired the passage of the Wheeler-Lea Act in 1938 (Kallet 1933/1976). This legislation gave the Federal Trade Commission the power to regulate false advertising in addition to advertisements for food, drugs, cosmetics, and therapeutic devices (Mayer 1989). Ironically, CRs' focus on the interests of consumers

---

[1] Parts of this section were previously published as "Contemporary Consumer Movement" in *The Wiley Blackwell Encyclopedia of Consumption and Consumer Studies*, March 2015.

was deemed too narrow by its own workers, who went on strike in 1935 after the organization fired three of them for trying to establish a chapter of the AFL's Technical, Editorial, and Office Assistants Union. Several of these workers decided to form their own consumer organization, CU. CU is best known today for its popular publication, *Consumer Reports,* a product testing guide (Glickman 2009; Hilton 2009; Mayer 1989).

The consumer movement gained momentum in the mid-1960s and early 1970s with the successful passage of federal legislation to protect consumers, including the Federal Cigarette Labeling and Advertising Act (1965), National Traffic and Motor Vehicle Safety Act (1966), and the Consumer Product Safety Act (1972). Ralph Nader emerged as the contentious leader of the consumer movement during this time with the publication of his book *Unsafe at Any Speed* (1965), which documented the human and social costs of dangerously designed automobiles. Nader stressed the unfair economic playing field that corporations created and was critical of how the federal government refused to challenge the concentration of corporate power. He assembled law students and undergraduates—known as "Nader's Raiders"—to investigate the failure of government agencies to protect consumers from dangerous products and founded the public interest group Public Citizen in 1972 to fight for food and environmental safety, product liability, and government accountability (Pertschuk 1982).

Political Consumerism: A New Era

The power of the consumer movement began to wane in the 1980s as corporations united in their "revolt against regulation" and defeated the efforts of the consumer movement to create a federal Consumer Protection Agency (Pertschuk 1982:59). According to Glickman (2009:279), this defeat signaled the triumph of free market ideology and coincided with the rise of neoliberalism in the West (see Chapter 9). While political consumerism has grown stronger in the context of neoliberalism because it uses free market ideology to further its goals, the consumer movement has not disappeared entirely. Recent legislation to help protect consumers from predatory financial practices has been passed, including the Credit Cardholders Bill of Rights Act in 2009, additionally to the creation of the Bureau of Consumer Financial Protection in 2010 (see Chapter 9). In addition, organizations are fighting for federal regulation for mandatory labels on food that contains genetically modified ingredients. However, political consumerism is more aligned with the neoliberal ideology that has come to dominate American society, especially its emphasis on individual choice and deregulation of the marketplace (Banet-Weiser and Mukherjee 2012; Littler 2009). This is especially true of the buycotts that characterize most political consumerism today—urging individuals to "consume better" instead of refraining from consuming at all.

One of the most salient indicators of the new era of political consumerism is the so-called certification revolution, which occurred in the 1990s (Micheletti and Stolle 2009). Labels are key components of this certification revolution, which are displayed on products to inform consumers at the point of purchase about their origins, including *who* produced the goods they want to buy, *where* they were made, and *how* they were grown or manufactured. This information is typically certified by an independent organization that guarantees its reliability and authenticity. According to Boström and Klintman (2008), the popularity of labels on consumer products reflects several trends, including individualization or consumers becoming more self-dependent, globalization and the increasingly complex biography of products, and standardization, which has emerged as a form of regulation in the global marketplace. Labels, of course, have been used for over a century as a buycott tactic. Like the NCL's white label and the AFL's union label, contemporary label campaigns connect consumer agency to more formal organizations that help coordinate the individual purchasing decisions of thousands of consumers. Hawken maintains that nongovernmental organizations "work toward amending the market policies of globalization because markets are not designed to be surrogates for ethics, values, and justice" (2007:126). With regard to political consumerism, these organizations help "make the ethical consumer visible" and "seek to connect the forms of care and concern already embedded in everyday consumption practices into wider networks of collective solidarity" (Barnett et al. 2011:97, 93). Today, these ethical consumers are more likely to be scattered around the world.

This global dimension of the new era of political consumerism presents both benefits and challenges. On one hand, the global consumer base is enormous, which means that there is a lot of purchasing power to mobilize. However, the diversity of these global consumers and their geographic distance may make them feel little solidarity with one another. Furthermore, if the ability to influence social change is based strictly on how much purchasing power one possesses, then wealthy consumers, especially those in developed countries, have more power to determine the agenda of organizations that coordinate political consumerism than poor ones. While the rich might want organic apples to protect themselves from pesticides, the hungry poor may be more concerned with simply having access to any apples. This dilemma, of course, is one of the main problems with using market-based tactics, like buycotts, whether they are local or global in scale. But, as we will see with the case of the fair trade movement, the global nature of political consumerism today means that the purchasing power of wealthy consumers can be used to directly help people in developing countries. Just as corporations and their brands have gained strength through globalization, so too can consumer activism.

The Fair Trade Movement

One of the most successful example of political consumerism today is the fair trade movement. **Fair trade** aims to "offer the most disadvantaged producers in developing countries the opportunity to move out of extreme poverty through creating market access (typically to Northern consumers) under beneficial rather than exploitative terms" (Nicholls and Opal 2005:6). It is based on the principle of cooperation rather than competition, supporting fair wages and the prohibition of child and slave labor through a monetary **social premium.** This social premium is added to the price of all fair trade products and must be used to fund development projects in local communities (Nicholls and Opal 2005:6–7). Fair trade products are among the fastest growing segments of the global food market, valued at approximately $1.6 billion per year, encompassing 58 developing countries and over 5 million farmers, farm workers, and their families (Murray and Raynolds 2007:3). Fair trade labels are one of the most recognizable labels in the marketplace today and can be found on a variety of products from coffee to bananas to chocolate. According to Fair Trade USA, the number of fair trade products for sale in the United Sates is currently over 10,000, and the sale of fair trade was up 63% in 2011. Global fair trade sales reached $3.3 billion in 2009 (Oosterveer and Sonnenfeld 2012:133). The success of fair trade has been attributed not just to consumer demand but to religious groups and humanitarian organizations like Oxfam that have coordinated grassroots campaigns to sell fair trade goods (Barnett et al. 2011; Micheletti and Stolle 2009). The participation of nongovernmental organizations in the fair trade movement is important to stress because its success is not simply the result of individual consumer decisions but more structured action. In other words, the success of fair trade depends on more than "the whims of consumer preferences" (Wilson 2010).

The first fair trade label, created in 1988 in the Netherlands, was placed on coffee. It was certified by the Max Havelaar Foundation, which developed guidelines for producers, traders, and roasters. In 1997, the Fairtrade Labelling Organization (FLO) was created to establish global standards for production and trade and coordinate national fair trade schemes, seeking to bring accountability and transparency into the certification process. Producers who want to be certified must apply and pay a fee of 500 euros. Next, they pay for an independent FLO certifier to conduct an on-site audit. Meetings with stakeholders, site visits and interviews, and a closing meeting take place before a decision is reached concerning a producer's compliance to certification standards. If compliance is satisfactory, then the producer is awarded the use of the fair trade label (Oosterveer and Sonnenfeld 2012:132–36). Other fair trade organizations, like TransFair USA, the European Fair Trade Association, and the Fair Trade Federation, certify their own labels as well. Today, towns and institutions such as universities can even obtain fair trade certification if they demonstrate a political, retail, media, and activist commitment to promoting fair trade products. Currently, over 300 towns in the United Kingdom have received fair trade certification (Micheletti and Stolle 2009:90).

According to Nicholls and Opal (2005:153), the greatest challenge facing fair trade groups today is "how to market their products to a wider audience beyond the naturally sympathetic segment of 'ethically aware' consumers and gain mainstream acceptance." One of the potential problems with becoming more mainstream is that growing demand can most likely only be accomplished by working with large-scale producers, traders, and retailers, which may undermine the original aim and principles of the fair trade movement (Murray and Raynolds 2007; Lyon and Moberg 2010). Can small farmers and their families compete with larger producers—perhaps even corporations—in developing countries? Will corporations attempt to appropriate fair trade to improve their public image, like Starbucks has done by claiming to be a fair trade company even though only 3.7% of its total coffee sales in 2007 were fair trade (Lyon and Moberg 2010:10)? Another problem that the fair trade movement needs to address is the high cost of fair trade products, which makes it difficult for lower-income consumers to support. Can the price of fair trade products be decreased without affecting the social premium? If yes, then how can the fair trade movement attract a less affluent consumer base? The answer to these questions will certainly inform the success of the fair trade movement in the future.

Culture Jamming

A provocative intersection between political consumerism and the consumer movement is **culture jamming,** a type of discursive action that parodies mass advertisements and slogans in an attempt to educate consumers about the extensive reach of corporate power. Culture jammers hope to reclaim public spaces to "propagate ideas instead of plugging products" and encourage "spontaneous acts of public art and mischief" (Bordwell 2002:238). In general, culture jammers want to make mass consumer culture and its individualistic, materialist ethic "uncool" and hope that consumers can learn to critically resist the pressure created by advertisers and the media to mindlessly buy whatever they are trying to sell (Lasn 1999). Two ways they try to do so is by creating subvertisements and spreading cultural memes. **Subvertisements** are artistic efforts to sabotage the meanings of popular corporate logos and advertising campaigns by co-opting them, such as imitating the hamburger logo for Burger King but replacing the name of the company with Murder King. Cultural jammers also create subversive **cultural memes,** or ideas and information that spread from one individual to another, to try to challenge the status quo (Lasn 2012). For example, the cultural meme "Media Carta" pushes people to understand that "every human being has the 'right to communicate'—to receive and impart information through any media" (Bordwell 2002:251). Control over our thoughts, ideas, and actions is what is at stake in the culture jammers' discursive battle with corporate logos, slogans, and catchphrases.

Adbusters Media Foundation, founded in 1989 in Canada, is one of the main organizations that advocates culture jamming and publishes a magazine called *Adbusters: Journal of the Mental Environment* that contains numerous subvertisements. Some of Adbusters' more infamous campaigns include Joe Chemo, a cartoon parody of the former "mascot" of Camel cigarettes in a hospital receiving chemotherapy treatment, and Absolute on Ice, a spoof on the famous Absolut Vodka advertisements that depicts a frozen foot on a morgue table. These subvertisments clearly attempt to provoke consumers into considering the health risks associated with smoking

(Continued)

(Continued)

cigarettes and consuming alcohol. In addition to publishing its magazine, Adbusters created "Buy Nothing Day," celebrated the day after Thanksgiving, to critique the commoditization of the holidays (Sommer 2012). It also initiated the Occupy Wall Street movement in 2011 to protest corporate power and its role in producing social inequality, organizing in Zuccotti Park to demonstrate the people's right to assemble and communicate in a public space.

Questions

1. If both corporate advertisements and Adbuster's subvertisements are trying to control our thoughts and behaviors, then do you think that there are any differences between them? If yes, what are some of these differences? If no, are subvertisements disingenuous?

2. Go to https://www.adbusters.org/spoofadsonline and browse through some of the subvertisements. Which one do you think is most effective? Why?

3. Do you think that social media can be used to create and promote subversive cultural memes? If so, how? Construct a cultural meme that you think would be effective in raising awareness about a particular social problem.

Green Consumerism

Scholars studying the environment have long been aware of the environmental impact of consumption, categorized as affluence in the influential IPAT model developed by Paul Erhlich and John Holdren in the late 1970s. The **IPAT model** posits that environmental impact (I) is a function of population (P), affluence (A), and technology (T). While much research has been conducted over the years studying the environmental impacts of population and technology, "consumption, by contrast, has neither well-defined and accepted units of measurement nor a scientific community devoted to studying its dynamics" (Stern et al. 1997:3). Although consumption or affluence is a distinct variable, much research has either reduced consumption to a function of population (more people equals more consumption) or reduced consumption to a function of technology (more efficient use of resources equals less waste). However, more recent studies have pointed out that population growth cannot explain significant increases in the consumption of forest products, food, or water (Princen, Maniates, and Conca 2002:6–7). The United States, for example, consumes far more natural resources in proportion to its population than China or India. Indeed, each baby born in the United States causes anywhere from 15 to 150 times more environmental damage than a baby born in a poor country (Ehrlich and Ehrlich 2004:115). The average American consumes 240 times as much gasoline than the average Indian, contributing more carbon dioxide emissions to the atmosphere (Myer and Kent 2004:6). Reducing consumption to technology is also problematic because technological improvements often encourage more consumption. For instance, increased fuel efficiency in automobiles has not resulted in people driving fewer miles and may convince consumers that purchasing fuel-efficient SUVs or owning more than one car has little impact on the environment (Princen, Maniates, and Conca 2002:9). As discussed in Chapter 1, technology often promotes planned obsolescence, which simply increases future consumption and waste.

Many pioneers in the field of environmental studies have recently turned their attention to the environmental impact of consumption. Paul Ehrlich, author of the popular books *The Population Bomb* (1968) and *Population Explosion* (with Anne Ehrlich 1990), has moved away from arguing that population is the most important environmental problem, positing that the "consumption factor" needs to be analyzed (Ehrlich and Ehrlich 2004). Environmental scientist Norman Myer has also turned his attention toward the environmental impact of consumption, claiming that we are "witnessing one of the biggest revolutions in history": the consumer boom in developing countries (Myer and Kent 2004). Myer and Kent state that the rise of these new consumers presents us with one of the greatest challenges of the future: "how to achieve ever-greater consumption—or, better consumption of alternative sorts—without grossly depleting the environmental underpinnings of our economies" (2004:7). They view **sustainable consumption** as a means toward improving quality of life, both materially and environmentally, and highlight the power of individual consumers to make this happen. Sustainable consumption embraces both technological innovations and marketplace initiatives and is based on the ideas that consumption should be

1. shared, ensuring basic needs for the global population;

2. strengthening or building human capital; and

3. socially responsible and equitably distributed (United Nations 1998).

According to the United Nations (UN), sustainable consumption is strongly connected to human development and should aim to support it, particularly through the inputs of goods and services from personal income, public provisioning, unpaid work, and natural resources (1998:38).

Unfortunately, global consumption patterns are currently unsustainable, creating extreme divisions between the wealthy and the poor and environmentally damaging patterns of development that will negatively affect future generations. Uneven growth and increasing inequalities are most apparent when comparing the consumption rates of developed and undeveloped nations. For example, the richest 20% of the global population consumes over 80% of global goods and resources, including automobiles, paper, meat, and electricity. Furthermore, wealthy nations are some of the largest contributors to global climate change, like the United States, which emits approximately 20 metric tons of carbon dioxide per year compared to the 3.9 metric tons emitted by Mexico and close to 0 metric tons emitted by sub-Saharan Africa (UN 1998:3). If developing nations hope to decrease poverty and improve their standards of living, then they will need to be able to consume more goods and resources. In order for this to occur in an equitable way, developed nations will need to start curbing their excess consumer spending. Telecommuting, skipping one beef meal a week, using energy-efficient lightbulbs, and installing water-efficient showerheads are all adjustments that individuals in developing countries can make without drastically changing their lifestyles (Myer and Kent 2004:134). Many mainstream environmental organizations, like the Environmental Defense Fund (EDF), endorse this idea that small personal adjustments made by consumers can help save the environment. EDF urges consumers to plant trees, purchase dolphin-safe tuna, and recycle newspapers to help "save the Earth" (Maniates 2002a:48).

One of the main problems with focusing on self-directed individual consumer decisions, or **individualization,** is the assumption that individuals or households are the primary culprits for environmentally destructive consumption. This ignores the consumption patterns of businesses and governments, which cause more environment damage than the activities of individual consumers combined (Stern 1997:16). Some of these very businesses intentionally engage in **greenwashing,** or trying to fool consumers into believing their policies and products are environmentally friendly even if they are not (Pierre-Louis 2012; Littler 2009). For example, British Petroleum (BP) tries to market itself as a green corporation through its "Beyond Petroleum" advertising campaign, while Toyota brands itself as a green corporation because it manufactures the Prius (Unruh 2011). While many consumers are clever enough not to be deceived by greenwashing, those who are not might mistakenly believe they are saving the environment every time they fill up their gas-guzzling Toyota Tundra at a BP station. Individualization neglects the need for better environmental regulations and standards at the structural level and places all the blame—and responsibility—for environmental change on consumers at the micro-level (Maniates 2002a). Basically, individualization promotes the ideology of political consumerism at the expense of the consumer movement.

Maniates (2002a) argues that proponents of the consumption angle need an alternative to the IPAT model to account for its failures. He proposes an **IWAC formula,** which stresses that environmental impact (I) is a function of W (quality of work), meaningful consumption alternatives (A), and political creativity (C). While Maniates is not entirely opposed to political consumerism, he does not think that individual consumer choices are enough to accomplish structural social change. In particular, the IPAT model does not adequately address the problem of overconsumption. For example, one explanation for overconsumption is that the routinization of work leaves people feeling powerless, positioning consuming goods as one of the few ways they can feel empowered. If quality of work is improved, compensation of power through consumption may be restrained and consumers may become more discriminating in the choices they make. However, in order for this to occur, social institutions need to begin providing meaningful consumption alternatives, like reliable public transportation and delineated bike lanes. At the same time, consumers need to recognize themselves as citizens, unite, and exercise political creativity that goes beyond recycling and changing lightbulbs (Maniates 2002a: 62–64). In other words, some aspects of the consumer movement need to be connected with political consumerism to achieve future sustainability. Eco-labels, consumption and eco-taxes, and cap and trade programs are a few ways that the market approach of political consumerism is intersecting with the more structural orientation of the consumer movement.

The World Wildlife Fund (WWF) has promoted consumer awareness and education by co-creating the Marine Stewardship Council (MSC) and the MSC **eco-label.** In 1997, WWF partnered with Unilever, one of the world's largest buyers of fish, to establish the MSC in an effort to promote sustainable fisheries. This partnership was due to the failure of national governments and international agencies to regulate global fisheries (Boström and Klintman 2008:56). Overfishing, wasteful fishing practices such as discarding by-catch, and habitat damage are the key environmental problems that the MSC works to ameliorate, focusing its efforts on the capture of wild fisheries that have been declining across the globe (May et al. 2003). The MSC eco-label identifies seafood products that have been caught in sustainable, certified fisheries. According to the MSC, a **sustainable fishery** is one that "can be continued indefinitely at a reasonable level" and "maintains and seeks to maximize ecological health and abundance" (May et al. 2003). Currently, 190 fisheries are MSC certified, including fisheries in the Arctic, Atlantic, Indian, and Pacific Oceans that maintain sustainable cod, hoki, rock lobster, salmon, and shrimp populations. Consumers can purchase MSC-certified seafood at popular restaurants, such as Mitchell's Fish Market, and retailers, including Wal-Mart; they can even purchase MSC-certified pet food and treats (http://www.msc.org/).

In addition to eco-labels, consumption and eco-taxes are being suggested by some environmentalists as ways to achieve environmental sustainability through the purchasing power of consumers. Taxing consumer goods and services—instead of or in addition to wages—might help solve the problem of overconsumption. While most states and cities have a sales tax on many goods and services already, a **consumption tax** would be an additional value added to the cost of goods and services at the point of purchase. Consumption taxes, popularly referred to as "sin taxes," are already collected for some harmful products, like tobacco and alcohol, to try to discourage consumers from purchasing them. Thus, individual consumers have the choice to reduce or limit their consumption if they do not wish to pay this type of tax. According to Ehrlich and Ehrlich (2004:232), implementing a consumption tax would be relatively easy because taxes are "familiar instruments with social structures already in place to collect them."

Eco-taxes attempt to incorporate principles of ecology into economic policy by ensuring that the price of a good reflects *all* of its costs, including its ecological ones (Brown 2001:4, 234). Nature's goods move through the market, but not nature's services. For example, some of the services of a tree include controlling floods, providing habitat for birds and animals, and protecting the soil from erosion. Brown (2001) argues that the price of these services needs to be signaled in products made from this tree and strongly supports restructuring the tax system as a way to help tell the ecological truth of all goods and services. Eco-taxes can communicate whether a product is environmentally destructive and can have a "systemic effect" by "steering millions of consumer decisions in an environmentally sustainable direction every day" (Brown 2001:239). Importantly, eco-taxes can capture the **negative externalities** or social costs associated with environmentally damaging production and consumption practices. For example, if a business releases excessive amounts of carbon dioxide into the atmosphere, it should have to pay a tax on its emissions. This tax should be high enough to capture the social costs associated with global climate change and should eventually provide an incentive for this business to reduce its carbon emissions over time if it wants to save money. Although eco-taxes are driven by the logic of a capitalist market, they would be executed and controlled by national governments or international governing bodies, like the UN.

Eco-taxes are supported by the **Kyoto Protocol,** an international agreement overseen by the UN Framework Convention on Climate Change that was adopted in 1997 and implemented in 2005. The goal of the protocol is to reduce greenhouse gas emissions through the creation of a carbon market, where greenhouse gases are treated as a commodity that can be traded. Popularly referred to as a **cap and trade program,** the protocol allows countries to sell their allotment of emission units if they do not use them to countries that have exceeded their emission targets. Currently, 191 countries have signed the protocol, but not all of them have implemented it, including most notably the United States (http://unfccc .int/kyoto_protocol/items/2830.php). A major reason why the United States has not implemented the protocol includes the fact that developed countries have more stringent emission targets than developing countries. This distinction, the UN argues, was necessary since developed countries are historically most responsible for the emission of greenhouse gases. However, in December 2015 at the UN Climate Change Conference in Paris, the United States along with 194 other countries agreed to cut carbon emissions to try to mitigate the effects of climate change. The **Paris Agreement** does not exempt developing countries from these emission reductions like the Kyoto Protocol did. While each nation can choose what kind of tactics it will use to reduce emissions, many of the largest polluters, including the United States and China, have committed to cap and trade programs. Interestingly, although it is not legally binding, the Paris Agreement includes in a preamble that rich countries should supply $100 billion annually to poor countries to help them manage the immediate and long-term effects of climate change (Davenport 2015).

Conclusion

The rise of political consumerism in the absence of the coordination of governments or nonprofit organizations is not without challenges. Those on the left consider it the triumph of neoliberal values and a sign of the decline of the state, while those on the right view it as a form of socialism that interferes with free trade (Micheletti 2003:3). Others posit that political consumerism may just be a "feel-good" game played by the wealthy who can afford fair trade and eco-friendly products and the highly educated who know what consumer labels represent. Some question whether the individual actions of consumers even constitute collective action or if changing individual shopping habits can "save the world" if existing institutions are not altered (Maniates 2002a). Purchasing eco-friendly laundry detergent does not challenge consumerism—we are still buying albeit with ethical considerations. Finally, some think that the political consumer is a "myth" because it is not so much consumer demand as corporate supply that makes political consumerism successful. In other words, corporations are making the decision to sell fair trade coffee, not individual consumers (Devinney, Auger, and Eckhardt 2010:3). Whether consumers are aware of purchasing ethical products, it is evident that most businesses are not threatened by it and seem happy to support political consumerism as long as it improves their reputations and profit margins.

Perhaps it is most useful to understand political consumerism as a form of **individualized collective action,** which is civic engagement that "combines self-interest with the general good" and "illustrates how private concerns" can have a "public face" (Micheletti 2003:25, 44). In the United States, this includes **citizen consumers,** individuals who "put the market power of consumers to work politically," and **purchasers as citizens,** or those who believe that "satisfying personal material wants actually served the national interest" (Cohen 2003:8). Citizen consumers are common during times of economic uncertainty and war, such as during the Great Depression and World War II. For example, during World War II, consumers were called upon to engage in citizenship duties through the act of consumption, including rationing and price controls. Purchasers as citizens came to dominate consumer activism after World War II when they were encouraged to shop for economic recovery (Cohen 2003; Deutsch 2010)—a message that may sound familiar today as it was employed by President George W. Bush after 9/11 and President Barack Obama during the 2008 recession. Similarly, the

consumer confidence index, which measures consumer perceptions of the labor market, seems to be almost as significant, if not more, in measuring the nation's economic strength as the unemployment rate.

Equating the identities and activities of consumers with those of citizens does not resonant well with those who feel like the focus on consumption undermines the democratic values of fairness, the importance of public goods, and democratic actions, like voting, petitioning, and other more traditional kinds of political protests. But others view consumer activism as an opportunity to use the marketplace to vote for political and social change. In an increasingly deregulated, neoliberal world, individual consumers instead of governments may hold the power to challenge corporations to improve unsafe working conditions, provide fair wages, and produce environmentally sustainable goods and services. Within this neoliberal context, the responsibility of the consumer to achieve social change may become even more significant if "individual rights and freedoms are guaranteed not by the state but rather by the freedom of the market and trade" (Banet-Weiser and Mukherjee 2012:9). As Schudson reminds us, "Both political behavior and consumer behavior can be either public-spirited or self-interested" (2007:236). Clearly, not all consumer choices are based on trying to achieve social justice or environmental sustainability; however, it would be remiss to ignore those that are.

9

Credit and Debt

Mass consumer society would be unfeasible without near-universal access to credit, which allows consumers to purchase goods and services beyond their savings—often unsecured and without collateral. On one hand, access to credit "allows people to smooth consumption over their lifetime" (Coggan 2012:183). Instead of having to save thousands of dollars to pay up front for homes and cars, consumers can borrow money, albeit with interest, and make monthly payments over a set number of years. As John Kenneth Galbraith argued, credit could perform quite an egalitarian function because "it allows the man with energy and no money to participate in the economy more or less on par with the man who has capital of his own" (Kuttner 2013:182). On the other hand, the consequence of easy access to credit is debt. According to Lazzarato, "Through consumption, we maintain an unwitting relationship with the debt economy" as credit habitually creates "permanent debtors" (2012:20). Disturbingly, increases in consumption have been "largely financed by debt, rather than by increases in wages or appreciation of asset" (Porter 2012:2). According to the Federal Reserve, consumer debt in the United States is over $11 trillion, including about $8 trillion in home mortgages, $1 trillion in student loans, $800 billion in automobile loans, and $700 billion in credit card debt (Schneider 2013:6). Given these numbers, it is perhaps not surprising that indebtedness has become normalized—at least for the middle classes (Peñazola and Barnhart 2011).

This chapter will discuss the liberalization of consumer credit over the past few decades, resulting in massive household debt that culminated in the 2008 recession. In doing so, it will explore the asymmetrical relationship between creditors and debtors and suggest that growing economic inequality should be understood as one between those who own financial capital, creditors, and those who do not and therefore are structurally forced to borrow money and become debtors. In addition, the morality of debtors and creditors will be analyzed in relation to this asymmetry, including a discussion of why debtors default on loans. This chapter will conclude with an examination of sovereign debt and review several solutions to indebtedness, including debt forgiveness programs.

Liberalization of Financial Markets and the Credit Industry

State policy "guided credit from the margin of the economy in the 19th century to its center in the 20th," helping to make the extension of credit profitable (Hyman 2012:40). Usury laws and social customs restricted lenders from charging interest on loans that were often made by small shopkeepers to regular customers who lacked access to bank capital. But in the 1920s, the financial company was created, which could mediate the relationship between retailers and banks by borrowing money from banks, lending it to retailers, who could then lend it to customers. Even after paying banks back, financial companies were able to profit from this economic arrangement, making personal debt a "good investment" (Hyman 2012:41). The rise of **securitization** for consumer debt in the 1970s allowed investors to resell consumer loans. This practice became so profitable that they began producing more loans, often using predatory tactics (Hyman 2012:44, 48).

Since the 1980s, the ideology of **neoliberalism** has come to dominate economic activity and policy initiatives in the United States and other countries around the world—some by choice, others by decree. According to Harvey, neoliberalism is

> in the first instance a theory of political economic practices that proposes that human well-being can best be advanced by liberating individual entrepreneurial freedoms and skills within an institutional framework characterized by strong private property rights, free markets and free trade. The role of the state is to create and preserve an institutional framework appropriate to such practices. (2005:2)

One key development of neoliberalism has been the ascendancy of financial markets over industrial production in developed economies. Stocks, bonds, and commodities traded on abstract algorithms made by "bots," or computerized software applications, characterize capitalism today (Arvidsson and Peitersen 2013:3). The accumulation of wealth is gained from investments and interest on loans and has become largely concentrated in the hands of those who have enough capital to participate in financial markets. At the same time, financial markets have become less regulated, making it easier for the average and even low-income consumer to obtain credit and loans. "Lending standards were steadily reduced" over the past few decades and the size required for down payments or deposits dropped from 20% to in some cases zero; in fact, some individuals can obtain "liar loans" without having to provide any proof of income at all (Coggan 2012:183). The expansion of subprime mortgage loans with adjustable and typically high interest rates to marginal borrowers helped many realize the American dream of homeownership but also caused U.S. mortgage debt to rise from 30% of gross domestic product (GDP) in 1983 to about 80% by 2006 (Coggan 2012:183; Mian and Sufi 2014:76). Between 2000 and 2007, mortgage application denial rates dropped to less than 30% from 42% in low credit-score zip codes at the same time that the average income dropped, creating a situation where "mortgage-credit and income growth became negatively correlated" (Mian and Sufi 2014:76). In addition, aggressive lending practices persuaded many homeowners to take out home equity loans, borrowing against a speculative bubble in their home values that burst during the recession (Mian and Sufi 2014:87). This resulted in millions of homeowners being "underwater," or having negative equity in their houses, which accounted for 23% of all mortgaged properties in 2011 (Mian and Sufi 2014:26). According to Vague (2014:6), U.S. mortgage debt grew from $5.3 trillion in 2001 to $10.6 trillion in 2007, doubling in only six years.

Neoliberalism has encouraged the growth of the credit card industry too, creating institutional arrangements and cultural practices that make swiping a piece of plastic for a can of soda at a vending machine both convenient and acceptable. Laws restricting the activities of credit card companies weakened after a 1978 Supreme Court decision that allowed them to charge interest rates in the state where they are located, not where customers reside. Predictably, this resulted in credit card companies establishing their offices in states with high interest rates to become more profitable and developing aggressive marketing campaigns, such as mailing preapproved credit card applications and promoting introductory 0% annual percentage rate offers (Vyse 2008:50, 25). Some companies engaged in ethically questionable practices, like arbitrarily increasing interest rates without notifying customers, unfairly allocating payments to balances on low interest rates first over higher ones, and issuing credit cards to individuals under the age of 21, many without steady incomes (Credit Cardholders Bill of Rights Act 2009). The primary way that credit card companies make money is through encouraging their customers to accrue and revolve debt over time, and once these customers reach their credit limits, many credit card companies will simply increase their lines of credit to allow them to continue consuming, effectively preventing them from paying off their debt. According to Vyse (2008:25), from the perspective of the credit industry, the "worst customer is one who never carries a balance on her credit card," who they refer to as "deadbeats." Structurally, credit card companies have created an economic environment that makes it incredibly difficult for individuals who either voluntarily choose not to have credit cards or are involuntarily denied access to them. One needs a credit history—and the all-important credit score—to obtain a standard automobile loan or home mortgage or, in some cases, even rent an apartment. Furthermore, many mobile phone services and travel reservations for hotel rooms require consumers to have a credit card with a high enough limit to cover incidental charges.

Of course, the late 1970s coincided with stagnant wages, the loss of industrial jobs overseas, and a decrease in welfare assistance, positioning the credit card as the "new safety net" (Vyse 2008:52). The rise of neoliberalism has cut public spending to such an extent that consumers are forced to use credit to finance goods and services, such as education, that were supported at least in part by state provisions and subsidies (Dienst 2011:60). As the household debt-to-income ratio spiked from 1.4 to 2.1 between 2001 and 2007, the average American had little or no savings to use to pay for unexpected events like the loss of a job, an automobile accident, or a medical emergency; however, he or she did have access to an average of four credit cards to choose from to pay for these events—and more (Botsman and Rogers 2010:30; Mian and Sufi 2014:4). Many consumers found themselves in a cat-and-mouse game of using one credit card to pay off another one and transferring balances from high-interest rate cards to new ones with temporary low or zero interest rates. Credit card debt tripled between 1989 and 2001 from $238 billion to $692 billion, peaking at $1.005 trillion in 2008 (Botsman and Rogers 2010:30; Miller and Washington 2014:55).

Neoliberal policies that have made home loans and credit cards more widely available certainly give many consumers the ability to purchase the American Dream they would otherwise not have. In doing so, they have helped to shift the view of debt from something that most consumers try to avoid into something that is, if not embraced, then at least acceptable (Peñaloza and Barnhart 2011). Indeed, consumer debt is currently the norm and has "become one of the most common shared qualities of middle-class Americans, usurping the fraction of the population that owns a home, is married, has graduated from college, or attends church regularly" (Porter 2012:5). The normalization of indebtedness has even shaped the practice of filing for personal bankruptcy in the past few decades. In 1978, the Bankruptcy Reform Act made filing for bankruptcy easier by allowing most debtors to file for **Chapter 7 bankruptcy,** which permits them to eliminate their consumer debt after liquidating nonexempt assets. In some cases, property, houses, and automobiles are considered nonexempt, so debtors can retain them at the same time they default on other types of debt, especially unsecured debt like credit card and medical debt. Debt is typically discharged four months after filing, there is little court involvement, and attorney fees average $1,000 to $1,500 (Porter 2012:18). Compared to **Chapter 13 bankruptcy,** which requires filers to establish a repayment plan to creditors but retain more of their assets. In light of the fact that Chapter 13 bankruptcy does not allow filers to discharge their debt until the end of repayment, and costs between $2,000 and $4,000, it is clear why more debtors would choose to file for Chapter 7, especially as most of them do not have anything of value to liquidate (Porter 2012:19; Vyse 2008:48).

Personal bankruptcy filing increased after 1978, reaching a record high of 1.6 million in 2003 (Vyse 2008:48; www.justice.gov). Policy makers argued the increase in personal bankruptcies indicated their normalization and consequent lack of social stigma. Representative Asa Hutchinson claimed that bankruptcy had become "a tool to avoid financial obligations rather than a measure of last resort" (Thorne and Anderson 2006:79), and Senator John Kerry stated that bankruptcy had lost so much of its stigma that it had become "a lifestyle choice" (Vyse 2008:47). Hutchinson and Kerry were not alone in calling for changes to the bankruptcy laws, which helped pass the **Bankruptcy Prevention and Consumer Protection Act of 2005** with strong bipartisan support. This act makes it more expensive to file for bankruptcy by increasing attorney fees and requiring new income limits (Vyse 2008:47). According to data from the U.S. Courts, the quarterly filing of bankruptcies dropped to around 200,000 in March 2006 from over 600,000 in December

2005 (Vyse 2008:54). Whether this sharp decline in bankruptcies can be entirely attributed to the 2005 act is debatable, but it appears that the 2008 recession blunted this decline, with approximately 1.5 million households filing for bankruptcy in 2012 (Porter 2012:2). Furthermore, the disappearance of the social stigma surrounding indebtedness is also questionable. One study of bankrupt debtors found that they tend to feel shame and humiliation; about 80% of them tried to conceal their bankruptcy from others, especially their parents, employers, and coworkers, even though the declaration of bankruptcy is a public act and is published in most city newspapers (Thorne and Anderson 2006:84). This same study also found that some bankrupt debtors feared stigmatization so much that they used avoidance techniques, like postponing filing and ignoring bill collectors (Thorne and Anderson 2006:86). In addition, the increase in bankruptcy filings after the 1978 Reform Act may not have been caused so much by easier filing requirements and lack of social stigma but by structural necessity as wages and job security declined and divorce rates increased (Vyse 2008:51–52). Thus, rather than becoming normalized, declaring bankruptcy could have continued to be associated with personal failure, lack of self-control, and even laziness, but economic necessity forced debtors to file anyway.

Debtor-Creditor Relationships

While indebtedness is certainly created by economic practices, like "the leveraging of values beyond belief," there are "social and psychic relations that make economic debt possible" (Dienst 2011:13). According to Susan Wilcox, "Debt is a social contract. . . . You don't enter it alone—it's relational and communal" (Steenland 2013). Historically, credit was a form of virtual currency that represented "a relation (of debt and obligation) between human beings" (Graeber 2009:3). While trust between creditor and debtor is a critical aspect of their relationship, especially before institutions such as churches or nation-states could provide "some sort of controls on the potentially catastrophic social consequences of debt," the threat of violence is also present as anyone who has watched *The Godfather* or *The Sopranos* can easily understand (Graeber 2009:8). Dating back at least to 1752 B.C. in the Code of Hammurabi of Mesopotamia, **debt bondage** or debt slavery remains one of the most hostile relationships between creditors and debtors. According to this code, men could pledge their wives, children, and even themselves into slavery to a merchant for money to pay off their debts (Atwood 2008:56). In

England during the seventeenth and into the early nineteenth century, creditors could have individuals who owed them money arrested and held in debtors' prisons until they paid their debts. Absurdly, debtors were required to pay for their room and board in these prisons, making it even more difficult to pay back the money they borrowed. Often the debtor's family had no choice but to live in prison with him and go out to work to pay for the cost of room and board (Atwood 2008:127–28). Indentured servitude was a common form of debt bondage in the United States during the 1600s when labor was in short supply. Immigrants, mostly from the British Isles, would be required to work a specified time for a creditor or master who fronted the money to pay for their passage across the Atlantic (Atwood 2008:130–31). While imprisoning people for indebtedness may seem like an archaic and inhumane practice, it has made a comeback in the United States, with some states, like Minnesota, increasing its use of arrest warrants against debtors by 60% between 2005 and 2009 (Graeber 2011:17). Recently, in the state of New York, some nursing homes are filing for legal guardianship of patients who owe them money (Bernstein 2015). Today, debt bondage is not uncommon in India, where Human Rights Watch estimates that 15 million children are forced to work to pay off their parents' debts (Atwood 2008:129).

Besides the threat of bondage, the behavior and lifestyle of debtors have been scrutinized by creditors as a way to discern who is worthy to receive loans and who is making a good-faith effort to pay loans back. In the words of Marx, "Credit is the economic judgment on the morality of a man" (Lazzarato 2012:59). According to Lazzarato (2012:3), "Debt produces a specific 'morality,'" such as the "promise" that one will honor his or her debt and at the same time is at "fault" for having entered into debt in the first place. Ross (2014:185) argues that the belief that loan repayment is "a highly moral test of personal responsibility" is the "glue that holds the financialized economy together." In particular an asymmetrical relationship exists between the debtor and the creditor, resulting in a situation where "the one who must accept credit (the debtor) submits to the judgment of the creditor" (Dienst 2011:148). Benjamin Franklin summed up this relationship in the following:

> The most trifling actions that affect a man's credit are to be regarded. The sound of your hammer at five in the morning, or eight at night, heard by a creditor, makes him easy six months longer; but if he sees you at a billiard-table, or hears your voice at a tavern, when you should be at work, he sends for his money the next day; demands it, before he can receive it, in a lump. (Weber 1992:15)

Thus, even the debtor's free time must meet the moral approval of his or her creditor. That is, if one is deemed to possess the moral character to borrow money in the first place. Simmel, quoting an English businessman, captures the sentiment of how the poor cannot be trusted with credit because they do not have enough honor or status: "The common man is one who buys goods by cash payment; a gentleman is one who I give credit to and who pays me every six months with a cheque" (Polletta and Tufail 2014:8). Today, new banks are trying to evaluate the character of potential borrowers by using digital software to track their household buying habits, social network connections, and even whether they use proper capitalization in their online correspondence—the assumption being that if they do not, they must be flippant or lazy and therefore unworthy of credit (Lohr 2015).

Ironically, the morality of money lenders used to be questioned more critically than that of borrowers. **Usury,** or the payment of interest on a loan by a borrower to a lender, was prohibited in Judaism and Christianity and remains forbidden in Islam. These religions found it objectionable that creditors could profit from debt, especially when creditors and debtors belonged to the same religion. The Torah allowed Jews to charge interest on money they lent to non-Jews, but Deuteronomy states that "thou shalt not lend upon interest to thy brother" (Jafri and Margolis 1999:372). The Catholic Church excommunicated usurers during the Middle Ages, positioning Jews as money lenders in Florence and other Catholic cities and countries at the same time they were denied access to other types of work (Graeber 2011:10; Jafri and Margolis 1999:373). As Graeber reminds us, the usurer is often depicted as the Devil, "an evil accountant with his books and ledgers" (2011:10), while Jesus instructed his disciples in the Lord's Prayer to "forgive us our debts as we forgive our debtors" (Atwood 2008:44). However, the Protestant Reformation signaled a shifting view of creditors as it did in making money and accumulating wealth more generally. As long as creditors viewed their job as a calling from God and kept interest rates reasonable, Martin Luther and John Calvin did not condemn them or view their actions as sinful (Jafri and Margolis 1999:374–75). Calvin went so far as to state that "capital and credit are indispensable; the financier is not a pariah, but a useful member of society" (Tawney 1954:95, quoted in Jafri and Margolis 1999:375). When the role of creditors became indispensable in the development of capitalism, "the moral stain was removed from the business of lending," and it was "shifted onto those who required its services" (Vyse 2008:34).

In addition to moral judgments, today debtors are forced to bear responsibility for most of the financial risk associated with debt. For example, a decline in housing values affects not lenders but borrowers as their home equity declines and net financial worth evaporates; the lender is still owed the remainder of the mortgage (Mian and Sufi 2014:12, 18). Perhaps the most glaring evidence of the current asymmetrical relationship between creditors and debtors is how the federal government favored the former in its economic stimulus plans to recover from the 2008 recession. The very Wall Street banks that were most responsible for causing the 2008 recession received "$700 billion in taxpayer aid and trillions more in Federal Reserve cash advances and bond purchases," while individual consumers received no such bailout for their homes that went into foreclosure or mortgages that were underwater (Kuttner 2013:206). Protecting the interests of creditors over those of the debtor is a recent development, part of the neoliberal policies enacted by nation-states and international organizations like the World Bank and the International Monetary Fund (IMF) in the 1980s (Graeber 2009:9). The trend can be observed in regards to public debt as well, which was directed in the past "toward socially necessary investments," like education and health care, but has been turned into "a subsidy program to increase the power of the private sector," the cost of which is "imposed on everybody" (Dienst 2011:28, 59). In other words, the taxpayers are asked to pay the cost of bailing out Wall Street at the expense of state services that could—and should—benefit them. They are obliged to do this without any guarantees of employment or wage increases from the private sector. Even more indicative of the power of creditors over debtors is that "even those too poor to have access to credit must pay interest to creditors through the reimbursement of public debt" (Lazzarato 2012:32).

This asymmetrical burden of debt risk and imposition of costs is not surprising given the rise in economic inequality since the late 1970s. Hyman captures this quite clearly when he explains that "whereas in the postwar period the 1 percent paid the 99 percent in wages, after 1970 the 1 percent increasingly just lent the 99 percent money" (Hyman 2012:48). According to Dienst (2011:151), this has created an economic situation where "there is credit without debt for the few (who can wield the power of investment without accountability) and debt without credit for many (who bear the hazards without exercising a choice)." Clearly, the 1% of creditors are growing extremely wealthy at the expense of the 99% of debtors, who, in the absence of government protections or religious doctrine, neither expect nor often experience fair money-lending terms, like reasonable interest rates or fair debt repayment schedules. Even Adam Smith, who professed the freedom of the market, understood the precarious position of debtors when he claimed that some government regulations were necessary to limit interest rates in "order to prevent the extortion of usury" (quoted in Clary 2011:421).

Debtor Default and Settlement

Given the unequal position of debtors in relation to creditors today, it is not shocking that many default on their consumer debt, including credit card debt, auto and medical loans, gym fees, and overdue utility and mobile phone bills. Banks often sell this unpaid consumer debt, or **bad paper,** to third-party collection agencies that purchase it for pennies but attempt to collect and make a profit off of the original amount of debt. This so-called bad paper is usually a simple spreadsheet that contains the personal information of the debtor and how much he or she owes. Problems arise when bad paper is duplicated and sold to different debt collectors, resold, or stolen; it becomes difficult to trace how much, if any, of the original debt has been paid, and debtors may be harassed by several collection agencies at once to make payments on the same debt that has been copied (Halpern 2014). Complicating matters, much resold debt is time-barred, or beyond the statute of limitations, to legally collect, which in most states is between three and six years. Controversial sewer services, like falsely claiming to have served papers on individuals that have been thrown away or using robo-signing to serve en-masse affidavits to individuals without verifying their accuracy, are additional problems that plague the debtor-creditor relationship (Turnbull 2013:339).

The purchasing of debt has grown considerably over the past decade, involving tens of billions of dollars annually (Turnbull 2013:339). "American consumers owe a grand total of $11.28 trillion, of which roughly $831 billion is delinquent or unpaid" (Halpern 2014:4). According to Porter (2012:6), the percentage of consumers who have experienced third-party debt collection activity doubled from 7% in 2000 to 14% in 2010. Given the bad practices of many debt collectors and the increasing number of people who must deal with them, it no surprise that the Federal Trade Commission ranks complaints against debt collectors second only to identity theft (Halpern 2014:7). However, many people do pay off their consumer debt, which begs the question why? According to one debt collector, most people actually want to pay off their debt, and he finds that talking to debtors as a therapist would talk to her patients works better at securing payment than harassing tactics (Halpern 2014:15). Perhaps the most telling evidence that the indebted feel an obligation and responsibility to pay off their debt is the growing popularity of debt refinancing and settlement agencies. Unlike the traditional debt collector who comes knocking on the debtor's door or calling the debtor's phone number, this newer form of collecting debt typically requires the debtor to contact the collector (Halpern 2014:218–19). Thus, instead of ignoring the knocking on the door or the ringing of the phone, the debtor is actively acknowledging his or her debt and pursuing payment options.

Even though most people pay off their debt, there are those who do not; some default entirely, while others settle their debt and agree to repay a reduced amount of their original balance. Just as creditors view the actions of debtors through a moral lens, so do debtors view the services performed by creditors. One study on debt settlement found that debtors were more likely to pay back debt in full when they felt like the creditor performed a valuable service for them. For example, debtors are more likely to pay back medical debt compared to credit card debt because they feel obligated to hospitals and doctors for saving or improving their lives, even though the amount of medical debt often surpasses credit card debt (Polletta and Tufail 2014). If debtors feel like creditors are using unscrupulous tactics, they may also feel justified in defaulting on their loans. Creditors consider debt "contaminated" after debtors resist aggressive "shakedown" measures to coerce them to pay, including threats to take them to court. Once debt is deemed contaminated, creditors generally give up on trying to collect, which happens most frequently with payday loans (Halpern 2014:221). It is easy to understand why debtors would be most likely to default on loans made by payday lenders, considering that their fees and interest rates are ridiculously and some might argue unethically high. Currently, the national average annual rate charged by payday lenders is over 400%, and the fee charged to borrow $100 is between $18.50 and $30 (Mayer 2013:515). In addition, the payday lending market might be interpreted by some debtors as unfair or coercive because they lack access to conventional banks and credit unions, and their immediate need for cash creates a situation where the price of the loan becomes extraneous (Mayer 2013:520). Therefore, even if payday lenders do perform a valuable service, their questionable tactics and unfair market advantage might induce some debtors to default.

Clearly, there is a critical need to establish some semblance of equity into the relationship between debtors and creditors. Atwood (2008) emphasizes that when the relationship between debtors and creditors is out of balance for too long, not only does animosity between them grow, but debt becomes "dirty," like the slates at pubs that were used to record the tabs of regular customers. When the slate became too dirty, "smeared all over with debts," it was "dirty for both debtors and creditors alike." To restore the relationship between debtors and creditors, the slate needed to be wiped cleaned (Atwood 2008:80). The same can be argued today—that the slate needs to be wiped clean to relieve the financial and moral burdens placed on debtors. The actions of creditors have been if not forgiven then at least somewhat alleviated through federal stimulus policies. In the context of the 2008 recession, they have escaped much of the blame as well for creating the conditions that encouraged overleveraging at the individual and household levels. However, debtors are still waiting for the slate to be wiped clean. According to Greider (2011:12), "Forgiving the debtors is the right thing to do, because the bankers have already been forgiven. The largest banks were in effect relieved of any guilt . . . when the government bailed them out, no questions asked."

Pawn Shops

Dating back to the Middle Ages in Europe, pawning household goods, clothing, jewelry, and other objects of consumption has been used by all classes of society—from the aristocracy trying to maintain their position of status to the impoverished trying to survive between harvests or paychecks. Even the Catholic Church, which viewed the interest charged by pawnbrokers as a sin, tolerated money lending as long as it was conducted between people of different religions. Since Jewish people were prohibited by law from working in most trades—and their religion did not condemn usury—many found an occupational niche as moneylenders and pawnbrokers (Woloson 2009:71–72). It became a weekly custom for some Christians to pawn their Sunday attire on Mondays and redeem it on Saturdays to budget household expenses between paydays (Calder 1999). Until the turn of the twentieth century when mass production made clothing less expensive and valuable, articles of clothing were the most popular possessions pawned (Caskey 1994:17).

Pawning is essentially collateralized lending. The object pawned, referred to as a pledge, is collateral, which is used to obtain a short-term monetary loan. These loans are subject to interest, which varies by law according to each state. Pawners receive a ticket that states the conditions of their loans, including the interest rate and when the loan is due. These pawn tickets must be presented by the pawner if he or she wants to retrieve the object that was pawned. Pawnbrokers often permit pawners to renew their loans if they pay the interest that they owe at the end of the initial loan term. If a pawner fails to reclaim his or her collateral, then it becomes the pawnbroker's property. Pawnbrokers can then sell these objects in their stores to recoup the loss of the loan in addition to a profit. Thus, although officially neither merchants nor bankers, pawnbrokers act as both (Woloson 2009:2).

Some argue that this type of collateralized lending is more transparent—and perhaps even fairer—than using credits cards, especially for low-income consumers. Pawners know upfront the conditions of their loans, they cannot be charged compound interest, and if they fail to reclaim their collateral, they simply lose possession of it instead of being subjected to harassing bill collectors and long-term low credit ratings (Woloson 2009:186; Krupnik 2009:55–56). Pawnshops also provide a space of consumption for people to shop for goods that might not otherwise be available in their neighborhoods. They circulate preowned goods through the local economy at prices low-income consumers can afford. However, others view pawning as a form of fringe banking that exploits low-income consumers, who lack access to mainstream banks, credit cards, or retail stores (Caskey 1994).

Questions

1. Discuss the different practices and stigmas surrounding obtaining a quick cash loan from a pawnshop and using a credit card. Does one type of loan seem more transparent than the other? Are you more likely to pawn one of your possessions or use a credit card to access money you need? Why?

2. Watch an episode of one of the popular pawn store reality shows, such *Pawn Stars* or *Hardcore Pawn*. What kinds of items are people trying to pawn? What reasons do they give for pawning their belongings? How are they treated by the employees and/or owners of these pawn stores? Do think that they are being victimized or being offered a helpful loan service? Why?

3. Would you ever consider shopping at a pawnshop? Why or why not?

Debt Forgiveness and Relief

The precedent for debt forgiveness has its roots in Mosaic law, whereby every seven years, debts were considered annulled, land would be returned to its original owners, and debt slaves would be freed (Atwood 2008:48). Referred to as a **Jubilee,** debt forgiveness found a more secularized audience in the late 1990s as a way to release poor countries from sovereign or **public debt** incurred mainly from loans by the World Bank and the IMF. Much of this sovereign debt was considered **odious debt** because it was acquired without the consent of the people by authoritarian rulers who used the money to benefit themselves and their supporters instead of improving the lives of the people. Some policy makers questioned whether this debt should be transferable to successor governments when these previously unscrupulous rulers were either overthrown or elected out of office (Jayachandran and Kremer 2006:216). Odious debt became particularly problematic in light of the **structural adjustment** policies imposed on loans by the World Bank and IMF. These policies required debtor nations to open up their markets to global free trade by eliminating trade barriers and subsidies that protected domestic markets and privatizing state services (Roodman 2006:18). The assumption behind structural adjustment policies was that they would encourage economic growth, which would both reduce poverty and provide the means for governments to pay back their loans. However, the structural reforms required by the World Bank and IMF as loan conditions were often at the expense of funding public services, such as education and health care. Instead of alleviating poverty, these reforms exacerbated it in many countries, especially when food prices increased as a result of the elimination of state subsidies. If debtor nations did begin to realize economic stability, then the IMF would demand debt repayments, which would in turn threaten this very stability (Sachs 2006:vii).

By the late 1990s, it was becoming distressingly evident that sovereign debt was overwhelming poor nations, motivating a diverse coalition of participants to organize a global campaign to forgive Third World debt. Jubilee 2000 mobilized faith-based groups, trade unions, celebrities, academics, and even businesspeople to pressure G8 countries to cancel the debt of **heavily indebted poor countries,** or HIPCs (Mayo 2005; Pettifor 2006). In exchange for debt relief, HIPCs were required to allocate money that they would have used for debt service payments to domestic poverty reduction programs. Organizers of Jubilee 2000 were able to frame debt forgiveness—or cancelation, as many supporters prefer to use since forgiveness connotes blaming the debtor instead of acknowledging the behavior of creditors in causing indebtedness as well—as a worthy goal to welcome the new millennium and one that would resonate with the religious audiences in Western nations. The movement's first popular success came during a protest at the 1998 G8 summit in Birmingham, England, when over 70,000 people joined together to form a 9-kilometer human chain, effectively putting debt cancelation on the international agenda (Pettifor 2006:301–2). Celebrities such as Bono joined protests at the 1999 G8 summit in Cologne in June, and in September 1999, Pope John Paul II endorsed Jubilee 2000, prompting President Bill Clinton to announce that the United States would cancel all debts owed by HIPCs (Pettifor 2006:304–5). Of the 40 countries identified as HIPCs, 36 qualified for debt relief by 2011 and received close to $100 billion in debt relief combined (Kuttner 2013:269).

Sovereign debt is not only a problem faced by HIPCs in Africa and South America. In 2008, the public debt in the United States totaled over $10 trillion, and the IMF estimates that "the average developed country will have government debt of more than 100 percent of GDP in 2015, compared with just 30 percent in emerging markets" (Coggan 2012:197). Currently, several European Union countries are experiencing postrecession debt burdens that are proving difficult to overcome, especially in the so-called PIGS countries (Portugal, Ireland, Greece, and Spain). Because these countries adopted the euro as their national currency, they are not free to devalue their currencies to try to stimulate economic growth. This has left them with few options but to implement **austerity measures** to try to relieve their debt burdens in exchange for bailout money from euro-zone countries, Britain, and the IMF. These austerity plans include severe cuts in domestic spending, especially to public-sector jobs and pensions (Coggan 2012:201, 206). Greece, for example, accepted a €110 billion bailout package in May 2010 and implemented harsh austerity measures, which not only failed to increase the international economic competitiveness of Greece but further contracted its domestic economy, producing more sovereign debt and the need for more bailout money in just over a year (Coggan 2012:207). With household budgets stretched to the brink, Greek citizens protested this new bailout because it meant accepting even more cuts to public services, which ultimately led to the election of Syriza, a radical, anti-bailout party, in 2015. Given that Greece's current sovereign debt load is the equivalent of 175% of its GDP, there is talk of European creditors relieving at least some of its debt burden to prevent the country from default (Eavis 2015).

Forgiving sovereign debt, especially if it is odious debt, is one thing, but what about cancelling personal debt? Unlike sovereign debt that can be blamed on abstract institutions and international policies, individuals are blamed for their own indebtedness because they are perceived to have been irresponsible with their money; thus, they are not easily understood as justified victims. Viewed as an individual problem, debtors are forced to face their debt and their creditors alone, a problem that one organiza-tion, Strike Debt, is trying to change. A debt resistance movement with its origins in the Occupy Wall Street movement, Strike Debt wants indi-vidual debtors to realize that their indebtedness is not their fault but the result of an economic system, or a **creditocracy**, that has made indebted-ness a "precondition not just for material improvements in the quality of life, but for the basic requirements of life" (Ross, quoted in Palumbo-Lui 2014). Its slogan "You Are Not a Loan" and its publication, the *Debt Resist-ance Operation Manual,* hope to educate the public that they are indeed not alone in being in debt and, moreover, that loan repayment is not a "moral test of personal responsibility"; therefore, debtors should not feel a moral obligation to pay their debt (Ross 2014:185). Some of Strike Debt's recent campaigns include Rolling Jubilee and trying to unionize college and university students. The goal of Rolling Jubilee is to raise money to pur-chase third-party medical debt. Instead of collecting this debt, it cancels it. So far, it has raised $700,000 and canceled approximately $20 million in medical debt (Ashton 2014). In addition to Rolling Jubilee, Strike Debt is attempting to organize college and university students into a union to protest the cost of higher education, which has resulted in massive stu-dent loan debt—over $1 trillion in the United States alone (Ashton 2014). Considering that the federal government made a profit of $41.3 billion in 2013 on student loans it originated and that student loan debt cannot legally be discharged if one declares bankruptcy, mobilizing students to fight for debt relief does not seem unreasonable (Jesse 2013). According to Andrew Ross, a sociology professor at New York University and par-ticipant in Strike Debt, the ultimate goal of this action is not simply debt forgiveness but a system of free higher education (Palumbo-Lui 2014). Ross argues that to be truly free of debt, cancellation campaigns are not enough to achieve structural change; an alternative to creditocracy must be established to prevent debt from accumulating yet again.

Conclusion

Since most Americans are in debt, some Marxists wonder if "there is a special role for debt in emancipatory thinking" that might accelerate financial crises and lead to if not direct revolution then at least the dissolution of capitalism (Dienst 2011:152). Historically, there is a significant correlation between debt and rebellion. According to Graeber, "For thousands of years, the struggle between rich and poor has largely taken the form of conflicts between creditors and debtors" (2011:8). If creditors were unwilling to wipe the slates of debt clean, then debtors were prepared to do so with force. "Popular insurrections have begun the same way: with the ritual destruction of the debt records" (Graeber 2011:8). From the French Revolution of 1789 to the Hungarian uprising of 1956, "one of the primary goals of the rebels was to destroy tax and debt records" (Atwood 2008:142–43).

Aside from debtors organizing a mass rebellion, the government could do a better job of protecting debtors from unfair practices of creditors. Most recently, the Croatian government implemented a program to cancel the debt of 60,000 of its poorest citizens, specifically those who have blocked bank accounts, owe less than $5,000, own no property except for their primary residence, and receive welfare (Orovic and Smale 2015). Some steps in this direction that have been made in the United States include the passage of the **Credit Cardholders Bill of Rights Act in 2009** and creation of the **Bureau of Consumer Financial Protection** (BCFT) in 2010. The former aims to protect credit cardholders from arbitrary rate increases, double-cycle billing, fees for regular processing services, and due date gimmicks. It also stipulates that anyone under the age of 21 can only acquire a credit card if they have a qualified co-signer or prove that they have the financial means to repay their credit card debt. The BCFT regulates consumer mortgage companies, payday lenders, and private education lenders (Mogilnicki and Malpass 2013:557). It also hopes to educate the public with its "Know Before You Owe" campaign, which provides consumers with clear disclosure information on the terms of mortgage loans. Most recently in 2015, the BCFT and the U.S. Department of Education forgave $480 million of debt owed by students who borrowed money through high-cost private student loans from Corinthian College, sending a clear signal that debt forgiveness for others is not out of the question.

Of course, there is another course of action available to current and potential debtors: stop borrowing and start saving. According to Porter, "The deleveraging process of paying down debt and increasing savings has just begun" (2012:2). Although indebtedness has become a norm over the past few decades, postrecession attitudes indicate that avoiding debt is becoming the "new normal" (Etzioni 2011). Chapter 10 will explore how this new normal is informing a variety of anticonsumption practices that can prevent individuals from having to rely so much on creditors— and therefore going into debt at all.

10

Alternative Forms of Consumption

Considering the social problems that mass consumer society has created, some consumers are making a deliberate effort to try to become less dependent on consumer goods and services and de-commoditize their lives by engaging in alternative forms of consumption. Some of these alternative consumers are choosing to reduce their overall consumption through reusing and repairing products they have already bought, while others are trying to avoid accumulating mass consumer goods by borrowing from and sharing with others. Voluntary simplicity consumers are reducing their hours at work to have more free time, do-it-yourself consumers are building their own furniture, and collaborative consumers are sharing cars, power tools, and even their couches for others to crash on instead of paying for a hotel room. Resisting the power of multinational corporations and the pressure of credit card companies, some alternative consumers have even created local currency that supports small businesses in their communities. Others have suggested that the focus on economic growth as an indicator of progress needs to be reevaluated given the social and environmental costs of consumer culture, advocating economic policies that emphasize degrowth. Each of these forms of alternative consumption will be examined in further detail throughout this chapter.

An additional perspective on alternative forms of consumption involves not the rejection of mass consumer culture but how consumers can be co-creators in the invention, design, use, and delivery of products and services. New legislation has even made it possible for them to be co-owners of these products and services through participating in various crowdfunding platforms. Co-creation activities have been characterized as types of prosumption because consumers are actively engaged in both production and consumption. Controversy over prosumption involves whether consumers are being exploited for their labor because they are not receiving any monetary compensation. Do consumers care if they are exploited if they are having fun offering companies new ideas or writing peer product reviews? This is a question that will be further explored later in this chapter.

Frugality, Sacrifice, Austerity, and Postmaterialism

Several alternative forms of consumption, including the voluntary simplicity movement, the do-it-yourself movement, and the local currency movement, can be situated within a theoretical framework that has its roots in the historical values of frugality and sacrifice, which have been more recently interpreted as postmaterialism. **Frugality,** or being thrifty and economical with material resources and money, has been condemned as a character flaw and celebrated as a moral virtue. On one hand, frugal characters in popular culture are portrayed as stingy, miserly, and selfish, like Ebenezer Scrooge in Charles Dickens's *A Christmas Carol* or Charles Montgomery Burns on *The Simpsons*. On the other hand, the virtue of frugality through consumer discipline, self-denial, and delayed gratification has been advocated by a variety of actors throughout American history (Witkowski 2010). During the colonial era, Puritans, Quakers, and Calvinists preached the moral imperative of frugality over a life of frivolous, sinful consumption, while the nonimportation movement mobilized colonists on the basis of self-denial and sacrificing "the joys of the marketplace" (Breen 2006:407; Witkowski 2010). The federal government used the virtue of frugality and the rhetoric of sacrifice during World War II to mobilize the home front (Deutsch 2010; Witkowski 2010; Young 2005). Although specific products were rationed by the state for the war effort, like tires, meat, and nylons, consumers were urged to view their consumer sacrifices and the thrift that it entailed as acts of patriotism. Instead of an act of humility, self-denial was understood as a source of pride and even gratification. Today, governments continue to use the rhetoric of consumer frugality and sacrifice, particularly by enacting **austerity** measures to reduce budget deficits. In fact, during the recession, austerity policies, such as decreasing government spending through reducing public-sector wages and jobs and increasing taxes, became so common that the Merriam-Webster dictionary named *austerity* the word of the year in 2010 (Contreras 2010). Consumer indebtedness was partially blamed for causing the 2008 recession, and many European governments opted to enact austerity measures to attempt to stabilize and eventually restore their economies, asking consumers to sacrifice their living standards for the greater good of their nations. According to the findings of one study in Portugal, as long as consumers have trust in their government and financial institutions, they are willing to avoid defaulting on their consumer loans by reducing their spending on entertainment and travel or relying on family and friends for financial support (Lopes and Frade 2012).

Frugality is associated with the concept of **sacrifice,** or the negation of self-interest. Being frugal, like sacrificing, can be understood as "a more expansive sense of self-interest" (Meyer 2010:14, 17). Wapner suggests that sacrifice can be "a potential avenue toward richer meanings toward life itself" (2010:36). Thus, sacrifice is not so much "a deprivation, but a provision—it involves feeding our moral selves" (Wapner 2010:53). Ralph Waldo Emerson and Henry David Thoreau viewed "frugality as a means to a higher end" and a way to achieve self-sufficiency and greater freedom (Witkowski 2010:241). In the words of Thoreau, "In proportion as he simplifies his life, the laws of the universe will appear less complex, and solitude will not be solitude, nor poverty poverty, nor weakness, weakness" (Hawken 2007:37). The idea of frugality as a source of personal pleasure and gratification continues today and may be best understood as a value of **postmaterialism,** or an "emphasis on the quality of life" (Inglehart 1990:5). Given the relative economic security experienced by most Americans, they are able to meet their basic material or physiological needs, like food and shelter, allowing them the privilege to focus on meeting their nonphysiological needs, like self-expression and aesthetic appreciation (Inglehart 1990:68). However, postmaterial values are not simply a product of current material security; they also reflect the material conditions during the time period one was socialized in, creating a lag time of adjustment (Ingelhart 1990:68). Thus, postmaterial values "reflect one's subjective sense of self," not necessarily one's economic position

(Inglehart 1990:68). A person who achieves wealth in adulthood but was raised in poverty as a child and involuntarily forced to live frugally might find it absurd to think of frugality as a value that people voluntarily pursue to attain self-expression.

The Voluntary Simplicity Movement

The virtue of frugality and the idea that sacrifice can enhance our lives inform the **voluntary simplicity movement**. Although the origins of this movement were in the late 1970s during the energy crisis—a time characterized as "an era of scarcity" (Elgin 1981:21)—it has become increasingly popular in affluent societies that are blessed with abundance yet plagued by overconsumption. Participants in the voluntary simplicity movement assert that "real reductions in consumption . . . bring real net benefits to be enjoyed rather than sacrifices to be endured" (Maniates 2002b:201) and hope to "cultivate non-materialistic sources of satisfaction and meaning" (Etzioni 1998:612). As the term *voluntary* implies, reducing consumption is a "deliberate choice," as are other lifestyle decisions made by participants, like riding bikes, using public transportation, gardening, and canning vegetables. According to Etzioni, there are three variations of voluntary simplifiers: (1) downshifters, who practice a moderate form of voluntary simplicity by giving up some but not all consumer goods and maintain a relatively affluent lifestyle; (2) strong simplifiers, who trade high income and often stressful jobs for more time and less income; and (3) individuals who belong to the simple living movement, changing their entire lives to follow a "coherently articulated philosophy" of anticonsumerism (1998:626).

An online survey of 2,268 voluntary simplifiers found that they had diverse motives for wanting to reduce their consumption, including saving money, self-sufficiency, environmental and personal health concerns, and a desire to spend more time on one's self and with one's family (Alexander and Ussher 2012). In terms of basic demographics, this survey discovered that voluntary simplifiers lived in both urban (28%) and rural (21%) areas, most owned their own homes (69%), 42% had no children, 27% had annual household incomes between $35,001 and $60,000, and 23% had annual household incomes between $60,000 and $100,000 (Alexander and Ussher 2012:73). While Alexander and Ussher found that most voluntary simplifiers identified as being part of a movement,

Zamwel, Sasson-Levy, and Ben-Porat (2014) learned that some individuals who voluntarily reduce their consumption do not identify with belonging to a movement. Instead, they viewed their daily consumer, or anticonsumer, activities as political, ongoing, and generally invisible to the public because they tend to take place in the private sphere of their homes (Zamwel, Sasson-Levy, and Ben-Porat 2014). Either way, individuals who choose this lifestyle are faced with similar challenges, including how to pay for health care and higher education on limited incomes and finding meaningful jobs that do not conform to the standard 40-hour workweek (Alexander and Ussher 2012:78).

Do-It-Yourself Movement

With more time and less income, some voluntary simplifiers engage in **do-it-yourself** (DYI) projects, like home remodeling and automobile repairs, "circumventing traditional marketplaces and improving well-being" (Wolf and McQuitty 2013:196). While not all DYI-ers are voluntary simplifiers, the movements intersect in terms of espousing self-sufficiency and "higher-order values that go beyond the financial benefits," such as mastering craft skills that they can use in the future and teach others (Wolf and McQuitty 2013:205). Some DYI-ers view mass-produced goods and services as inferior in quality or cannot find what they want in the mass consumer marketplace, so have to make it themselves (Hornik and Feldman 1982:45; Wolf and McQuitty 2013:198). Other DYI-ers are motivated to avoid the high cost of mass-produced goods and services, trading their "leisure time" for "homework" to save money (Hornik and Feldman 1982). Most DYI-ers are homeowners with above-average incomes and educations who have the perceived skills, physical ability, and knowledge to repair leaky faucets, flat tires, and broken appliances (Hornik and Feldman 1982:54, 60).

Clearly, many consumers feel that they have at least some perceived home improvement skills as sales at retailers that cater to this movement, like Home Depot and Lowes, have increased from $22.5 billion in 1978 to $38.5 billion in 1987 to $300 billion in 2006 (Wolf and McQuitty 2013:195). Part of this growth has been fueled by lower prices for basic tools, like power drills, and the invention of new materials, like fast-drying water-based paints, that have expanded the projects that the average DIY-er is willing to attempt (Watson and Shove 2008:73). Obviously, many DIY-ers do not subscribe to the anticonsumerism of the voluntary simplicity movement, although their know-how may be part of what Leadbetter and Miller (2004) call the "pro-am revolution" and "constitute a form of everyday resistance to the alienating effects of contemporary society" (Watson and Shove 2008:75). By doing things for themselves, these professional amateurs experience personal autonomy; they control their labor and their time and own what they make. They may also overcome social forms of alienation as many DIY-ers rely on personal networks of family, friends, and neighbors for advice and physical help (Watson and Shove 2008:74). Of course, these nonalienating effects of DIY projects may only be realized by those who view this so-called homework as enjoyable and not as a burdensome chore.

Local Currency Movement

Perhaps the ultimate do-it-yourself venture has been the creation of local currency mediated through **Local Exchange Trading Systems** (LETS), which are "local associations whose members list their offers of, and requests for, goods and services in a directory and then exchange them priced in a local unit of currency" (Williams 1996:85). Local currency is not convertible to national currency, although it is often based on units equivalent to national currency or measured in labor hours regardless of the skills or services exchanged. Most associations use volunteers to keep records of all transactions, crediting and debiting member accounts, and often issuing them monthly statements. Some LETS have opted to organize as nonprofits with professional administrative support (Schwartz 2009). No interest is accrued or owed, making wealth accumulation or "surplus money" irrelevant (Helleiner 2002; Williams 1996).

One of the main economic objectives of a LETS is to build sustainable, local economies that are "less reliant on outside sources for goods and services" and keep money within communities (Williams 1996:87). A 2008 study by Civic Economics found that just a 10% shift in consumer spending from chain stores to independent stores could create 1,600 new jobs and bring $137 million into the local economy (Schwartz 2009). Another economic advantage of a LETS is that it can empower those marginalized by the official labor market, including the poor and individuals who are "retired, unemployed, and underemployed," by using their human capital and providing them access to credit or even tools they can loan (Collom 2011:146; Williams 1996). Indeed, during economic crises, like the Great Depression, the creation and use of local money often increase to provide access to and a more equitable distribution of financial resources

(Gatch 2008). In one study of a LETS in Great Britain, participants from low-income households were able to earn 3% to 7% of their household income, and 44% of them claimed that participating in LETS allowed them to increase their standard of living (Williams 1996:91–92).

In addition to economic objectives, LETS hope to build **social capital,** or "social networks, norms, and trust that facilitate coordination and cooperation for mutual benefit" (Putnam 1995:67) within local communities. Economic inclusion fosters social inclusion that connects strangers and encourages the "re-embedding of markets within social relationships" (North 2006:5). According to Purdue et al. (1997:655), LETS help to build social solidarity and protect participants "against the anomic effects of global exchange." The reciprocity expected of participants provides a means of integration, and the obligation of providing a good or service after accepting one "binds the LETS community together" (Purdue et al. 1997:657). Helleiner argues that trust is a key component of alternative currencies since their market value "depends entirely on the willingness of members to accept them," which in turn "may encourage a sense of collective identity among users" (2002:269). North argues that local currency schemes like LETS promote a different kind of spatial and temporal dimension to market transactions compared to the formally rationalized, anonymous global capitalist market—creating an economy that is coordinated around "slower, local, and community rhythms" (North 2006:6).

In the past 20 years, over 200 LETS have been initiated in the United States, and interest in the local currency movement has increased since the 2008 recession (Collom 2011:145; Schwartz 2009). BerkShares, the largest local currency system in the United States, has circulated over $2.5 million through 400 businesses in Berkshire County, Massachusetts, since it began in 2006. Currency is printed by a local paper store on colorful bills that feature famous people from Berkshire like Norman Rockwell. One incentive used to attract participants is providing a bonus of additional BerkShares in exchange for national currency at local banks, such as $100 BerkShares for $95 U.S. dollars (Schwartz 2009). The longest running local currency system in the United States is located in Ithaca, New York (Schwartz 2009). Unlike BerkShares, Ithaca Hours is a time-based currency, printed on notes in various time denominations, including one-tenth and one-quarter hours (North 2006:4). Businesses that accept Ithaca Hours pay $10 to be listed in a print and web directory and in return receive two Hours worth $20. Consumers can purchase Ithaca Hours at a local credit union, where participating businesses can apply for interest-free loans that, if approved, they receive in Hours (ithacahours.info).

Bitcoin

Alternative currencies are not just restricted to the boundaries of local communities; thus, they do not always keep money circulating within a local economy. Furthermore, they need not be issued or printed in a material medium. For example, Bitcoin is a digital or virtual currency that has extended alternative currency to the global level and is accepted by international companies, like CVS, Dish Network, Expedia, Dell, Amazon.com, and Home Depot. While technologically savvy consumers can attempt to accrue Bitcoins through data mining, most consumers obtain them through a Bitcoin exchange, where they open an account and create a digital wallet that they can then transfer money into and use to transact with businesses or other people who accept Bitcoins for goods and services. More recently, Bitcoin ATMs have been created that participants who have a digital wallet can use to deposit cash into their Bitcoin accounts (Ember 2014). Bitcoin users can visit websites such as CoinMap.org and Coindesk.com to find thousands of places that accept this alternative currency.

Created in 2008, over 41 million Bitcoin accounts have been opened around the world. Similar to local currency arrangements, Bitcoin is decentralized and run by volunteers, although in addition to keeping track of all transactions, Bitcoin volunteers must authenticate encrypted electronic signatures to validate them (Kharif 2014). While the early adopters of Bitcoin tended to be "tech geeks" who love all things digital, libertarians and anarchists who privilege personal autonomy over government control, and even criminals who can use the anonymity of Bitcoin to launder dirty money, mainstream users have become increasingly common, from parents paying their children allowance in Bitcoins to roommates paying their share of rent with them (Kharif 2014). One recent study on Bitcoin users found that they are becoming less politicized: in 2013, 43% of respondents identified as libertarians or anarchists, while in 2014, only 22% identified as such (Kharif 2014).

Questions

1. If you have not used Bitcoin, would you consider using it? Why? What kind of purchases do you think you would most likely make using Bitcoin? Where would you most likely use it (visit CoinMap.org or Coindesk.com for places that accept Bitcoin)?

2. Do you think that Bitcoin should be regulated—or even prohibited—by the federal government? Why or why not?

3. Do you think that virtual currencies like Bitcoin will ever become as popular as government-issued currencies? Why or why not? What advantages might a digital, global currency like Bitcoin have over a government-issued currency?

Consumer Cooperatives

Established in 1844 in the English town of Rochdale by a group of weavers, consumer cooperatives embrace the idea that "those who use what is sold from a store or made in a factory own the store and the factory" (Cowling 1942). If workers did not possess the power to own and control the means of production, they could at least attempt to own and control their means of consumption. The Rochdale consumer cooperative was based on several key principles of cooperation that continue to be practiced today, including democratic control, open membership, education, the return of net profit to members, fair market prices for goods, and political nonpartisanship (Sekerak and Danforth 1980). Some cooperatives even allow individuals to trade their labor performed within them for the products that they carry. According to French economist Charles Gide (1847–1932), the consumer could "assert his supremacy through the establishment of consumer cooperatives," which could serve as "an instrument of social justice and moral transformation" (Williams 1982:283, 286). Similar to the local currency movement, many consumer cooperatives operate in local communities, keeping money within the community and bolstering the local economy. W. E. B. DuBois even advocated consumer cooperatives as a strategy of economic development for African Americans who voluntarily practiced self-segregation (Carreiro 2015). Throughout American history, marginalized racial and ethnic groups have built a way not only to economically survive but also to strengthen communal solidarity through participating in consumer cooperatives as a result of both voluntary and forced residential segregation.

Consumer cooperatives are well positioned to handle situations that involve food scarcity and the potential for price inflation, such as economic depressions and wars. For instance, in the United States, consumer cooperatives have been most popular during such times. Consumer cooperatives grew dramatically after the Great Depression with 1.5 million members nationwide by 1944, which was an 800% increase since 1929. During

World War II, consumer-controlled co-ops "seemed to exemplify the consumer-regulated economy" that the federal government agency, the Office of Price Administration (OPA), "was fostering." The OPA was created to establish price control policy and coordinate the wartime rationing of food and other consumer necessities, like gasoline. Like co-ops, the OPA had a decentralized structure, working at the local level to mobilize consumers on the home front to support the war and often recruiting its volunteers from the consumer cooperative movement (Deutsch 2010:116, 174).

Today, consumer cooperatives have abandoned much of their working-class roots in the United States. Most co-op members are affluent and college educated and apt to "focus on conscience consumption and identity politics through food" at the expense of the concerns of working-class consumers (Carreiro 2009; Sekerak and Danforth 1980). For example, contemporary consumer food cooperatives often stock products that do not correspond with the tastes of working-class consumers, such as kale and tofu, and that are likely priced outside of their budgets. However, other types of consumer cooperatives, like credit unions, have a more inclusive membership in terms of socioeconomic class. As of 2010, approximately one in four Americans belonged to some type of cooperative (Knupfer 2013).

Collaborative Consumption and the Sharing Economy

One of the most recent trends in alternative forms of consumption is **collaborative consumption,** or "traditional sharing, bartering, lending, trading, renting, gifting, and swapping, redefined through technology and peer communities" (Botsman and Rogers 2010:xv). Collaborative consumption is part of what is being referred to as the **sharing economy** that encompasses both traditional nonmonetary sharing and more entrepreneurial activities, like when individuals rent out their unused camping equipment. While families, friends, and neighbors have been sharing everything from lawnmowers to pet sitting services for years, technology, in particular the Internet, has redefined the "scope, meaning, and possibility" of what we share, how we share it, and with whom we can share things, including strangers across the world (Botsman and Rogers 2010:55).

Collaborative consumption has its origins in sharing computer code through the open-source movement, "a model of software development in which the underlying code of the program . . . is by definition made freely available to the general public for modification, alteration, and endless redistribution" (Leonard, quoted in Terranova 2000:49). The generation of Web 2.0 services, spaces, and products (such as Facebook, eBay, YouTube) has popularized collaboration on the Internet because they rely on users to cooperate with each other and share a variety of services and activities for free in addition to being relatively easy to navigate (Denergi-Knott and Zwick 2012:441–42). Furthermore, in this high-tech gift economy of the Internet, where users "give and receive information without thought of payment," copyright protection is either absent or at times violated, making the value of private ownership negligible to many users (Barbrook 2005).

According to Botsman and Rogers, collaborative consumption is organized into three systems: product service systems, redistributive markets, and collaborative lifestyles. **Product service systems** involve consumers "paying for the benefit of a product . . . without needing to own the product outright" (Botsman and Rogers 2010:71), such as paying to rent a car or a bicycle for a few hours or days. Consumers can benefit from not owning products because they do not have to pay for them outright, for their upkeep, or for places to store them. Buying, selling, or just giving away preowned goods that are redistributed to those who need them from those who do not characterizes **redistributive markets.** Websites like Ebay, Craigslist, thredUP, and freecycle.com help connect consumers who want to participate in redistributive markets and facilitate their transactions as do traditional rummage sales, flea markets, antique stores, and secondhand retailers. Sharing time, space, and skills to build social relationships are important values to those who follow **collaborative lifestyles.** Planting community gardens, cooking in collectively rented kitchen spaces, traveling via couch surfing, and establishing daycare cooperatives are activities that allow consumers to escape the materialism of mass consumer culture.

In order for collaborative consumption to be successful, enough consumers need to participate; a critical mass not only provides social proof that this type of consumption can work but also allows for more choice and convenience (Botsman and Rogers 2010:75). For example, critical mass is important for a redistributive market in clothing in order to have a variety of sizes and for a product service system of bicycle sharing to have bicycles in a variety of locations for convenience. Botsman and Rogers further argue that consumers need to believe in the Internet as a commons—a place to build community and, most important, trust strangers—in order for collaborative consumption to flourish. As collaborative consumption is primarily based on the self-governance and coordination of peer relationships, they stress that reputation can help build trust between strangers. **Reputation capital** is accumulated via peer reviews and ratings that are posted on websites by peer providers and consumers and can be used to flag those who are not trustworthy (Botsman and Rogers 2010:217–19). For example, drivers and customers of Uber, a peer taxi service, can rate one another. A driver who is late picking up a customer or a customer who is rude to a driver might receive a low rating, which is shared on the digital Uber platform. Enough low ratings and a driver or customer will not have enough reputation capital to continue participating in Uber. Reputation might also provide a psychological motivation for consumers to participate in the sharing economy as higher ratings confer higher status.

However, reputation capital has not replaced economic capital entirely in the sharing economy. Many of the "micro-jobs" found in the sharing economy are being performed by "part-time entrepreneurs" or "rentreprenuers" who are making some income by renting their unused musical instruments or mailing packages for people (Geron 2013:58; Baedeker 2011). According to Forbes, the sharing economy was estimated to grow over 25% in 2013, with revenues in excess of $3.5 billion (Geron 2013:60). Even corporations are starting to pay attention to collaborative consumption, like General Motors, which invested $3 million in the RelayRides car-renting scheme (Geron 2013:66). Some companies like Airbnb (worth about $10 billion in 2013) are making money by being brokers, connecting users and sellers in the sharing economy. In 2011, over 2 million total nights were booked using Airbnb, which takes a 3% commission from those who want to rent out their rooms, apartments, or houses and a 6% to 12% cut from travelers in exchange for handling services like payments and customer support (Geron 2013:62). Other companies, like Facebook, are making money (about $1 billion per quarter) from consumers who freely share posts and photos by collecting and selling their personal data to advertising firms, who pay to have their advertisements strategically pop up on users' timelines and feeds (Ritholtz 2013). Thus, while the sharing economy is clearly open to anyone who wishes to participate, some actors have better reputations than others and are accumulating more money as well.

Another way that money is being generated in the sharing economy is through **freemiums,** or providing basic content and services for free but charging for the premium versions; in this way, paying consumers subsidize free consumers (Anderson 2010). For example, LinkedIn, a professional networking website, offers its basic services for free but charges users who want premium features, like additional InMails and the capacity to view search results outside of their own network. Direct cross-subsidies are another type of freemium used when companies offer complementary goods to try to entice consumers to pay for other ones. This is an old marketing tactic first used by Gillette at the turn of the twentieth century when it gave away free disposable razors with chewing gum and coffee purchases with the hope of introducing—and hooking—consumers to its new product (Anderson 2010). Today, examples of direct cross-subsidies abound from mobile communication providers offering free smartphones with two-year contracts to Zygna giving away free coins, puzzle pieces, and farm animals for its virtual games, which often can be continued only if users purchase more of these items to level up. Clearly, these examples demonstrate the "paradox of free" as "people are making lots of money charging nothing" (Anderson 2010:3).

Co-Creation, Presumers, and Prosumption: Free Consumer Labor

Besides selling personal data and website space to advertisers, businesses are also able to profit from the sharing economy through the free, voluntary labor of consumers. **Co-creation** is when companies work "with and through the freedom of the consumer" to development new products and services or help market those that do exist (Zwick, Bonsu, and Darmody 2008:163). Consumers are understood as partners, who can realize a sense of empowerment by using their "technical, social, and cultural competence" to add value to businesses (Zwick, Bonsu, and Darmody 2008:166). For example, Frito Lay has an annual contest on Facebook that asks consumers to create new flavors for its potato chips. Consumers vote on their favorite flavors, and Frito Lay creates new potato chips from the flavors that receive the most votes. For Frito Lay, co-creation is a way to not only profit from the free ideas and inventions of consumers but also from the purchases of the products created from free consumer labor. For consumers, co-creation is a way to influence what products are being made and to purchase goods in the marketplace that they have always desired.

Co-creation is situated in the **expectation economy,** where consumers not only want new products and services fast but also want to be the first ones to purchase and experience a new product or service. Consumers actively engaged in the expectation economy are called **presumers,** who "push, fund, and promote products and services before they are realized" ("Trend Briefing" 2012). Presumers are "consuming in the future tense" and are motivated to prelaunch new products and services because it "makes for a great status story" that they can share via social media. This provides an opportunity for them to belong to a broader movement ("Trend Briefing" 2012). **Crowdfunding**—the funding of a project, idea, or product by raising money from a large number of people—is one of the main ways that consumers can become presumers. Via crowdfunding platforms, entrepreneurs can present a project or invention to consumers, who back it by prepurchasing it. Parameters to meet funding goals include a specified amount of money and a time period, which are presented on the crowdfunding platform in addition to how many presumers have backed the project and their comments. Some crowdfunding platforms, like Kickstarter, are based on donations and rewards, while others, like Crowd Supply, offer e-commerce services for products after they have reached funding goals ("Trend #2" 2013). Interestingly, equity-based crowdfunding is now a possibility as a result of the 2012 JOBS legislation, which eliminated many regulations on unaccredited small investors and entrepreneurs. According to a recent report, the fastest growing sector of crowdfunding is equity-based platforms ("Massolution Report" 2012). Presumers can become custowners, owning equity in the products, projects, and services they support ("Trend Briefing" 2012). With over 450 crowdfunding platforms worldwide, crowdfunding is exploding in popularity, with some predicting that it will exceed raising $6 billion worldwide, up from $1.5 billion in 2011 (Drake 2013; "The New Thundering Herd" 2012). On Kickstarter alone, over $1 billion has been pledged by 7.3 million people since it was launched in 2009 (kickstarter.com).

While it is clear why businesses are embracing co-creation and presumers, the question of whether the labor of consumers is being exploited by them is debatable. Zwick, Bonsu, and Darmody (2008) argue that co-creation is just a new way to discipline the actions of consumers and take advantage of their free labor. Humphreys and Grayson (2008) agree, claiming that consumer input in the production process results in "exploitation twice over, once when the object is produced, and twice when it is sold back for a profit." Others, like Arvidsson, understand co-creation, or what he calls customer coproduction, as part of an ethical economy "where value is related to social impact rather than monetary accumulation" (2008:326). Consumers benefit from "socially recognized self-expression" when they contribute to the "coproduction of brands, experiences, design, market strategies, and even product development" (Arvidsson 2008:326). When consumers like a brand on Facebook or tweet about it on Twitter, they create value for the brand but also self-recognition and reputation capital for themselves (Arvidsson 2013). According to Dujarier (2014:10), when debating whether consumers are exploited, a distinction should be made between companies that *require* consumers to perform labor and companies that *offer* them opportunities to do so. The former is more likely to be considered exploitation because companies impose work as a condition of being able to consume a product or service.

Ritzer and Jurgenson situate consumer labor within the economic system of **prosumer capitalism,** which involves consumers both producing and consuming goods and services and is characterized "by unpaid labor and free products" (Ritzer and Jurgenson 2010:14). For example, consumers who engage in extreme couponing spend countless hours searching through newspaper inserts and websites clipping and printing coupons, shopping on double coupon days, and matching local store coupons with national manufacturers' coupons to either obtain items completely free or buy them at significantly reduced prices (Fortini 2012). Although consumers have been engaged in prosumer activities for some time, including pumping their own gasoline and bagging their own groceries, they argue that the Internet and Web 2.0 sites have facilitated their growth. Unlike traditional capitalism, they argue that prosumer capitalism is based on postscarcity or abundance, effectiveness, and quality of content instead of efficiency. This makes sense in connection to reputational capital—it does not matter how much *time* a person spends writing product reviews, suggesting new ways to improve existing services, or posting comments on social media, but the *distinction* of his or her efforts. Although Ritzer and Jurgenson think that "it is difficult to think of prosumers as being exploited" because so many of them seem to truly enjoy what they are doing, they acknowledge that they may be taken advantage of if Web 2.0 sites start charging them for specific content or selling their personal data to third parties (2010:22). But the quality and effectiveness of prosumers may begin to diminish over time when what once felt like fun becomes routinized. For example, the initial enchantment that entices prosumers to participate on eBay often weakens after they realize how time-consuming and laborious the auction-style activities on eBay are (Denergi-Knott and Zwick 2012).

Reduce, Reuse, and Dematerialism

Possibly the most alternative form of consumption is to just stop consuming. **Waste recovery,** also known as dumpster diving and trash trolling, is an anti-consumption tactic used by individuals to reclaim "useable resources from the waste of a hyperconsumption society" (Weissman 2006:128). Scavenging for curbside furniture and appliances or fresh food discarded by restaurants in dumpsters at the end of the day, some waste foragers eliminate purchasing consumer goods altogether. **Freegans** use waste reclamation in combination with other alternative consumer strategies like squatting in abandoned houses, using modes of transportation that do not rely on automobiles, like biking and skating, and community gardening in their attempts to "boycott an economic system where the profit motive has eclipsed ethical considerations" ("What Is a Freegan?" http://freegan.info/). Those not inclined to rummage through outdoor waste can hone their scavenging skills indoors at secondhand thrift stores. While goods in these stores, such as clothing, handbags, and dishware, are not free, they are typically priced at nominal amounts and allow individuals to reduce their ecological footprint by reusing goods that might otherwise end up as garbage. Waste recovery challenges the ideology of consumer culture that new is best and that sacrifice is an obligation to be endured instead of enjoyed. Indeed, one study on thrift shoppers found that they experience pleasure searching in these often disorderly spaces for "gems" and the unpredictability of what they would find (Bardhi 2003). Of course, waste recovery practices cannot truly be divorced from mass consumer culture, especially because most depend on planned obsolescence.

Consumers who cannot abandon the culture of novelty can potentially reduce their consumption of physical items by engaging in **digital materialism,** or bookmarking consumer goods on websites like Pinterest. According to Tackett (2012), the instant gratification that some people feel from pinning goods they want on virtual corkboards may provide enough of a rush that they do not feel the need to actually purchase and physically possess the goods. Filling up virtual shopping carts online without ever purchasing the goods in them may also help consumers feel the satisfaction of shopping without spending any money. While not all virtual materialism is anticonsumerist, much does involve **dematerialism,** eliminating the need and desire to own tangible goods. Millennials, in particular, seem more comfortable streaming music on Pandora and videos on YouTube than owning physical collections of CDs and DVDs (Geron 2013). They also are less likely to own a car or a house than previous generations (J. Davidson 2014; Weissman 2012). According to Geron, dematerialism "could prove to be the longest-lasting legacy of the Great Recession" as everyone, not just the Millennials, has been challenged to critically examine the costs and benefits of the culture of mass consumption. Etzioni (2011) argues that the Great Recession created a norm of austerity—what he calls the "**new normal**"—that persists even though the worst of the economic crisis is over. The "new normal" includes deriving happiness from personal relationships and religious and spiritual pursuits instead of material goods. It also emphasizes saving money and living within one's means instead of being burdened with consumer debt. For example, in a 2010 PEW research study, more than 70% of Americans reported purchasing less expensive brands, 44% were eating out less often, 30% reduced alcohol and cigarette purchases, and 20% cancelled or reduced cable television after the recession (Etzioni 2011:780). In addition, a 2010 Euro RSCG Worldwide Report found that 67% of Americans "felt the recession had served to remind people of what is really important in life," and 87% stated that "saving money made them feel good about themselves" (Etzioni 2011:781). Interestingly, many of the values that inform alternative consumption movements and practices may become increasingly normalized; however, the voluntary aspects of the "new normal" need to be taken into account. Millennials may be purchasing fewer houses than previous generations not because they do not want to own a house but because they do not have enough money for a down payment or a strong credit history to qualify for a loan (J. Davidson 2014).

Conclusion

As much as individuals and communities turn to alternative forms of consumption to try to resist the problems associated with mass consumer society, solving these problems requires structural change. Alexander and Ussher (2012:69) suggest that one of the only ways to reduce consumption is if wealthy countries implement **degrowth** policies centered on "planned economic contraction" and stop measuring progress through economic growth, like gross domestic product (GDP). According to Eisenstein (2011:259), a shrinking economy may actually produce abundance, particularly in regards to leisure time, while eliminating the need for increasing amounts of money. Over time, economic degrowth will reduce our use of raw materials, decrease air and water pollution, and free us from working jobs that are not personally fulfilling (Eisenstein 2011). Degrowth policies also have the potential to decrease economic inequality if consumer spending and private affluence are redistributed into public spending to fund collective affluence. Implementing economic degrowth policies involves imagining a different way to measure development instead of GDP. Pirgmaier and Hinterberger (2012) claim GDP is a narrow measure that does not take into account overconsumption, job-related stress, environmental destruction, or inequality. Paradoxically, a high GDP is not necessarily correlated with human or social development. While the United States ranks high in terms of GDP, it "has the worst social record of any developed country in the world," including the largest prison population; the highest rates of childhood hunger, drug use, illiteracy, and use of antidepressants; and the most teenage pregnancies (Hawken 2007:118). Some degrowth advocates support adopting the genuine progress indicator (GPI) to measure quality of life and well-being. Composed of 26 indicators, including the cost of underemployment, water and air pollution, commuting, crime, the value of parenting, volunteer work, and higher education, the GPI is an attempt to account for environmental and social variables that are excluded from a strict economic growth model of progress (http://genuineprogress .net/genuine-progress-indicator/).

Perhaps if less emphasis is put on valuing economic growth at the expense of societal well-being, the value of materialism will begin to lose its currency and Etzioni's "new normal" will have the space to flourish. Numerous studies support the view that materialism is responsible for undermining personal well-being, leading to depression, anxiety, insecurity, and even physical health problems (Kasser 2002:22). Materialistic people tend to be possessive of the goods they own and unwilling to share them with others as well as envious of others' possessions, causing them to report lower levels of happiness and satisfaction with their lives (Kasser 2002:18–19). Thus, instead of increasing our personal freedom, materialism is coercive; people work long hours and are saddled with debt just to own possessions that encumber their personal happiness and their social relationships.

11

Conclusion

The Globalization of Mass Consumer Culture

Although this book has focused primarily on the development and effects of mass consumption in the United States, it would be unfortunate not to provide some insight into how mass consumption has become a truly global phenomenon. According to Gabriel and Lang (2006:8–10), "contemporary consumerism is global in nature" and has become the "economic ideology of global development" since the collapse of the Soviet Union. Leslie Sklair (2002:62) situates mass consumerism within what he calls the **cultural-ideology sphere** of global capitalism that attempts "to persuade people to consume not simply to satisfy their biological and other modest needs but in response to artificially created desires in order to perpetuate the accumulation of capital for private profit." Powerful global actors, including multinational corporations (MNCs), international finance organizations like the World Bank, and G-8 countries, actively endorse this cultural ideology through international trade agreements, new information and communication technologies, immigration policies, and intercontinental travel (Gabriel and Lang 2006; Ger and Belk 1996; Sklair 2002). As a consequence, globalization has resulted in "a greater exposure of developing countries to products and product innovations occurring in the developed countries" and often "entails a change in the preferences among consumers in developing countries in favor of such products" (James 2000:11).

This concluding chapter will explore how mass consumer culture has traveled beyond the borders of the United States to developing countries. It will begin by presenting the debate over whether globalization is a form of **cultural imperialism,** which forces other countries to adopt Western mass consumerism at the expense of their own cultural traditions, or is characterized more by **creolization** or **localization,** where different cultures appropriate Western mass consumer goods to reflect local meanings and uses (Ger and Belk 1996; Watson 2006). Next, it will analyze these understandings of globalization in relation to the development of mass consumerism in China and India. The vast populations in these two countries represent the world's largest emerging consumer markets. Although most Chinese and Indians are currently poor, especially compared to the American standard of living, a growing middle class with increasing purchasing power exists in both countries. Even relatively poor consumers in these developing countries often possess some discretionary earnings. While the amount of this money may be modest for the individual consumer—perhaps enough for an occasional stick of chewing gum or bottle of soda—from the perspective of a multinational corporation, capitalizing on even small amounts of discretionary income can be extremely profitable given the sheer volume of people in China and India, 1.3 billion and 1.1 billion, respectively. Undoubtedly, "international capital has a lot at stake in seducing the displaced peasant and exploited workers of the Third World and converting them into consumers aspiring after Western standards" (Gabriel and Lang 2006:11).

Globalization and Localization

Although **globalization** became a popular topic of study by academics in the mid-1990s, the idea that the world is becoming increasingly compressed in terms of space and that there is an "intensification of consciousness of the world as a whole" is not an entirely new phenomenon (Robertson 1992:8). In 1848, Karl Marx and Friedrich Engels wrote in *The Communist Manifesto* about the global nature of capitalist production and consumption. In reference to **spatial compression,** they suggested that "[i]n place of the old wants, satisfied by the production of [a] country, we find new wants, requiring for their satisfaction the products of distant lands and climes." Marx and Engels described how the bourgeoisie formed a capitalist world economy by "expanding markets for its products" through exploitative international trade. They also alluded to the notion of a **global consciousness,** using the example of the globalization of literature to explain how "from the numerous national and local literatures, there arises a world literature," which they argued made "national one-sidedness and narrow-mindedness become more and more impossible." Marx and Engels viewed the globalization of capitalism by the bourgeoisie as a force that would "compel" all nations to "adopt" a capitalist economy and civilization to survive.

Taking a contemporary Marxist perspective on globalization, **world-system theorists** elaborate on the spatial compression component of globalization, proposing that an international division of labor connects and integrates different nation-states or geographic areas into the capitalist world economy (Chase-Dunn and Grimes 1995; Emmanuel 1972; Wallerstein 1979). These nation-states or geographic areas are categorized into three economic zones based on their division of labor: the core, the semi-periphery, and the periphery. The division of labor in core zones is capital intensive, involving the use of advanced technologies by high-wage workers, while the division of labor in periphery zones is labor intensive, dependent on low-wage workers using unsophisticated technologies in the production process. The division of labor in semi-periphery zones is characterized as possessing qualities of both core and periphery zones (Shannon 1996:33). The relationship between these economic zones is exploitative, with core areas extracting profits from periphery areas. Arrighi Emmanuel describes this relationship as one of **unequal exchange** because core areas are able to take advantage of inexpensive products made by workers in periphery areas who make low wages. If these same goods were produced in the core, they would be much more expensive given the higher wages that core workers can command compared to periphery workers. Perversely, these same periphery workers often have little choice but to purchase expensive products made by relatively highly compensated workers in the core because the inexpensive products they produce are exported to the core (Emmanuel 1972; Shannon 1996:34). An additional way to understand how economic zones in the capitalist world system are spatially compressed is via a **commodity chain,** or "a network of labor and production processes whose end result is a finished commodity" (Hopkins and Wallerstein 1994:17). Each link within a commodity chain represents a specific input that is needed to complete a finished commodity, including raw materials, labor power, transportation, distribution, advertising, and consumption. Commodity chains tend to be global, with each link located in a different geographical area or economic zone; higher valued links, such as advertising and consumption, most often located in core regions (Gereffi, Korzeniewicz, and Korzeniewicz 1994:2). In fact, the finished commodities themselves may only be realized in the core, where they are finally assembled, advertised, and consumed.

While world-system theorists focus mostly on the economy and how production processes are shaped by globalization, others are more concerned with the cultural implications of globalization, including the intensification of a global consciousness. On one hand, some fear that this global consciousness is becoming homogenized through cultural imperialism as American mass consumer culture invades and destroys indigenous or local cultures. The assumption behind cultural imperialism is that it is unilateral insofar as the Americanization of global culture is imposed on the world without invitation and often by brute force, such as when countries are enticed to liberalize their trade policies and allow MNCs access to their markets in exchange for loans from the World Bank or International Monetary Fund (IMF). The global extension of American mass consumer culture is typically understood to be "a one-way street" that positions the United States as the "origin and centre" of global consciousness (Trentmann 2009:189–90). Brand-name American products, in particular, are at the center of this global consciousness. Levi blue jeans, Marlboro cigarettes, Coca-Cola beverages, and McDonald's fast food are just a few American objects of consumption that are easily recognizable to individuals around the world and often desired for the alleged "first world" or "Western" status that they symbolize. Benjamin Barber goes so far as to argue that these brands are beginning to constitute the universal language of the world as a "brand name-trademark lexicon" that crosses international borders quite fluidly (2001:84). An American may not be able to speak Mandarin and an Indian might not be able to speak French, but they can all communicate with each other through the language of brand names.

On the other hand, global consciousness may not be so much homogenized as **creolized** as people appropriate mass consumer goods for different uses and give them different meanings, while maintaining their own cultural values and practices (Ger and Belk 1996). For example, in Turkey, some women use dishwashers to wash dirty spinach instead of dirty dishes and use ovens to dry clothes (Ger and Belk 1996:289). In India, top-loading style washing machines are used to make *lassi*, a type of yogurt (Mazzarella 2003:282). James Watson (2006) describes creolization in terms of localization to explain how American mass consumer goods and stores adapt to local tastes and customs. Students and the elderly in China use McDonald's as a type of leisure center or youth club where they are encouraged to spend time and socialize, and in India, McDonald's was forced to change most of its menu to reflect the vegetarian diet and spicy tastes of Indian consumers (Borkar et al. 2010; Watson 2006). Consumers in other cultures are certainly viewed as having agency when they localize American consumer goods and places, instead of passively accepting them as cultural imperialism suggests. However, similar to the cultural imperialism thesis, localization often assumes that the United States is the origin of global consumer culture. Culture from other places is rarely viewed as having an influence on global consumer culture, much less American culture.

In an attempt to decenter the United States as sole creator and distributor of global consumer culture, Frank Trentmann (2009:189) argues that we should recognize that "Americanization and global consumerism are not necessarily the same thing." First, other cultures, including non-Western ones, also influence global consumer culture such as Japanese manga and Brazilian jiu jitsu. Second, the United States has localized and incorporated other cultures into its own, including objects that have become part of its consumer culture, like fried potatoes from France, pizza from Italy, and tacos from Mexico. Thus, one could argue that American consumer culture may be characterized more by hybridity than standardization. Third, we should recognize that indigenous cultures are often hybrids as well and perhaps should be understood as "synthetic products of multiple global influences" instead of ahistoric, static entities. For example, the beads used in South African Ndebele art are not an artifact of traditional African culture but Czech in origin (Cowen 2004:7–8; Lyman 2015). Finally, some global goods are transnational and cannot be "identified with a single place of origin" (Watson 2006:11). This happens when a foreign brand becomes so firmly established in another country that it is no longer understood as foreign but as indigenous to that culture. Children in China who have grown up their entire lives eating at McDonald's do not view it as American but as Chinese, just as children in the United States probably view French fries, pizza, and tacos as American instead of foreign (Watson 2006). Likewise, The Fédération Internationale de Football Association (FIFA) can be understood as a transnational

Mecca Cola

Mecca Cola was launched in 2002 in France to combat "America's imperialism and Zionism by providing a substitute for American goods" (Murphy 2003). To support campaigns against American imperialism and Zionism, Mecca Cola contributes 10% of its revenues to fund humanitarian projects in Palestine and another 10% to nonprofits in countries where it is sold, including those in the European Union. Like its American counterpart, Mecca Cola is primarily sugar and water—albeit holy water sourced in Mecca is used to make Mecca Cola. The various messages displayed on Mecca Cola bottles and cans, including the slogans "Don't Drink Stupid," "Drink with Discipline," and "Don't Shake Me. Shake Your Conscience" are intended to motivate Muslims to purposefully choose a Halal beverage that complies with their religious beliefs and political ideologies (Echchaibi 2011; Littler 2009).

According to Ram (2007:465), Mecca Cola occupies a provocative position in the global consumer marketplace—between the "global" and the "local" and the "West" and the "rest." Ram suggests that Mecca Cola conforms to the structural homogenization of the Coca-Cola product that it imitates but with a symbolism that makes it heterogeneous, or diverse (2007:466). Littler (2009:39) situates Mecca Cola as not so much against American imperialism but "part of a quasi-globalized campaign 'for' an alternative to US-oriented neo-imperialism." If drinking Coca-Cola is emblematic of global consumerism, then drinking Mecca Cola can be a way for the world's Muslim population to both embrace Islam and global consumerism—unlike purchasing traditional Halal items, like prayer mats, that eschew global consumerism (Echchaibi 2011:31).

Questions

1. Are there any products where you live that have been "localized"? If yes, what are they and how have they been altered to accommodate local preferences?

2. Have you ever found yourself intentionally purchasing (or refraining from purchasing) a product because of where it was made? If yes, what was the product and what specifically motivated your actions? How are your motivations similar to or different from consumers of Mecca Cola?

3. For the past few years, ABC News has been airing a series called "Made in America." Go the following website (http://abcnews.go.com/WN/MadeInAmerica) and research at least one product that is made in the United States. You can also take quizzes on what brands are made in the United States and your car's history.

phenomenon. Even though teams and their fans are associated with specific nations, members of these teams are often from a variety of different countries and the matches are followed by a global audience.

Clearly, globalization has resulted in both cultural imperialism and localization. According to Appadurai, "The central problem in today's global interactions is the tension between cultural homogenization and cultural heterogenization" (1996:32). Rather than accept this tension as a binary opposition, Tyler Cowen suggests that we should recognize that "cultural homogenization and heterogenization are not alternatives or substitutes; rather, they tend to come together" (Cowen 2004:16). For example, globalization tends to increase cultural diversity within societies, while decreasing it across societies (Cowen 2004). In the United States, growing cultural diversity can be observed by the increasing variety of foods from around the world. A person can eat French cuisine on Monday, Thai on Tuesday, Vietnamese on Wednesday, Ethiopian on Thursday, and Colombian on Friday. However, across societies, one can witness that the options available to consumers are becoming more and more similar. A consumer in France or China or Russia might also be able to eat the same cuisines listed above as an American. The following sections of this chapter will examine in more detail the interplay between cultural homogenization and heterogenization in the context of two countries, China and India. American consumer culture has challenged and transformed some cultural practices and values in China and India, while at the same time being forced to adjust itself to localize to their respective cultural customs and preferences.

China: Global Brands and Belonging

The growth of mass consumerism in China is quite astonishing since it was not that long ago during the 1949 Chinese Revolution that the communist leader, Mao Zedong, banned foreign products, prohibited the sale of so-called bourgeois goods like jewelry and makeup, and either closed or demanded that the central government take over department stores (Comor 2008:122). Shopping consisted of standing in line and using coupons at state-run stores for basic, yet scarce, necessities (Yu 2014:10). According to Tsang, Maoist China was a "relatively classless yet impoverished society" that "had no culture of consumption and no landholdings or private property" (2014:4). Production was privileged at the expense of consumption as Mao's economic policies, referred to as the Great Leap Forward, aimed at industrializing a predominately agrarian country. The emphasis on production, especially the economic dependence on exports that characterized much of the 1970s and 1980s, has shifted since the mid-1990s, when the Chinese government started to promote consumption as a way to stimulate economic growth and prove that it is on par with modern, developed countries like the United States (Comor 2008; Gerth 2010; Ngai 2003). In 1995, the Chinese government instituted a 40-hour workweek, creating a 2-day weekend to entice its population to "travel, shop, and enjoy a restaurant meal," and in 1997, official government holidays, including National Day on October 1 and International Labor Day on May 1, were extended to last an entire week and broadcast in the media as "golden consumer days" and "golden travel days" (Ngai 2003:471). In addition to increasing leisure time, the government has been attempting to cultivate a consumer ethos that challenges the traditional Chinese value of saving money by convincing banks to increase consumer lending, especially with credit cards (Gerth 2010). It has also been trying to attract foreign retail chains as a way to "help the country modernize its distribution infrastructure" (Comor 2008:122). As former premier Zhu Rongji declared at the Ninth People's Congress in 2002, "We need to eliminate all barriers to consumption by deepening reform and adjusting polities" (Yu 2014:13).

Creating government policies to encourage consumption is nothing new in China. During the early twentieth century, the **National Products Movement** positioned consumer goods as a way Chinese people could identify as citizens belonging to a modern nation (Gerth 2003:3). Because China was an imperial power, it could not restrict imports through high tariffs, which resulted in a deluge of foreign goods (Gerth 2003:5–6). To discourage the consumption of these imports, products were labeled as either "national" or "foreign." These labels explicitly differentiated consumer goods as "patriotic" or "treasonous," while government propaganda pushed the ideology that "Chinese People Ought to Buy Chinese Products" (Gerth 2003:3, 13). The four key factors that determined whether a product could be labeled as "national" were raw material, labor, management, and capital—the content of all or most of which had to be Chinese in origin (Gerth 2003:21). By investing commodities with a national identity, the National Products Movement hoped to protect if not strengthen Chinese culture from foreign influences and reassert to the Chinese people that their civilization was not eroding (Gerth 2003:29). Ironically, today the Chinese government is pursuing just the opposite policy by encouraging foreign imports to demonstrate that its citizens have the purchasing power to participate in global mass consumerism. However, the demand for foreign products and brands does not signify a desire to identify with or emulate the nation from which they originate but a yen to be "part of a global consuming class" ("Doing It Their Way" 2014). Doctoroff (2012) explains that to be successful in China today, Western brands need to define themselves as global instead of foreign, "so that they can become vessels of Chinese culture."

The Chinese government is not the only actor trying to promote mass consumerism to the Chinese people. MNCs have been entering China not just to manufacture mass consumer goods but also to establish retail chains, including McDonald's and Wal-Mart. As any American consumer who has bothered to examine the labels on the clothing, shoes, or electronic devices that he or she purchases is aware, relatively inexpensive products "Made in China" make global mass consumerism possible. However, since most of the mass-produced goods in China are exported, many MNCs ignored until recently the approximately 430 million Chinese, about one-third of the population, who can be classified as middle class. Residing in a household that owns at least six electronic products, such as refrigerators, washing machines, air-conditioners, mobile telephones, microwaves, stereos, and DVD players, are indicators that one is a member of the middle class (Gerth 2010:14). These purchases have fueled Chinese household consumption, which reached $3.3 trillion in 2014, overtaking Japan as the second largest consumer market behind the United States ("Doing It Their Way" 2014). China is currently the largest car market in the world, the world's largest McDonald's is located in Beijing with 700 seats, Ikea has opened over 700 stores nationwide, and the Chinese are the largest consumers in the world of Bordeaux wine and Cognac ("Doing It Their Way" 2014; Yan 2006; Yu 2014:4,33).

Internal demand in China for Western brands that are often manufactured in China, like Apple iPads, is growing at the same time young people have more discretionary money to spend. An unintended consequence of China's one-child policy implemented in 1979 to control population growth has been the transformation of children into consumers, who have been empowered to not only make autonomous choices in the marketplace but also occupy a privileged position in the family as the singular center of attention. Watson (2006) describes the children of the one-child policy generation as "emperors" and "empresses" who, because they do not have any siblings, are doted on by their two parents and four grandparents both emotionally and monetarily. According to Wang and Fong (2009:1137), these so-called singletons are "lavished with parental attention, luxuries, and opportunities not experienced by any previous Chinese generation."

Curiously, given Mao's former restrictions on luxury goods, today the Chinese are the world's largest consumers of expensive luxury items, accounting for 29% of all purchases in 2013 ("Doing It Their Way" 2014). Chinese consumers are especially brand conscious, turning China into what Tsang describes as "a battleground for international brands" (2014:89). However, the increasing presence of Western brands and retail outlets is not simply a result of the Chinese wanting to emulate Western mass consumer culture. MNCs and foreign retail chains have had to localize some of their marketing and products to complement the cultural norms and values of Chinese society. BMW has developed a sedan to meet the Chinese consumer preference of a larger backseat since many hire drivers and desire more room in the back for themselves, while Western-style supermarkets are trying to adjust to the fact that many Chinese equate meat that is still alive and vegetables with traces of dirt with freshness (Yu 2014:5; Comor 2008:125).

Western companies in particular are being challenged to understand consumerism through the lens of the collectivist values in China compared to the individualist values in most Western societies. Tsang stresses that in China, the "primary forces shaping an individual's identity, choices, and biography" are "the traditional and communal bonds of the extended family, neighborhood, and wider communities" (2014:15). During Mao's regime, the workplace, or *danwei*, determined one's standard of living, including housing, social welfare provisions, entertainment, and even holiday treats; consumption decisions were based on communal decision making (Yu 2014:10). Understood communally, the current Chinese passion for brands may not signify a desire to identify as Western so much as "characterize emerging social ties" within Chinese consumer culture (Yu 2014:23). Instead of using brands to differentiate themselves and stand out, the Chinese interpret brands as a way to symbolize belonging. According to Yu (2014:64), Chinese consumers use brands, especially luxury ones, "in order to demonstrate their participation in China's consumer culture." Doctoroff (2012) concurs with Yu, stating that in China, "individuals have no identity apart from obligations to, and acknowledgement by, others." This is why, Doctoroff argues, products that can be consumed in public and made visible to the approval of others can command price premiums. Thus, the Chinese fascination with expensive luxury goods is more about the external acceptance of others than about the internal happiness of the individual consumer.

The need of approval by others has shaped the development of e-commerce in China (Doctoroff 2012). Currently, China is the world's largest e-commerce market, with an estimated $540 billion in spending in 2015, and the total number of Internet users has increased from 2.1 million in 2000 to 600 million in 2013 ("Doing It Their Way" 2014; KPMG International 2014). Transactions on Alibaba, China's largest e-commerce company that accounts for 80% of online shopping, totaled $284 billion in 2013, more than eBay and Amazon.com combined (Lajoie and Shearman 2014). Much of the initial success of e-commerce has been attributed to reliance on product peer reviews by Chinese online consumers. Chinese consumers trust their peers more than government officials to provide reliable product information, using social media platforms for "buy/don't buy" advice from friends and to post product reviews. Approximately 40% of Chinese online consumers read and post reviews about consumer goods, which is more than twice the amount in the United States ("Doing It Their Way" 2014; KPMG International 2014). Product peer reviews provide a means to both seek and gain social approval and recognition or reputational capital, making online consumption more personal and communal.

The growth of e-commerce in China is significant in managing one of the key obstacles to further develop consumer society: inclusion of the rural population. During his administration, Mao instituted a household registration system, *hukou*, as a mechanism of population control to prevent rural peasants from migrating to overcrowded cities and abandoning agricultural food production for the country. According to *hukou*, households are registered as either rural or urban, and it continues to prevent rural residents from permanently relocating to urban areas where higher wage jobs and most of the consumer retail stores are located (Hsu 2014). Although 2011 marked the year that more Chinese lived in urban areas than rural ones, the need remains to improve the standard of living in rural areas. E-commerce is being proposed as one way to build the rural consumer marketplace. About 30% of the rural population, or 177 million people, has access to the Internet, and online purchases are expected to grow from 180 billion yuan in 2014 to 460 billion yuan in 2016 (Jiayi 2015).

India: Nationalism and Resistance

Compared to China, the introduction of mass consumerism in India has been more contested as the country has "historically actively resisted global cultural homogenization" (Eckhardt and Mahi 2004:138). This resistance was shaped in part against past colonialism, which inspired the formation of the **swadeshi movement** to challenge British power by boycotting British products. Swadeshi, or "of one's own country," is a nationalist ideology that values independence, self-reliance, and strong statist policies aimed at protecting the domestic market from foreign influences and preserving traditional culture (Comor 2008:108, 119; Mazzarella 2003:4–5). Mahatma Gandhi was a strong proponent of swadeshi, advocating the value of frugality over Western materialism and elevating homespun cloth, or *khadi,* into a symbol of resistance (Varman and Belk 2009; White 2008). According to Varman and Belk (2009:687), "Gandhi interpreted consumption of machine-manufactured products from outside India as sinful" and endorsed the purchasing of homespun clothes over machine-made ones even though the former were often more expensive than the latter. Swadeshi informed economic policy so strongly that before 1991, most if not all consumer goods available in India were made there (Mazzarella 2003). Import barriers and high tariffs prevented most foreign goods from entering the country, direct investments by foreign companies in Indian companies were restricted, and foreign companies were prohibited from owning majority shares in Indian companies (White 2008). These protectionist policies were viewed by some as contributing to stagnant economic growth from the 1950s through the 1980s, disparagingly called the "Hindu rate of growth," and doing little to alleviate widespread poverty in the country. Facing bankruptcy, the Narasimha Rao government was required to remove many economic protectionist policies and liberalize its economy in 1991 as a condition of an IMF bailout. Since joining the World Trade Organization (WTO) in 1997, the Indian economy has moved away from swadeshi principles, yet culturally, Indian consumers are reluctant to abandon indigenous preferences to Western tastes, and some remain committed to Gandhi's asceticism and frugality.

When India opened its economy, MNCs were eager to enter one of the potentially largest consumer markets in the world with a total population of 1.1 billion people. Since the late 2000s, India's GDP has been growing by more than 7% per year, and private consumption now accounts for 64% of its GDP, which is higher than China (42%). More important for the development of a mass consumer society, the standard of living in India has been increasing over time. Currently, 26% of the Indian population is classified as living below the poverty line compared to 50% in the 1970s (Dayal-Gulati and Jain 2010:vii–viii). Approximately, 67% of the Indian population—about 700 million people—possess enough discretionary income to make regular purchases (Borkar et al. 2010:1). However, just because many Indians can now be considered consumers does not mean that MNCs should assume that they will act like Western or even Chinese consumers. The first wave of MNCs that tried to capitalize on the Indian market in the early 1990s was not very successful because they failed to take into account local tastes and customs (White 2008:134). Kellogg's learned that to sell cereal, it had to localize its product to fit into a culture that preferred hot milk instead of cold milk, while Whirlpool had to redesign its refrigerators to fit into small spaces and contain doors that could easily accommodate 1.5-liter bottles since many Indians buy bottled water and need space to store it. McDonald's understood that to attract Indian consumers, it had to localize its menu to reflect the dietary restrictions of Hindus who do not eat beef and the cultural preferences for spicy food and vegetarian options (Borkar et al. 2010:9–12).

Another reason why the first wave of MNCs in India did not meet with immediate success is because they ignored the price consciousness of Indian consumers (Borkar et al. 2010; Srinivas 2008). On one hand, low-income consumers face budgetary constraints and often do not have enough money to make bulk purchases in terms of quantity of goods or the volume size of a particular product. For example, shampoo sales expanded significantly in India after the product was downsized from large bottles to single-use sachets, even though shampoo in sachets costs more per unit of volume than in bottles (Borkar et al. 2010:17). On the other hand, Indian consumers with higher levels of purchasing power tend to privilege price and bargains over novelty and brands. According to Borkar et al. (2010:7), MNCs tried to "sell global products at global prices, assuming their brands were strong enough to draw enough customers." But many discovered that unlike in China, brands do not hold the same esteem in India. Indeed, some global brands, like Coca-Cola and Kentucky Fried Chicken (KFC), have been condemned as cultural imperialists trying to erode traditional Indian values, exploit the environment, and undermine consumer preferences for healthy and natural indigenous products (Varman and Belk 2009). In the words of Bijapurkar, (2007:3), the Indian marketplace is "rebellious about what it will embrace and what it will not," and the Indian consumer is "no walkover for global big brands." The inability of global brands to easily manipulate the average Indian consumer is in part a legacy of swadeshi economic policies. By preventing the importation of foreign products, "robust and sophisticated Indian brands were built" by highly developed Indian advertising and marketing agencies that provided initial consumer socialization for Indians instead of MNCs and their marketing of their global brands (Bijapurkar 2007:5; Mazzarella 2003).

Another legacy of swadeshi is that conspicuous consumption in general is viewed through the lens of "debased materialism" in India, conflicting with traditional values and "ideals of community and family" (Van Wessel 2004:98). Some MNCs have realized this and adjusted their marketing messages accordingly. Given that many marriages in India are arranged, De Beers changed the symbolic meaning of its diamond rings from romance between a bride and a groom to close ties between extended families—and targeted grooms and their mothers, who play a larger role in selecting an engagement ring than they do in other cultures (Borkar et al. 2010:8). But conspicuous consumption is not entirely unheard of in India. Similar to Chinese consumers, Indian consumers will purchase ostentatious products if they are deemed worthy of enhancing their personal relationships, keeping up with their social peers, or reflecting "the desires and expectations of important others" (Eckhardt and Mahi 2012:288). Furthermore, the younger generation is "projecting" themselves with consumer goods more than the older generation that views such ostentation as an affront to "Gandhian asceticism and Nehruvian socialism" (Mazzarella 2003:272–73). The "luxury fever" for elite, international brands that is sweeping China has yet to definitively arrive in India due not just to a cultural suspicion of an acquisitive lifestyle but probably because India has a much larger percentage of low-income consumers and a smaller middle class (Walia 2015).

The adherence to frugality is strong in India, especially for the generations who lived before market liberalization (Eckhardt and Mahi 2012:285). Srinivas (2008:7) states that the typical consumer attitude in Indian is one of "if it isn't broke don't fix it," which makes the strategy of planned obsolescence to stimulate consumer demand and spending difficult at best to implement. This attitude can be challenging in terms of marketing new products to Indian consumers because they have "a set way of doing things that works pretty well" so will not change their behaviors without a lot of persuasion, especially if it means spending money for products or services that are inexpensive or free (Bijapurkar 2007:5). For example, efforts to try to sell water purification systems to Indian consumers have not met with much commercial success in the past because Indian consumers resisted paying for something that was if not entirely sanitary at the source then at least free. Indians were also reluctant to change their everyday routine of boiling water instead of adding even relatively inexpensive packets of powder to water to purify it (Simanis 2009; Strom 2014). But paradoxically, frugality is inspiring mass consumerism through bargain hunting in the more than 12 million retail outlets that currently exist in India (Srinivas 2008:125). Although most of these outlets are neighborhood mom-and-pop convenience stores, shopping at larger malls is becoming popular. Srinivas (2008:129–32) describes the typical Indian mall as chaotic and crowded, like a bazaar with a jumble of stores that offer an unorganized assortment of random goods and require consumers to explore and discover the lowest prices. Indian consumers assume a crowd signifies a great bargain, which is why these spaces of consumption are intentionally designed to appear and feel filled to attract more customers (Srinivas 2008:132). Many places of consumption of India have found a clever way to bring together family, community, and frugality all under one roof.

Interestingly, the same crowds that make brick-and-mortar retail establishments popular may hinder the success of e-commerce. While e-commerce is growing in India compared to other countries, it ranks low in the percentage of Internet users, fast and reliable delivery services, and access to credit cards or other forms of online payments (Thoppil 2015). One of the biggest difficulties for e-commerce is actual street traffic in crowded cities, which makes the delivery of online purchases difficult (Rai 2015). Flipkart, India's largest online retailer, is working with a network of around 5,000 Dabbawallas to deliver e-commerce packages by foot, bicycle, and train. Dabbawallas organized over a hundred years ago to deliver hot lunches in boxes to workers from their homes, and today they continue to deliver about 150,000 lunches daily in addition to products ordered online (Rai 2015). According to McClain (2015), these so-called backpack men represent the "foot soldiers on the front lines of India's e-commerce revolution" and, unlike delivering hot lunches to workplaces, often encounter difficulties delivering e-commerce packages because home address numbers are not always arranged sequentially. Besides delivery problems, to become successful, e-commerce must figure out efficient payment methods given that India is predominantly a cash-based economy where less than 2% of the population has access to a credit card. Currently, 80% of online purchases are paid for in cash when they are delivered (Thoppil 2015).

Similar to China, the development of mass consumerism in India must address ways to include the rural population. Currently, 70% of the population lives in rural areas, and rural consumers account for more than $100 billion in consumer spending (Borkar et al. 2010:4). Rural consumers spend more money on nonessential items than urban ones, especially on expenses associated with traditional ceremonies like dowries for weddings (Srinivas 2008:4). The per-capita income in rural India is growing at the same rate as urban India but represents three times as many people—a little over half of India's GDP. Given that the rural population is expected to grow in the future, improvements in product delivery and distribution are needed in addition to reliable, permanent electricity and indoor plumbing (Borkar et al. 2010:23; Srinivas 2008:9). However, it continues to be underserved by most businesses, which continue to view it as agricultural with archaic lifestyles and fail to recognize the "pent-up" demand for goods and services (Bijapurkar 2007:180–84). The potential for e-commerce to supply some of this demand in the future is likely, especially now that some e-commerce firms are in collaboration with the postal service to deliver and collect payments for online packages. Since 90% of all post offices in India are located in rural areas, this partnership will provide the opportunity for communities traditionally overlooked by businesses to participate more fully in mass consumer culture (Rai 2015).

Conclusion

Although there are varying degrees of cultural acceptance and localization of Western mass consumerism in China and India, neither country is aggressively hostile to it, finding it a practical way to improve the standard of living of its citizens, signify its acceptance of modernity, and actively participate in the global economy. However, mass consumerism has not been welcomed by everyone around the world. Instead of a unified global consciousness, mass consumer culture may be encouraging fragmentation and a reassertion of parochial identities and cultural traditions. Religious fundamentalism has been identified as one such response to the perceived threat of Western cultural imperialism. Benjamin Barber (2001) describes this fundamentalist response as a jihad force of tribal identifications that mobilizes in reaction to what he calls the McWorld forces of global cultural uniformity and neoliberal economic policies. According to Barber, jihad forces are personal, violent, and bloody reactions to impersonal McWorld forces because what is at stake for fundamentalists is the destruction of an entire way of life, including their culture, their communities, their families, and their identities. Samuel Huntington (2011) frames this potential for global conflict in terms of the clash of civilizations, arguing that future wars will be fought over cultural differences that are becoming more acute as global spatial compression increases the awareness of the differences between civilizations, such as the West and Islam. Similar to the National Products Movement and swadeshi ideology of the past, the rejection of Western mass consumerism and foreign goods may strengthen preferences for local products and national or communal identities today (Ger and Belk 1996).

Oddly, it is in the West, especially within the United States, where one can encounter some of the most vocal opponents to the globalization of mass consumer culture. Critics of mass consumer culture argue that it results in a variety of social problems, such as egoism, greed, alienation, a loss of community, waste, the reckless depletion of natural resources, and the exploitation of labor. While it is important to acknowledge that American mass consumerism "depends on the poverty of others" (Wilk 2001:257), Daniel Miller reminds us that "we live in a time when most human suffering is the direct result of the lack of goods" and advises that "what most of humanity desperately needs is more consumption (2001:227–28). Thus, attacking the materialism, and what many moralize as the associated greed and individualism attached to it, is to deny that poverty "is constituted by a lack of material resources" (Miller 2001:241). In particular need of more consumption are those referred to as **bottom of the pyramid** (BOP) consumers, the "4–5 billion poor who are unserved or underserved by the large organized private sector, including multinational firms" (Prahalad 2011:6). Integrating BOP consumers into mass consumer society is not simply a matter of charity or social justice but also a potential means to alleviate poverty by turning millions of people into entrepreneurs in their own communities (Prahalad 2011:6). Some will be able to use micro-finance loans to open their own stores, and others will have the opportunity to become distributors for MNCs in rural areas or get involved in direct sales. Although most BOP consumers live in developing countries, such as India and China, low-income consumers in the United States are also underserved or neglected by the private sector. Like their counterparts abroad, they are in need of the three "As" of consumer capacity: affordability, access, and availability (Prahalad 2011:42–43). So, while the affluent have the luxury of condemning mass consumer culture, they at least have the means to afford a wider variety of options in the marketplace—or even escape it.

References

Abramovitz, Mimi. 2010. "Women, Social Reproduction, and the Neo-Liberal Assault on the U.S. Welfare State," in *The Legal Tender of Gender*. Edited by Shelley Gavigan and Dorothy Chunn. Oxford, UK: Hart Publishing, pp. 15–46.

Adorno, Theodor. 1991. *The Culture Industry: Selected Essays on Mass Culture*. Edited by J. M. Bernstein. London: Routledge.

Aldridge, Alan. 2003. *Consumption*. Cambridge, UK: Polity.

Alexander, Samuel, and Simon Ussher. 2012. "The Voluntary Simplicity Movement: A Multi-National Survey Analysis in Theoretical Context." *Journal of Consumer Culture* 12(1): 66–86.

Alkon, Alison Hope, et al. 2012. "Foodways of the Urban Poor." *Geoforum* 48: 126–35.

Amin, Ash, ed. 1994. *Post-Fordism: A Reader*. Oxford, UK: Blackwell.

Anderson, Chris. 2010. *Free*. New York: Hyperion.

Andreasen, A. 1975. *The Disadvantaged Consumer*. New York: Free Press.

Appadurai, Arjun. 1986. "Introduction: Commodities and the Politics of Value," in *The Social Life of Things: Commodities in Cultural Perspective*. Edited by Arjun Appardurai. Cambridge, UK: Cambridge University Press, pp. 3–63.

Appadurai, Arjun. 1996. *Modernity at Large: Cultural Dimensions of Globalization*. Minneapolis: University of Minnesota Press.

Armstrong, Elizabeth, and Laura Hamilton. 2013. *Paying for the Party: How College Maintains Inequality*. Cambridge, MA: Harvard University Press.

Arnould, Eric. 2007. "Should Consumer Citizens Escape the Market?" *Annals of the American Academy of Political and Social Science* 611: 96–111.

Arum, Richard, and Josipa Roksa. 2010. *Academically Adrift: Limited Learning on College Campuses*. Chicago: University of Chicago Press.

Arvidsson, Adam. 2008. "The Ethical Economy of Customer Coproduction." *Journal of Micromarketing* 28(4): 326–38.

Arvidsson, Adam. 2013. "The Potential of Consumer Publics," *Ephemera: Theory & Politics in Organization* 13(2): 367–91.

Arvidsson, Adam, and Nicolai Peitersen. 2013. *The Ethical Economy: Rebuilding Value after the Crisis*. New York: Columbia University Press.

Ashley, Bob, et al. 2005. *Food and Cultural Studies*. London: Routledge.

Ashton, Jerry. 2014. "Yesterday: The Factory Floor, Today: The Campus Commons." *Huffington Post*, December 29.

Associated Press. 2014. "Coke, Pepsi Dropping Controversial BVO from all Drinks." *USA Today*, May 5.

Atwood, Margaret. 2008. *Payback: Debt and the Shadow Side of Wealth*. Toronto: Anansi.

Avineri, Shlomo. 1968. *The Social and Political Thought of Karl Marx*. Cambridge, UK: Cambridge University Press.

Baedeker, Rob. 2011. "How to Make Money When Economy Is Failing." *Newsweek*, November 21.

Banet-Weiser, Sarah, and Roopali Mukherjee. 2012. "Introduction: Commodity Activism in Neoliberal Times," in *Commodity Activism: Cultural Resistance in Neoliberal Times*. Edited by Roopali Mukherjee and Sarah Banet-Weiser. New York: New York University Press, pp. 1–17.

Barber, Benjamin. 2001. *Jihad vs. McWorld: Terrorism's Challenge to Democracy*. New York: Ballantine Books.

Barbrook, Richard. 2005. "The Hi-Tech Gift Economy." *First Monday: Peer Reviewed Journal on the Internet*. December.

Bardhi, Fleura. 2003. "Thrill of the Hunt: Thrift Shopping for Pleasure." *Advances in Consumer Research* 30: 375–76.

Barnett, Clive, Paul Cloke, Nick Clarke, and Alice Malpass. 2011. *Globalizing Responsibility: The Political Rationalities of Ethical Consumption*. Chichester, UK: Wiley-Blackwell.

Baudrillard, Jean. 1975. *The Mirror of Production*. St. Louis, MO: Telos Press.

Baudrillard, Jean. 1981. *For a Critique of the Political Economy of the Sign*. St. Louis, MO: Telos Press.

Baudrillard, Jean. 1998. *The Consumer Society*. London: Sage.

Bauman, Zygmunt. 1989. *Globalization: The Human Consequence*. New York: Columbia University Press.

Bauman, Zygmunt. 1992. *Imitations of Postmodernity*. London: Routledge.

Bauman, Zygmunt. 2007. *Consuming Life*. London: Polity.

Beckham, J. Nichol. 2014. "Drinking Local: Sustainable Brewing, Alternative Food Networks, and the Politics of Valuation," in *Food and Everyday Life*. Edited by Thomas Conroy. Lanham, MD: Lexington Books, pp. 105–26.

Belk, Russell. 1979. "Gift Giving Behavior." *Research in Marketing* 2: 95–126.

Belk, Russell. 1988. "Possessions and the Extended Self." *Journal of Consumer Research* 15: 139–68.

Bell, Daniel. 1976. *The Cultural Contradictions of Capitalism*. New York: Basic Books.

Bellafante, Ginia. 2012. "The New Frontier of New York Tourism? It Might Just Be Your House." *New York Times*, July 8.

Benjamin, Walter. 1969. *Illuminations*. New York: Schocken Books.

Benson, Susan Porter. 1986. *Counter Cultures: Saleswomen, Managers, and Customers in American Department Stores, 1890–1940*. Urbana: University of Illinois Press.

Berstein, Nina. 2015. "To Collect Debts, Nursing Homes Are Seizing Control Over Patients." *New York Times*, January 25.

Bidwell, Allie. 2014. "Report: Nearly 1 in 10 Community College Transfers Lose Nearly All Course Credit." *U.S. News & World Report*, March 19.

Bijapurkar, Rama. 2007. *Winning in the Indian Market: Understanding the Transformation of Consumer India*. Singapore: John Wiley.

Bloch, Linda-Renee, and Dafna Lemish. 1999. "Disposable Love: The Rise and Fall of a Virtual Pet." *New Media & Society* 1(3): 283–303.

Blumer, Herbert. 1969. "Fashion: From Class Differentiation to Collective Selection." *Sociological Quarterly* 10: 275–91.

Bobrow-Strain, Aaron. 2013. *White Bread: A Social History of the Store-Bought Loaf.* Boston: Beacon Press.

Bok, Derek. 2004. "The Benefits and Costs of Commercialization of the Academy," in *Buying In or Selling Out? The Commercialization of the American Research University.* Edited by Donald Stein. New Brunswick, NJ: Rutgers University Press, pp. 32–47.

Bok, Derek. 2005. *Universities in the Marketplace: The Commercialization of Higher Education.* Princeton, NJ: Princeton University Press.

Bordwell, Marilyn. 2002. "Jamming Culture: Adbusters' Hip Media Campaign against Consumerism," in *Confronting Consumption.* Edited by Thomas Princen, Michael Maniates, and Ken Conca. Cambridge, MA: MIT Press, pp. 237–53.

Borkar, Shilpa, et al. 2010. "The Emergence of the Indian Consumer," in *Winning Strategies for the Indian Market.* Edited by Anuradha Dayal-Gulati and Dipak Jain. Evanston, IL: Northwestern University Press, pp. 1–29.

Boström, Magnus, and Mikael Klintman. 2008. *Eco-Standards, Product Labelling and Green Consumerism.* Hampshire, UK: Palgrave.

Botsman, Rachel, and Roo Rogers. 2010. *What's Mine Is Yours: The Rise of Collaborative Consumption.* New York: HarperCollins.

Bourdieu, Pierre. 1984. *Distinction: A Social Critique of the Judgment of Taste.* Cambridge, MA: Harvard University Press.

Bourdieu, Pierre. 1992. "The Practice of Reflexive Sociology (The Paris Workshop)." In *An Invitation to Reflexive Sociology.* Chicago: University of Chicago Press, pp. 217–60.

Bourdieu, Pierre, and Loïc Wacquant. 1992. *An Invitation to Reflexive Sociology.* Chicago: University of Chicago Press.

Bowles, Samuel, and Herbert Gintis. 1975. "The Problem with Human Capital Theory—A Marxian Critique." *American Economic Review* 65(2): 74–82.

Bowles, Samuel, and Herbert Gintis. 2002. "Schooling in Capitalist America Revisited." *Sociology of Education* 75(1): 1–16.

Brandt, Richard. 2011. *One Click: Jeff Bezos and the Rise of Amazon.com.* New York: Penguin.

Braungart, Michael, and William McDonough. 2002. *Cradle to Cradle.* New York: North Point Press.

Breen, T. H. 2004. *The Marketplace of Revolution: How Consumer Politics Shaped American Independence.* Oxford, UK: Oxford University Press.

Breen, T. H. 2006. "Will American Consumers Buy a Second American Revolution?" *Journal of American History,* September, pp. 404–8.

Breneman, David, Brian Pusser, and Sarah Turner. 2006. "The Contemporary Provision of For-Profit Higher Education: Mapping the Market," in *Earnings from Learning.* Edited by David Breneman, Brian Pusser, and Sarah Turner. Albany: State University of New York Press.

Briggs, Bill. 2010. "National Parks Feel the Effects of Human, Environmental Threats." *MSNBC,* August 30.

Brown, David. 2011. "The Social Sources of Educational Credentialism: Status Cultures, Labor Markets, and Organizations." *Sociology of Education*, Extra issue, pp. 19–34.

Brown, Lester. 2001. *Eco-Economy*. New York: W. W. Norton.

Bryman, Alan. 1995. *Disney and His Worlds*. London: Routledge.

Bryman, Alan. 2004. *The Disneyfication of Society*. London: Sage.

Buckingham, David. 2011. *The Material Child: Growing Up in a Consumer Culture*. Cambridge, UK: Polity.

Butcher, Jim. 2003. *The Moralisation of Tourism: Sun, Sand . . . and Saving the World?* London: Routledge.

Butler, R. W. 1980. "The Concept of a Tourist Area Cycle of Evolution." *Canadian Geographer* 24(1): 5–12.

Calder, Lendol. 1999. *Financing the American Dream: A Cultural History of Consumer Credit*. Princeton, NJ: Princeton University Press.

Campbell, Colin. 1989. *The Romantic Ethic and the Spirit of Modern Consumerism*. Oxford, UK: Blackwell.

Campbell, Colin. 1999. "Consuming Goods and the Good of Consuming," in *Consumer Society in American History: A Reader*. Edited by Lawrence Glickman. Ithaca, NY: Cornell University Press, pp. 19–32.

Campbell-Smith, Graham. 1967. *The Making of the Meal Experience*. Guildford, UK: University of Surrey Press.

Carey, Kevin. 2015a. "In-State Tuition, a Disappearing Bargain." *New York Times*, May 19.

Carey, Kevin. 2015b. *The End of College: Creating the Future of Learning and the University of Everywhere*. New York: Riverhead Books.

Carreiro, Joshua. 2009. "The Consumer Cooperative Movement: An Analysis of Class and Consumption." Paper presented at the American Sociological Conference, August 8, San Francisco, CA.

Carreiro, Joshua. 2015. *Consumer Cooperatives in the Early Twentieth Century: An Analysis of Race, Class and Consumption*. Dissertation. University of Massachusetts–Amherst.

Carrier, James. 1995. *Gifts and Commodities: Exchange and Western Capitalism since 1700*. London: Routledge.

Caskey, John. 1994. *Fringe Banking: Check-Cashing Outlets, Pawnshops, and the Poor*. New York: Russell Sage Foundation.

Chase, Stuart, and Frederick Schlink. 1936. *Your Money's Worth*. New York: Macmillan.

Chase-Dunn, Christopher, and Peter Grimes. 1995. "World-Systems Analysis." *Annual Review of Sociology* 21: 387–417.

"Chernobyl: Tourism Hot Spot." 2010. *Centralian Advocate*, December 17.

Chin, Elizabeth. 2001. *Purchasing Power: Black Kids and American Consumer Culture*. Minneapolis: University of Minnesota Press.

Clapp, Jennifer. 2002. "The Distancing of Waste: Overconsumption in a Global Economy," in *Confronting Consumption*. Edited by Thomas Princen, Michael Maniates, and Ken Conca. Cambridge, MA: MIT Press, pp. 155–76.

Clarke, John, et al. 1975. "Subcultures, Cultures and Class," in *Resistance through Rituals: Youth Subcultures in Post-War Britain*. Edited by Stuart Hall and Tony Jefferson. London: Routledge, pp. 9–74.

Clary, Betsy Jane. 2011. "Presidential Address: Institutional Usury and the Banks." *Review of Social Economy* 69(4): 419–38.

Clifford, Stephanie. 2012. "Retailers' Idea: Think Smaller in Urban Push." *New York Times*, July 26.

Clifford, Stephanie, and Claire Cain Miller. 2012. "Online Shoppers Are Rooting for the Little Guy." *New York Times*, January 15.

Clifford, Stephanie, and Quentin Hardy. 2013. "Attention, Shoppers: Store Is Tracking Your Cell." *New York Times*, July 14.

Clift, Stephen, and Simon Carter. 2000. "Tourism, International Travel and Sex: Themes and Research," in *Tourism and Sex: Culture, Commerce, and Coercion*. Edited by Stephen Clift and Simon Carter. London: Pinter, pp. 1–19.

Coggan, Philip. 2012. *Paper Promises: Money, Debt and the New World Order*. New York: Public Affairs.

Cohen, Erik. 1984. "The Sociology of Tourism: Approaches, Issues, and Findings." *American Review of Sociology* 10: 373–92.

Cohen, Lizabeth. 2003. *A Consumers' Republic: The Politics of Mass Consumption in Postwar America*. New York: Knopf.

Cohen, Margaret. 2004. *Brave New Neighborhoods: The Privatization of Public Space*. New York: Routledge.

Collins, Randall. 1979. *The Credential Society: An Historical Sociology of Education and Stratification*. New York: Academic Press.

Collom, Ed. 2011. "Motivations and Differential Participation in a Community Currency System: The Dynamics within a Local Social Movement Organization." *Sociological Forum* 26(1): 144–68.

Comor, Edward. 2008. *Consumption and the Globalization Project*. New York: Palgrave Macmillan.

Contreras, Russell. 2010. "Austerity Named Word of the Year 2010." *Huffington Post*, December 20.

Cook, Daniel Thomas. 2004. *The Commodification of Childhood: The Children's Clothing Industry and the Rise of the Child Consumer*. Durham, NC: Duke University Press.

Cowen, Tyler. 2004. *Creative Destruction*. Princeton, NJ: Princeton University Press.

Cowling, Ellis. 1942. *A Short Introduction to Consumers Cooperation*. Chicago: Cooperative League of the U.S.A.

Cross, Gary. 2000. *An All-Consuming Century: Why Commercialism Won in Modern America*. New York: Columbia University Press.

Csikszentmihalyi, Mihaly, and Eugene Rochberg-Halton. 1981. *The Meaning of Things: Domestic Symbols and the Self*. Cambridge, UK: Cambridge University Press.

Davenport, Coral. 2015. "Nations Approve Landmark Climate Accord in Paris." *New York Times*, December 13.

Davidson, Adam. 2014. "Hi, Mom, I'm Home!" *New York Times Magazine*, June 23.

Davidson, Jacob. 2014. "10 Things Millennials Won't Spend Money On." *Time*, July 16.

Davidson, Julia O'Connell. 2000. "Sex Tourism and Child Prostitution," in *Tourism and Sex: Culture, Commerce, and Coercion*. Edited by Stephen Clift and Simon Carter. London: Pinter, pp. 54–73.

Davis, Fred. 1992. *Fashion, Culture and Identity*. Chicago: University of Chicago Press.

Dawson, Michael. 2005. *The Consumer Trap: Big Business Marketing in American Life*. Urbana: University of Illinois Press.

Dayal-Gulati, Anuradha, and Dipak Jain. 2010. "Introduction," in *Winning Strategies for the Indian Market*. Edited by Anuradha Dayal-Gulati and Dipak Jain. Evanston, IL: Northwestern University Press.

de Certeau, Michel. 1984. *The Practice of Everyday Life*. Berkeley: University of California Press.

Debord, Guy. 1994. *The Society of the Spectacle*. New York: Zone Books.

DeCarlo, Jacqueline. 2010. *Fair Trade*. Oxford, UK: Oneworld.

Deitch, Lewis. 1989. "The Impact of Tourism on the Arts and Crafts of the Indians in the Southwestern United States," in *Hosts and Guests*. Edited by Valene Smith. Philadelphia: University of Pennsylvania Press, pp. 223–35.

Delbanco, Andrew. 2012. *College: What It Is, Was, and Should Be*. Princeton, NJ: Princeton University Press.

Denergi-Knott, Janice, and Detlev Zwick. 2012. "Tracking Prosumption Work on eBay: Reproduction of Desire and the Challenge of Slow McDonaldization." *American Behavioral Scientist* 56(4): 439–58.

Dépret, Molly Hurley. 2007. "Troubles Tourism: Debating History and Voyeurism in Belfast, Northern Ireland," in *The Business of Tourism: Place, Faith, and History*. Edited by Philip Scranton and Janet Davidson. Philadelphia: University of Pennsylvania Press, pp. 137–64.

DeSoucey, Michaela. 2010. "Gastronationalism: Food Traditions and Authenticity Politics in the European Union." *American Sociological Review* 75(3): 432–55.

Deutsch, Tracy. 2010. *Building a Housewife's Paradise*. Chapel Hill: University of North Carolina Press.

DeVault, Marjorie. 1991. *Feeding the Family*. Chicago: Chicago University Press.

Devinney, Timothy, Pat Auger, and Giana Eckhardt. 2010. *The Myth of the Ethical Consumer*. Cambridge, UK: Cambridge University Press.

Dienst, Richard. 2011. *The Bonds of Debt*. London: Verso.

Doctoroff, Tom. 2012. *What Chinese Want: Culture, Consumerism and China's Modern Consumer*. New York: Palgrave Macmillan.

"Doing It Their Way." 2014. *Economist*, January 1.

Donati, Kelly. 2005. "The Pleasure of Diversity in Slow Food's Ethics of Tastes." *Food, Culture and Society: An International Journal of Multidisciplinary Research* 8(2): 227–42.

Douglas, Mary, and Baron Isherwood. 1996. *The World of Goods: Towards an Anthropology of Consumption*. London: Routledge.

Drake, Samantha. 2013. "Crowdsource Your Next Delivery." June. http://www.entrepreneur.com/article/226976

Dreier, Peter. 2013. "Labor Board Sides with Workers." *The Nation*, November.

Dujarier, Marie-Anne. 2014. "The Three Sociological Types of Consumer Work." *Journal of Consumer Culture*, October, pp. 1–17.

Dynarksi, Susan. 2014. "Where College Ratings Hit the Wall." *New York Times,* September 21.

Eavis, Peter. 2015. "As Greece Rebels, the Notion of Debt Forgiveness Returns." *New York Times,* February 5.

Echchaibi, Nabil. 2011. "Mecca Cola and Burqinis: Muslim Consumption and Religious Identities," in *Religion, Media, and Culture: A Reader.* Edited by Gordon Lynch and Jolyon Mitchell. London: Routledge, pp. 31–39.

Eckhardt, Gianna, and Humaira Mahi. 2004. "The Role of Consumer Agency in the Globalization Process of Emerging Markets." *Journal of Macromarketing* 24(2): 136–46.

Eckhardt, Gianna, and Humaira Mahi. 2012. "Globalization, Consumer Tensions, and the Shaping of Consumer Culture in India." *Journal of Macromarketing* 32(3): 280–94.

Ehrenreich, Barbara. 2001. *Nickel and Dimed.* New York: Holt.

Ehrlich, Paul. 1968. *The Population Bomb.* New York: Ballantine.

Ehrlich, Paul, and Anne Ehrlich. 1990. *The Population Explosion.* New York: Simon & Schuster.

Ehrlich, Paul, and Anne Ehrlich. 2004. *One with Nineveh: Politics, Consumption, and the Human Future.* Washington, DC: Island Press.

Eisenstein, Charles. 2011. *Sacred Economies: Money, Gift & Society in the Age of Transition.* Berkeley, CA: Evolver Editions.

Elgin, Duane. 1981. *Voluntary Simplicity: Toward a Way of Life That Is Outwardly Simple, Inwardly Rich.* New York: William Morrow & Co.

Elias, Norbert. 2000. *The Civilizing Process.* Hoboken, NJ: Blackwell.

Eligon, John, and Richard Pérez-Peña. 2015. "University of Missouri Protests Spur a Day of Change." *New York Times,* November 9.

Ember, Sydney. 2014. "On To-Do List: Deposit Cash in Bitcoin A.T.M." *New York Times,* August 25.

Emmanuel, Arghiri. 1972. *Unequal Exchange: A Study of the Imperialism of Trade.* New York: Monthly Review.

Environmental Protection Agency (EPA). 2011. *Electronics Waste Management in the United States through 2009: Executive Summary.* EPA 530-S-11–001. Washington, DC: EPA.

Etzioni, Amitia. 1998. "Voluntary Simplicity: Characterizations, Select Psychological Implications, and Societal Consequences." *Journal of Economic Psychology* 19: 619–43.

Etzioni, Amitia. 2011. "The New Normal." *Sociological Forum* 26(4): 779–89.

Ewen, Stuart. 1976. *Captains of Consciousness.* New York: McGraw Hill.

Featherstone, Mike. 1991. *Consumer Culture & Postmodernism.* London: Sage.

Fine, Gary Alan. 2008. *Kitchens: The Culture of Restaurant Work.* Berkeley: University of California Press.

Finkelstein, Joanne. 1989. *Dining Out: A Sociology of Manners.* New York: New York University Press.

Firat, A. Fuat, and Alladi Venkatesh. 1995. "Liberatory Postmodernism and the Reenchantment of Consumption." *Journal of Consumer Research* 22: 239–67.

Fischler, Claude. 1988. "Food, Self, and Identity." *Social Science Information* 27(2): 275–93.

Fisher, Anne. 2015. "Why Don't Americans Take More Time Off? *Forbes,* June 28.

Fishman, Charles. 2006. *The Wal-Mart Effect.* New York: Penguin.

Fiske, John. 1989. *Understanding Popular Culture.* London: Routledge.

Fortini, Amanda. 2012. "Honey, I Got a Year's Worth of Tuna Fish." *New York Times Magazine,* May.

Frank, Dana. 1994. *Purchasing Power: Consumer Organizing, Gender, and the Seattle Labor Movement, 1919–1929.* Cambridge, UK: Cambridge University Press.

Frank, Dana. 1999. *Buy American: The Untold Story of Economic Nationalism.* Boston: Beacon.

Frank, Thomas. 1997. *The Conquest of Cool.* Chicago: University of Chicago Press.

Franklin, Adrian. 2003. *Tourism: An Introduction.* London: Sage.

Frederick, Christine. 1919. *Household Engineering: Scientific Management in the Home.* Chicago: American School of Home Economics.

Friedman, Milton. 1999. *Consumer Boycotts: Effecting Change through the Marketplace and Media.* New York: Routledge.

Fromartz, Samuel. 2006. *Organic, Inc.* Orlando, FL: Harcourt.

Furstenberg, Frank, et al. 2004. "Growing Up Is Harder to Do." *Contexts* 3(3): 95–102.

Gabaccia, Donna. 2000. *We Are What We Eat: Ethnic Food and the Making of Americans.* Cambridge, MA: Harvard University Press.

Gabriel, Yiannis, and Tim Lang. 2006. *The Unmanageable Consumer.* London: Sage.

Galbraith, John Kenneth. 1958. *The Affluent Society.* New York: Mentor Books.

Gatch, Lorin. 2008. "Local Money in the United States during the Great Depression." *Essays in Economic and Business History* 26: 47–61.

Ger, Guliz, and Russell Belk. 1996. "I'd Like to Buy the World a Coke: Consumptionscapes of the Less Affluent World." *Journal of Consumer Policy* 19: 271–304.

Gereffi, Gary, Miguel Korzeniewicz, and Patricio Korzeniewicz. 1994. "Introduction: Global Commodity Chains," in *Commodity Chains and Global Capitalism.* Edited by Gary Gereffi and Miguel Korzeniewicz. Westport, CT: Praeger, pp. 1–14.

Geron, Tomio. 2013. "The Share Economy." *Forbes,* February 11.

Gerth, Karl. 2003. *China Made: Consumer Culture and the Creation of the Nation.* Cambridge, MA: Harvard University Press.

Gerth, Karl. 2010. *As China Goes, So Goes the World: How Chinese Consumers Are Transforming Everything.* New York: Hill and Wang.

Gibson, James Williams. 2009. *A Reenchanted World: The Quest for a New Kinship with Nature.* New York: Picador.

Giroux, Henry. 1993. "Beyond the Politics of Innocence: Memory and Pedagogy in the 'Wonderful World of Disney.'" *Socialist Review* 23(2): 79–107.

Giroux, Henry. 2014. *Neoliberalism's War on Higher Education.* Chicago: Haymarket Books.

Gladwell, Malcolm. 1997. "The Coolhunt." *The New Yorker,* March 17.

Glickman, Lawrence. 1997. *A Living Wage: American Workers and the Making of Consumer Society.* Ithaca, NY: Cornell University Press.

Glickman, Lawrence. 1999. "Introduction: Born to Shop? Consumer History and American History," in *Consumer Society in American History: A Reader.* Edited by Lawrence Glickman. Ithaca, NY: Cornell University Press, pp. 1–16.

Glickman, Lawrence. 2009. *Buying Power: A History of Consumer Activism in America.* Chicago: University of Chicago Press.

Goeldner, Charles, and J. R. Brent Ritchie. 2009. *Tourism: Principles, Practices, and Philosophies.* Hoboken, NJ: John Wiley.

Goltz, Jay. 2013. "For Local Businesses, the Internet Threat Isn't Just the Sales Tax." *New York Times,* May 14.

Goodyear, Dana. 2012. "Raw Deal." *New Yorker,* April 30.

Gottdiener, Mark. 1982. "Disneyland: A Utopian Urban Space." *Journal of Contemporary Ethnography* 11(2): 139–62.

Gottdiener, Mark. 1995. *Postmodern Semiotics.* Hoboken, NJ: Wiley Blackwell.

Gottdiener, Mark. 2001. *The Theming of America.* Boulder, CO: Westview.

Gould, Eric. 2003. *The University in a Corporate Culture.* New Haven, CT: Yale University Press.

Graeber, David. 2009. "Debt: The First Five Thousand Years." *Mute.* February. http://www.metamute.org/editorial/articles/debt-first-five-thousand-years

Graeber, David. 2011. "Consumption." *Current Anthropology* 52(4): 489–511.

Grandclément, Catherine. 2009. "Wheeling One's Groceries around the Store: The Invention of the Shopping Cart, 1936–1953," in *Food Chains: From Farmyard to Shopping Cart.* Edited by Warren Belasco and Roger Horowitz. Philadelphia: University of Pennsylvania Press, pp. 233–51.

Greenwood, Davydd. 1989. "Culture by the Pound: An Anthropological Perspective on Tourism as Cultural Commoditization," in *Hosts and Guests.* Edited by Valene Smith. Philadelphia: University of Pennsylvania Press, pp. 171–85.

Greider, William. 2011. "Debt Jubilee, American Style." *The Nation,* November 14.

Guptill, Amy, Denise Copelton, and Betsy Lucal. 2013. *Food & Society.* Cambridge, UK: Polity.

Habermas, Jürgen. 1991. *The Structural Transformation of the Public Sphere.* Cambridge, MA: MIT Press.

Hahn, Laura, and Micahel Bruner. 2012. "Politics on Your Plate," in *The Rhetoric of Food.* Edited by Joshua Frye and Michael Bruner. London: Routledge, pp. 42–55.

Hall, C. M. 1996. "Gender and Economic Interests in Tourism Prostitution: The Nature, Development, and Implications of Sex Tourism in Southeast Asia." *Tourism: A Gender Analysis.* Edited by V. Kinnaird and D. Hall. Chichester, UK: John Wiley, pp. 142–63.

Hall, Stuart, and Tony Jefferson, eds. 1975. *Resistance through Rituals: Youth Subcultures in Post-War Britain.* London: Routledge.

Halpern, Jake. 2014. *Bad Paper: Chasing Debt from Wall Street to the Underworld.* New York: Farrar, Straus and Giroux.

Halweil, Brian. 2000. "Where Have All the Farmers Gone?" *World Watch Magazine,* September/October.

Hamilton, Shane. 2009. "Analyzing Commodity Chains: Linkages or Restraints?" in *Food Chains: From Farmyard to Shopping Cart.* Edited by Warren Belasco and Roger Horowitz. Philadelphia: University of Pennsylvania Press, pp. 16–25.

Hannigan, John. 1998. *Fantasy City.* Routledge: New York.

Hansmann, Henry. 1999. "Higher Education as an Associative Good." Yale Law School Working Paper No. 231.

Harris, Elizabeth. 2013. "The Social Showroom" *New York Times*, November 27.
Hartocollis, Anemona, and Jess Bidgood. 2015. "Racial Discrimination Protests Ignite at Colleges across the U.S." *New York Times*, November 11.
Harvey, David. 1990. *The Condition of Postmodernity.* Cambridge, UK: Blackwell.
Harvey, David. 2005. *A Brief History of Neoliberalism.* Oxford, UK: Oxford University Press.
Haug, W. F. 1986. *Critique of Commodity Aesthetics: Appearance, Sexuality and Advertising.* Cambridge, UK: Polity Press.
Hawken, Paul. 2007. *Blessed Unrest.* New York: Viking.
Hayden, Dolores. 2006. "Building the American Way: Public Subsidy, Private Space," in *The Politics of Public Space.* Edited by Setha Low and Neil Smith. London: Routledge, pp. 35–48.
Heath, Joseph, and Andrew Potter. 2004. *Nation of Rebels: Why Counterculture Became Consumer Culture.* New York: HarperBusiness.
Hebdige, Dick. 1979. *Subculture: The Meaning of Style.* London: Routledge.
Helleiner, Eric. 2002. "Think Globally, Transact Locally: The Local-Currency Movement and Green Political Economy," in *Confronting Consumption.* Edited by Thomas Princen, Michael Maniates, and Ken Conca. Cambridge, MA: MIT Press, pp. 255–73.
Hill, Ronald Paul. 2002. "Stalking the Poverty Consumer: A Retrospective Examination of Modern Ethical Dilemmas." *Journal of Business Ethics* 37: 209–19.
Hill, Ronald Paul. 2007. "Disadvantaged Consumers: An Ethical Approach to Consumption by the Poor." *Journal of Business Ethics* 80: 77–83.
Hilton, Matthew. 2009. *Prosperity for All: Consumer Activism in an Era of Globalization.* Ithaca, NY: Cornell University Press.
Himmelman, Jeff. 2013. "Buy It Now." *New York Times Magazine*, December 19.
Hirsch, Fred. 1978/2015. *Social Limits to Growth.* London: Routledge.
Hoang, Kimberly Kay. 2015. *Dealing in Desire: Asian Ascendancy, Western Decline, and the Hidden Currencies of Global Sex Work.* Berkeley: University of California Press.
Hochschild, Arlie Russell. 1983. *The Managed Heart.* Berkeley: University of California Press.
Hochschild, Arlie Russell. 2012. *The Outsourced Self: Intimate Life in Market Times.* New York: Metropolitan Books.
Honoré, Carl. 2004. *In Praise of Slowness.* San Francisco: Harper.
Hoose, Jayne, Stephen Clift, and Simon Carter. 2000. "Combating Tourist Sexual Exploitation of Children," in *Tourism and Sex: Culture, Commerce, and Coercion.* Edited by Stephen Clift and Simon Carter. London: Pinter, pp. 74–90.
Hopkins, Terrence, and Immanuel Wallerstein. 1994. "Commodity Chains in the Capitalist World-Economy Prior to 1800," in *Commodity Chains and Global Capitalism.* Edited by Gary Gereffi and Miguel Korzeniewicz. Westport, CT: Praeger, pp. 17–34.
Horkheimer, Max, and Theodor Adorno. 1993. *Dialectic of Enlightenment.* New York: Continuum.
Hornik, Jacob, and Laurence Feldman. 1982. "Retailing Implications of the Do-It-Yourself Consumer Movement." *Journal of Retailing* 58(2): 44–63.

Hsu, Sara. 2014. "China's Urbanization Plan—Sustainable Development?" *The Diplomat*, April 16.

Humphreys, Ashlee, and Kent Grayson. 2008. "The Intersecting Role of Consumer and Producer: A Critical Perspective on Co-Production, Co-Creation, and Prosumption." *Sociological Compass* 2(3): 963–80.

Huntington, Samuel. 2011. *The Clash of Civilizations*. New York: Simon & Schuster.

Huxley, Aldous. 1932/2006. *Brave New World*. New York: Harper Perennial Modern Classics.

Hyman, Louis. 2012. "The Politics of Consumer Debt: U.S. State Policy and the Rise of Investment in Consumer Credit, 1920–2008." *ANNALS of the American Academy of Political and Social Science* 644: 40–49.

Inglehart, Ronald. 1990. *Culture Shift in Advanced Industrial Society*. Princeton, NJ: Princeton University Press.

Isalska, Anita. 2015. CNN. April 14. http://www.cnn.com/2015/04/14/travel/chernobyl-tourism

Jackson, Anita, Aaron Shuman, and Gopal Dayaneni. *Toxic Sweatshops*. October 2006. http://www.ceh.org/legacy/storage/documents/toxicsweatshops.pdf

Jackson, T. J., and Richard Lears. 1983. *The Culture of Consumption: Critical Essays in American History, 1880–1980*. New York: Pantheon.

Jafri, Syed Hussain, and Lawrence Margolis. 1999. "The Treatment of Usury in the Holy Scriptures." *Thunderbird International Business Review* 41(4/5): 371–79.

James, Jeffery. 2000. *Consumption, Globalization, and Development*. New York: St. Martin's.

Jameson, Fredrick. 1984. "Postmodernism and the Consumer Society," in *Postmodern Culture*. Edited by H. Foster. London: Pluto Press.

Jayachandran, Seema, and Michael Kremer. 2006. "Odious Debt," in *Sovereign Debt at the Crossroads: Challenges and Proposals for Resolving the Third World Debt Crisis*. Edited by Chris Jochnick and Fraser Preston. Oxford, UK: Oxford University Press, pp. 215–25.

Jesse, David. 2013. "Government Books $41.3 Billion in Student Loan Profits." *USA Today*, November 25.

Jiayi, Liu. 2015. "E-Commerce Business Expansion Planned for Rural China." *ZDNet*, April 23.

Johnson, Nathanael. 2008. "The Revolution Will Not Be Pasteurized." *Atlantic Monthly*, April.

Johnson, Steven. 2015. "Creative Accounting." *New York Times Magazine*, August 23, pp. 30–37, 48–51.

Johnston, Josée, and Shyon Baumann. 2010. *Foodies: Democracy and Distinction in the Gourmet Foodscape*. New York: Routledge.

Kallet, Arthur, and Frederick Schlink. 1933/1976. *100,000,000 Guinea Pigs: Dangers in Everyday Foods, Drugs, and Cosmetics*. New York: Arno Press.

Karpyn, Allison, and Sarah Treuhaft. 2010. *The Grocery Gap*. PolicyLink and the Food Trust. http://thefoodtrust.org/uploads/media_items/grocerygap.original.pdf

Kasser, Tim. 2002. *The High Price of Materialism*. Cambridge, MA: MIT Press.

Kelley, Florence. 1899. "Aims and Principles of the Consumers' League." *American Journal of Sociology* 5: 289–304.

Khan, Shamus. 2012. "The New Elitists." *New York Times,* July 8.

Kharif, Olga. 2014. "Not Just for Libertarians and Anarchists Anymore." *Bloomberg,* October 9.

Kilbourne, Jean. 2010. *Killing Us Softly 4.* Video recording.

King, Margaret, and J. G. O'Boyle. 2011. "The Theme Park: The Art of Time and Space," in *Disneyland and Culture: Essays on the Parks and Their Influence.* Edited by Kathy Merlock Jackson and Mark West. Jefferson, NC: McFarland & Co., pp. 5–18.

King, Samantha, and Sheila Slaughter. 2004. "Sports 'R' Us: Contracts, Trademarks, and Logos," in *Academic Capitalism and the New Economy.* Edited by Sheila Slaughter and Gary Rhoades. Baltimore: Johns Hopkins University Press, pp. 256–78.

Kivisto, Peter, and Dan Pittman. 2010. "Goffman's Dramaturgical Sociology: Personal Sales and Service in a Commodified World," in *Illuminating Social Life: Classical and Contemporary Theory Revisited.* Edited by Peter Kivisto. Thousand Oaks, CA: Pine Forge Press, pp. 327–48.

Klein, Naomi. 1999. *No Logo.* New York: Picador.

Klein, Naomi. 2014. *This Changes Everything: Capitalism vs. The Climate.* New York: Simon & Schuster.

Knox, F. 2005. "The Doctrine of Consumers' Sovereignty." *Review of Social Economy* 63(3): 383–94.

Knupfer, Anne Meis. 2013. *Food Co-ops in America: Community, Consumption, and Economic Democracy.* Ithaca, NY: Cornell University Press.

Koch, Shelley. 2012. *The Theory of Grocery Shopping.* London: Berg.

Kopytoff, Igor. 1986. "The Cultural Biography of Things: Commoditization as Process," in *The Social Life of Things: Commodities in Cultural Perspective.* Edited by Arjun Appardurai. Cambridge, UK: Cambridge University Press, pp. 64–91.

Kousis, M. 1996. "Tourism and the Family in a Rural Cretan Community," in *The Sociology of Tourism: Theoretical and Empirical Investigations.* Edited by Yiorgos Apostolopoulos, Stella Leivadi, and Andrew Yianakis. London: Routledge, pp. 219–32.

Kowinski, William. 1985. *The Malling of America.* New York: William Morrow.

KPMG International. 2014. "E-Commerce in China: Driving a New Consumer Culture." https://www.kpmg.com/CN/en/IssuesAndInsights/Articles Publications/Newsletters/China-360/Documents/China-360-Issue15-201401-E-commerce-in-China.pdf

Krupnik, Stephen. 2009. *Pawnonomics: A Tale of the Historical, Cultural, and Economic Significance of the Pawnbroking Industry.* Mishawaka, IN: Cloud Ten.

Kuttner, Robert. 2013. *Debtors' Prison: The Politics of Austerity versus Possibility.* New York: Knopf.

Labaree, David. 1997. *How to Succeed in School without Really Learning: The Credentials Race in American Education.* New Haven, CT: Yale University Press.

Lajoie, Marc, and Nick Shearman. 2014. "What Is Alibaba?" *Wall Street Journal.* http://projects.wsj.com/alibaba/

Lamont, Michele, and Annette Lareau. 1988. "Cultural Capital: Allusions, Gaps and Glissandos in Recent Theoretical Development." *Sociological Theory* 6: 153–68.

Langman, Lauren. 1992. "Neon Cages: Shopping for Subjectivity," in *Lifestyle Shopping: The Subject of Consumption*. Edited by Rob Shields. London: Routledge, pp. 40–82.

Lash, Scott, and John Urry. 1994. *Economies of Signs and Space*. London: Sage.

Lasn, Kalle. 1999. *Culture Jam: The Uncooling of America*. New York: William Morrow.

Lasn, Kalle. 2012. *Meme Wars*. New York: Seven Stories Press.

Lawson, Neal. 2009. *All Consuming*. London: Penguin.

Lazzarato, Maurizio. 2012. *The Making of Indebted Man*. Los Angeles: Semiotext(e).

Leach, William. 1993. *Land of Desire: Merchants, Power and the Rise of a New Culture*. New York: Pantheon.

Leadbetter, Charles, and Paul Miller. 2004. *The Pro-Am Revolution*. London: Demos.

Lee, Martyn. 1993. *Consumer Culture Reborn*. London: Routledge.

LeGreco, Marianne, Stephanie Greene, and Derek Shaw. 2014. "Healthy Eating on a Budget: Negotiating Tensions between Two Discourses," in *Food and Everyday Life*. Edited by Thomas Conroy. New York: Lexington, pp. 231–56.

Lennon, John, and Malcolm Foley. 2000. *Dark Tourism*. London: Continuum.

Levi-Strauss, Claude. 1974/1983. *The Raw and the Cooked*. Chicago: University of Chicago Press.

Lewin, Tamar. 2013. "Students Rush to Web Classes, but Profits May be Much Later," *New York Times*, January 6.

Lewin, Tamar. 2014. "Most Don't Earn Degree in 4 Years Study Finds." *New York Times*, December 2.

Lichtenstein, Nelson. 2010. *The Retail Revolution*. New York: Picador.

Lindholm, Charles, and Siv Lie. 2013. "You Eat What You Are: Cultivated Taste and the Pursuit of Authenticity in the Slow Food Movement," in *Culture of the Slow*. Edited by Nick Osbaldiston. London: Palgrave, pp. 52–70.

Lipovetsky, Gilles. 2011. "The Hyperconsumption Society," in *Beyond the Consumption Bubble*. Edited by Karin Ekström and Kay Glans. London: Routledge, pp. 25–36.

Littler, Jo. 2009. *Radical Consumption: Shopping for Change in Contemporary Culture*. Berkshire, UK: Open University Press.

Lohr, Steve. 2015. "New Banks Sift Unusual Data to Make Loans." *New York Times* January 19.

Lopes, C. Abreu, and C. Frade. 2012. "The Way into Bankruptcy: Market Anomie and Sacrifice among Portuguese Consumers." *Journal of Consumer Policy* 35: 477–96.

Lorin, Janet. 2014. "You Mean I Have to Pay That Back?" *Bloomsberg*, July 17.

Loss, Christopher. 2012. *Between Citizen and State: The Politics of American Higher Education in the 20th Century*. Princeton, NJ: Princeton University Press.

Lowry, Brian. 1998. "*Seinfeld*'s Finale Ends Up Sixth Place of All Time." *Los Angeles Times*, May 16.

Lury, Celia. 1997. "The Objects of Travel," in *Touring Cultures: Transformations of Travel and Theory*. Edited by Chris Rojek and John Urry. London: Routledge, pp. 75–95.

Lyman, Rick. 2015. "Glass Beads Made in Czech Village Adorn Bodies of the World's Tribes." *New York Times,* January 13.

Lyon, Sarah, and Mark Moberg. 2010. "What's Fair? The Paradox of Seeking Justice through Markets," in *Fair Trade and Social Justice.* Edited by Sarah Lyon and Mark Moberg. New York: New York University Press, pp. 1–23.

Lyotard, Jean-François. 1984. *The Postmodern Condition.* Minneapolis: University of Minnesota Press.

MacCannell, Dean. 1999. *The Tourist.* Berkeley: University of California Press.

MacCannell, Dean. 2001. "Remarks on the Commodification of Cultures," in *Hosts and Guests Revisited: Tourism Issues of the 21st Century.* Edited by Valene Smith and Maryann Brent. Elmsford, NJ: Cognizant Communication Corporation, pp. 380–90.

Macnaghten, Phil, and John Urry. 1998. *Contested Natures.* London: Sage.

Maguire, Jennifer Smith. 2014. "Bourdieu on Cultural Intermediaries," in *The Cultural Intermediaries Reader.* Edited by Jennifer Smith Maguire and Julian Matthews. London: Sage, pp. 15–24.

Maniates, Michael. 2002a. "Individualization: Plant a Tree, Buy a Bike, Save the World?" in *Confronting Consumption.* Edited by Thomas Princen, Michael Maniates, and Ken Conca. Cambridge, MA: MIT Press, pp. 43–66.

Maniates, Michael. 2002b. "In Search of Consumptive Resistance: The Voluntary Simplicity Movement," in *Confronting Consumption.* Edited by Thomas Princen, Michael Maniates, and Ken Conca. Cambridge, MA: MIT Press, pp. 199–235.

Manno, Jack. 2002. "Commoditization: Consumption Efficiency and an Economy of Care and Connection," in *Confronting Consumption.* Edited by Thomas Princen, Michael Maniates, and Ken Conca. Cambridge, MA: MIT Press, pp. 67–100.

Marcuse, Herbert. 1964. *One Dimensional Man.* Boston: Beacon.

Marx, Karl. 1859/1970. *A Contribution to the Critique of Political Economy.* New York: International Publishers.

Marx, Karl. 1867/1967. *Capital: A Critique of Political Economy.* Vol. 1. New York: International Publishers.

Marx, Karl. 1932/1975. "The Economic and Philosophic Manuscripts of 1844," in *Karl Marx: Early Writings.* New York: Penguin Books.

Massolution Report. 2012. http://www.crowdsourcing.org/editorial/crowd-funding-market-grew-81-in-2012-finds-massolution-industry-report/25049

Matthews, Steve, Kathleen Howley, and Clea Benson. 2015. "Owning Your Home Is Good for the Kids." *Bloomberg,* May 11.

Mauss, Marcel. 1923/1967. *The Gift.* New York: W. W. Norton.

May, Brendan, et al. 2003. "The Marine Stewardship Council Background, Rationale, and Challenges," in *Eco-Labelling in Fisheries: What Is It All About?* Edited by Bruce Phillips, Trevor Ward, and Chet Chaffee. Oxford, UK: Blackwell, pp. 14–33.

May, Elaine Tyler. 1999. "The Commodity Gap: Consumerism and the Modern Home," in *Consumer Society in American History: A Reader.* Edited by Lawrence Glickman. Ithaca, NY: Cornell University Press, pp. 298–315.

Mayer, Robert. 1989. *The Consumer Movement: Guardians of the Marketplace.* Boston: Twayne.

Mayer, Robert. 2013. "When and Why Usury Should Be Prohibited." *Journal of Business Ethics* 116: 513–27.

Mayo, James. 1993. *The American Grocery Store: The Business Evolution of an Architectural Space.* Westport, CT: Greenwood.

Mayo, Marjorie. 2005. *Global Citizens: Social Movements and the Challenge of Globalization.* New York: Zed Books.

Mazzarella, William. 2003. *Shoveling Smoke: Advertising and Globalization in Contemporary India.* Durham, NC: Duke University Press.

McClain, Sean. 2015. "Why E-Commerce Can Be a Big Pain for India's Deliverymen." *Wall Street Journal,* March 29.

McCracken, Grant. 1990. *Culture and Consumption.* Bloomington: University of Indiana Press.

McGovern, Charles. 2006. *Sold American: Consumption and Citizenship, 1890–1945.* Chapel Hill: University of North Carolina Press.

McNamee, Stephen, and Robert Miller. 2009. *The Meritocracy Myth.* Lanham, MD: Rowman & Littlefield.

McRobbie, Angela. 1991. *Feminism and Youth Culture: From Jackie to Just Seventeen.* London: Macmillan.

Mettler, Suzanne. 2014. *Degrees of Inequality: How the Politics of Higher Education Sabotaged the American Dream.* New York: Basic Books.

Meyer, John. 2010. "A Democratic Politics of Sacrifice?" in *The Environmental Politics of Sacrifice.* Edited by Michael Maniates and John Meyer. Cambridge, MA: MIT Press, pp. 13–32.

Mian, Atif, and Amir Sufi. 2014. *House of Debt.* Chicago: University of Chicago Press.

Micheletti, Michele. 2003. *Political Virtue and Shopping: Individuals, Consumerism, and Collective Action.* New York: Palgrave.

Micheletti, Michele, and Dietlind Stolle. 2009. "Consumers as Political Actors," in *Critical Food Issues: Problems and State-of-the-Art Solutions.* Edited by Lynn Walter and Laurel Phoenix. Westport, CT: Greenwood, pp. 85–99.

Miles, Steven. 2010. *Spaces for Consumption.* Thousand Oaks, CA: Sage.

Miller, Claire Cain. 2013. "Wal-Mart Introduces Lockers as It Battles Amazon in E-Commerce." *New York Times,* March 27.

Miller, Claire Cain, and Stephanie Clifford. 2013. "To Catch Up, Walmart Moves to Amazon Turf." *New York Times,* October 19.

Miller, Daniel. 1987. *Material Culture and Mass Consumption.* Oxford, UK: Basil Blackwell.

Miller, Daniel. 1998. *A Theory of Shopping.* Cornell, NY: Cornell University Press.

Miller, Daniel. 2001. "The Poverty of Morality," *Journal of Consumer Culture* 1(2): 225–43.

Miller, Daniel. 2008. *The Comfort of Things.* Cambridge, UK: Polity.

Miller, Daniel, et al. 1998. *Shopping, Place and Identity.* London: Routledge.

Miller, Michael. 1994. *The Bon Marché: Bourgeois Culture and the Department Store, 1869–1920.* Princeton, NJ: Princeton University Press.

Miller, Richard, and Kelli Washington. 2014. *Consumer Marketing 2014–2015.* Loganville, GA: RKMA Publications.

Mintz, Sidney. 2002. "Food and Eating: Some Persisting Questions," in *Selling Taste in Consumer Societies.* Edited by Warren Belasco and Philip Scranton. New York: Routledge, pp. 24–33.

Mitchell, Wesley. 1912. "The Backward Art of Spending Money." *American Economic Review* 2: 269–81.

Mogilnicki, Eric, and Melissa Malpass. 2013. "The First Year of the Consumer Financial Protection Bureau: An Overview." *The Business Lawyer* 68: 557–70.

Moisio, Risto, Eric Arnould, and Linda Price. 2004. "Between Mothers and Markets: Constructing Family Identity through Homemade Food." *Journal of Consumer Culture* 4(3): 361–84.

Moore, Oliver. 2006. "Understanding Postorganic Fresh Fruit and Vegetable Consumers at Participatory Farmers' Markets in Ireland: Reflexivity, Trust, and Social Movements." *International Journal of Consumer Studies* 30(5): 416–26.

Moreton, Bethany. 2009. *To Serve God and Wal-Mart.* Cambridge, MA: Harvard University Press.

Moss, Michael. 2013. *Salt Sugar Fat: How the Food Giants Hooked Us.* New York: Random House.

Muller v. Oregon, 208 U.S. 412 (1908).

Mullings, Beverley. 2000. "Fantasy Tours: Exploring the Global Consumption of Caribbean Sex Tourisms," in *New Forms of Consumption.* Edited by Mark Gottdiener. Lanham, MD: Rowman & Littlefield, pp. 227–50.

Murphy, Verity. 2003. "Mecca Cola Challenges US Rival." *BBC News,* January 8.

Murray, Douglas, and Laura Raynolds. 2007. "Globalization and Its Antimonies: Negotiating a Fair Trade Movement," in *Fair Trade: The Challenges of Transforming Globalization.* Edited by Laura Reynolds and Douglas Murray. London: Routledge, pp. 3–14.

Myer, Norman, and Jennifer Kent. 2004. *The New Consumers: The Influence of Affluence on the Environment.* Washington, DC: Island Press.

Nader, Ralph. 1965. *Unsafe at Any Speed.* New York: Grossman.

National Association for the Advancement of Colored People v. Claibourne Hardware Co., 458 U.S. 886 (1982).

Nestle, Marion. 2013. "Today's "Eat More" Environment: The Role of the Food Industry," in *A Place at the Table.* Edited by Peter Pringle. New York: Participant Media, pp. 95–106.

"The New Thundering Herd." 2012. *Economist,* June 16.

Ngai, Pun. 2003. "Subsumption or Consumption? The Phantom of Consumer Revolution in 'Globalizing' China." *Cultural Anthropology* 18(4): 469–92.

Nicholls, Alex, and Charlotte Opal. 2005. *Fair Trade: Market-Driven Ethical Consumption.* London: Sage.

North, Peter. 2006. *Alternative Currency Movements as a Challenge to Globalisation?* Hants, UK: Ashgate.

Oldenberg, Ray. 1989. *The Great Good Place.* New York: Paragon House.

Oosterveer, Peter, and David Sonnenfeld. 2012. *Food, Globalization, and Sustainability.* London: Earthscan.

Orovic, Joseph, and Alison Smale. 2015. "Croatia Forgiving Debt of Some of Its Poorest Citizens." *New York Times,* February 4.

Outram, Dorinda. 2013. *The Enlightenment.* Cambridge, UK: Cambridge University Press.

Packard, Vance. 1970. *The Waste Makers*. New York: Pocket Books.

Palumbo-Lui, David. 2014. "Student Loan Debt: The Need for a Mass Movement." *Huffington Post*, July 20.

Parkins, Wendy, and Geoffrey Craig. 2009. "Culture and Politics of Alternative Food Networks." *Food, Culture, and Society* 12(1): 76–103.

Patten, Simon. 1907. *The New Basis of Civilization*. New York: Macmillan.

Peñaloza, Lisa, and Michelle Barnhart. 2011. "Living U.S. Capitalism: The Normalization of Credit/Debt." *Journal of Consumer Research* 38: 743–62.

Pendergrast, Mark. 2010. *Uncommon Ground: The History of Coffee and How It Transformed the World*. New York: Basic Books.

Pertschuk, Michael. 1982. *Revolt against Regulation: The Rise and Pause of the Consumer Movement*. Berkeley: University of California Press.

Peterson, Richard, and Roger Kern. 1996. "Changing Highbrow Taste: From Snob to Omnivore." *American Sociological Review* 61: 900–7.

Pettifor, Ann. 2006. "The Jubilee 2000 Campaign: A Brief Overview," in *Sovereign Debt at the Crossroads: Challenges and Proposals for Resolving the Third World Debt Crisis*. Edited by Chris Jochnick and Fraser Preston. Oxford, UK: Oxford University Press, pp. 297–317.

Pierre-Louis, Kendra. 2012. *Green Washed*. New York: Ig Publishing.

Pietrykowski, Bruce. 2004. "You Are What You Eat: The Social Economy of the Slow Food Movement." *Review of Social Economy* 62(3): 307–21.

Pietrykowski, Bruce. 2009. *The Political Economy of Consumer Behavior: Contesting Consumption*. London: Routledge.

Piore, Micahel, and Charles Sabel. 1984. *The Second Industrial Divide*. New York: Basic Books.

Pirgmaier, Elke, and Friedrich Hinterberger. 2012. "What Kind of Growth Is Sustainable? A Presentation of Arguments," in *Growth in Transition*. Edited by Friedrich Hinterberger, et al. New York: Earthscan, pp. 13–54.

Pi-Sunyer, Oriol, and R. B. Thomas. 1997. "Tourism, Environmentalism, and Cultural Survival in Quintana Roo," in *Environmental Sociology: From Analysis to Action*. Edited by Leslie King and Deborah McCarthy. Lanham, MD: Rowman & Littlefield, pp. 43–61.

Pollan, Michael. 2006. *The Omnivore's Dilemma*. New York: Penguin.

Polletta, Francesca, and Zaibu Tufail. 2014. "The Moral Obligations of Some Debts." *Sociological Forum* 29(1): 1–28.

Pomerantz, Dorothy. 2013. "*Breaking Bad* Finale Is Big but Not AMC's Biggest." *Forbes*, September 30.

Porter, Katherine. 2012. "Driven by Debt: Bankruptcy and Financial Failure in American Families," in *Broke: How Debt Bankrupts the Middle Class*. Edited by Katherine Porter. Stanford, CA: Stanford University Press, pp. 1–21.

Prahalad, C. K. 2011. *The Fortune at the Bottom of the Pyramid: Eradicating Poverty through Profits*. Upper Saddle, NJ: Pearson Education.

Princen, Thomas, Michael Maniates, and Ken Conca. 2002. "Confronting Consumption," in *Confronting Consumption*. Edited by Thomas Princen, Michael Maniates, and Ken Conca. Cambridge, MA: MIT Press, pp. 1–20.

Probyn, Elspeth. 1998. "Mc-Identities: Food and the Familial Citizen." *Theory, Culture & Society* 15(2): 155–73.

Pruitt, D., and S. Lafont. 1995. "For Love and Money: Romance Tourism in Jamaica." *Annals of Tourism Research* 22(2): 422–40.

Purdue, Derrick, et al. 1997. "DIY Culture and Extended Milieux: LETS, Veggie Boxes, and Festivals." *The Sociological Review* 45(4): 645–67.

Pusser, Brian. 2006. "Higher Education, Markets, and the Preservation of the Public Good," in *Earnings from Learning: The Rise of For-Profit Universities*. Edited by David Breneman, Brian Pusser, and Sarah Turner. Albany: State University of New York Press, pp. 23–43.

Putnam, Robert. 1995. "Bowling Alone: America's Declining Social Capital." *Journal of Democracy* 6(1): 65–78.

Putnam, Robert. 2000. *Bowling Alone: The Collapse and Revival of American Community*. New York: Simon & Schuster.

Rai, Saritha. 2015. "From Dabbawallas to Kirana Stores, Five Unique E-Commerce Delivery Innovations in India." *Forbes*. April 15. www.forbes.com/sites/saritharai

Ram, Uri. 2007. "Liquid Identities: Mecca Cola versus Coca-Cola." *European Journal of Cultural Studies* 10(4): 465–84.

Rawlins, Roblyn, and David Livert. 2014. "The Dilemma of Dinner: The Practice of Home Cooking in Everyday Life," in *Food and Everyday Life*. Edited by Thomas Conroy. Lanham, MD: Lexington Books, pp. 185–214.

Redmond, William. 2000. "Consumer Rationality and Consumer Sovereignty." *Review of Social Economy* 58(2): 177–96.

Reekie, Gail. 1993. *Temptations: Sex, Selling, and the Department Store*. St. Leonards, Australia: Allen & Unwin.

Ritholtz, Barry. 2014. "How Does Facebook Make Its Money?" February 23. http://www.ritholtz.com/blog/2014/02/how-does-facebook-make-its-money/

Ritzer, George. 2009. *Contemporary Sociological Theory and Its Classical Roots: The Basics*. New York: McGraw-Hill.

Ritzer, George. 2010. *Enchanting a Disenchanted World: Revolutionizing the Means of Consumption*. Thousand Oaks, CA: Pine Forge Press.

Ritzer, George. 2013. *The McDonaldization of Society*. Thousand Oaks, CA: Sage.

Ritzer, George, and Nathan Jurgenson. 2010. "Production, Consumption, and Prosumption: The Nature of Capitalism in the Age of the Digital 'Prosumer.'" *Journal of Consumer Culture* 10(13): 13–36.

Ritzer, George, Doug Goodman, and Wendy Wiedenhoft. 2001. "Theories of Consumption," in *Handbook of Social Theory*. Edited by George Ritzer and Barry Smart. London: Sage.

Ritzer, George, James Murphy, and Wendy Wiedenhoft. 2001. "Thorstein Veblen in the Age of Hyperconsumption," in *Explorations in the Sociology of Consumption*. Edited by George Ritzer. London: Sage, pp. 203–21.

Rivera, Lauren. 2015. "Guess Who Doesn't Fit in at Work." *New York Times*, May 31.

Rivoli, Pietra. 2009. *The Travels of a T-Shirt in the Global Economy*. Hoboken, NJ: John Wiley.

Robertson, Roland. 1992. *Globalization: Social Theory and Global Culture*. London: Sage.

Rojek, Chris. 1993. *Ways of Escape: Modern Transformation in Leisure and Travel.* New York: Rowman & Littlefield.

Roodman, David. 2006. "Creditor Initiatives in the 1980s and 1990s," in *Sovereign Debt at the Crossroads: Challenges and Proposals for Resolving the Third World Debt Crisis.* Edited by Chris Jochnick and Fraser Preston. Oxford, UK: Oxford University Press, pp. 13–34.

Rosenberg, Marjorie. 1985. "A Sad Heart at the Department Store." *American Scholar* 54(20): 183–93.

Rosenbloom, Stephanie. 2013. "Let the Games Begin." *New York Times,* June 2.

Rosin, Hanna. 2012. *The End of Men and the Rise of Women.* New York: Riverhead.

Ross, Andrew. 2014. "You Are Not a Loan: A Debtors Movement." *Culture Unbound* 6: 179–88.

Ross-Bryant, Lynn. 2013. *Pilgrimage to the National Parks: Religion and Nature in the United States.* New York: Routledge.

Royte, Elizabeth. 2005. *Garbage Land.* New York: Little, Brown.

Ryan, Chris, and C. Michael Hall. 2001. *Sex Tourism: Marginal People and Liminalities.* London: Routledge.

Ryan, John, and Alan Thein Durning. 1997. *Stuff: The Secret Lives of Everyday Things.* Seattle, WA: Northwest Environment Watch.

Sachs, Jeffrey. 2006. "Forward," in *Sovereign Debt at the Crossroads: Challenges and Proposals for Resolving the Third World Debt Crisis.* Edited by Chris Jochnick and Fraser Preston. Oxford, UK: Oxford University Press, pp. vii–xi.

Sack, Robert David. 1992. *Place, Modernity, and the Consumer's World.* Baltimore: Johns Hopkins University Press.

Sandel, Michael. 2012. *What Money Can't Buy: The Moral Limits of Markets.* New York: Farrar, Straus and Giroux.

Sassatelli, Roberta. 2007. *Consumer Culture: History, Theory and Politics.* Thousand Oaks, CA: Sage.

Schlosser, Eric. 2001. *Fast Food Nation.* Boston: Houghton Mifflin.

Schneider, Dan. 2013. "No Payment Required." *Dollars & Sense,* January/February.

Schor, Juliet. 1998. *The Overspent American.* New York: HarperPerennial.

Schor, Juliet. 2004. *Born to Buy: The Commercialized Child and the New Consumer Culture.* New York: Scribner.

Schor, Juliet. 2007. "In Defense of Consumer Critique: Revisiting the Consumption Debates of the Twentieth Century." *Annals of the American Academy of Political and Social Science* 611: 16–30.

Schrank, Zack. 2014. "Cultivating Localization through Commodity De-Fetishism," in *Food and Everyday Life.* Edited by Thomas Conroy. Lanham, MD: Lexington Books, pp. 147–72.

Schudson, Michael. 1999. "Delectable Materialism: Second Thoughts on Consumer Culture," in *Consumer Society in American History: A Reader.* Edited by Lawrence Glickman. Ithaca, NY: Cornell University Press, pp. 341–58.

Schudson, Michael. 2007. "Citizens, Consumers, and the Good Society." *Annals of the American Academy of Politics and Social Sciences* 611: 236–49.

Schwartz, Judith. 2009. "Tough Times Lead to Local Currencies." *Time Magazine,* July 13.

Schwartzkopf, Stefan. 2011. "The Political Theology of Consumer Sovereignty." *Theory, Culture & Society* 28(3): 106–29.

Scibelli, Cathy. 2011. "Forget the Prozac, Give Me a Dose of Disney," in *Disneyland and Culture: Essays on the Parks and Their Influence.* Edited by Kathy Merlock Jackson and Mark West. Jefferson, NC: McFarland & Co., pp. 215–22.

Seabrook, Jeremy. 2001. *Travels in the Skin Trade: Tourism and the Sex Industry.* London: Pluto.

Sekerak, Emil, and Art Danforth. 1980. *Consumer Cooperation: The Heritage and the Dream.* Santa Clara, CA: Consumers Cooperative Publishing Association.

Selingo, Jeffrey. 2014. "Demystifying the MOOC." *New York Times,* October 29.

Shah, Dhavan, et al. 2007. "Political Consumerism: How Communication and Consumption Orientations Drive 'Lifestyle Politics.'" *Annals of the American Academy of Politics and Social Sciences* 611: 217–35.

Shannon, Thomas. 1996. *An Introduction to the World-System Perspective.* Boulder, CO: Westview.

Shull, Kristina Karin. 2005. "Is the Magic Gone? Weber's 'Disenchantment of the World' and Its Implications for Art in Today's World." *Anamesa* 3(2): 61–73.

Silva, Jennifer. 2015. *Coming Up Short: Working-Class Adulthood in an Age of Uncertainty.* Oxford, UK: Oxford University Press.

Silverbush, Lori, and Kristi Jacobson, directors. 2013. *A Place at the Table.* DVD.

Silverstein, Michael, and Neil Fiske. 2008. *Trading Up: Why Consumers Want New Luxury Goods—and How Companies Create Them.* New York: Portfolio.

Simanis, Erik. 2009. "At the Base of the Pyramid." *Wall Street Journal,* October 26.

Simmel, Georg. 1903/1971. "The Metropolis and Mental Life," in *Georg Simmel.* Edited by D. Levine. Chicago: Chicago University Press, pp. 324–39.

Simmel, Georg. 1904/1957. "Fashion." *American Journal of Sociology,* May, pp. 541–58.

Simmel, Georg. 1907/1990. *Philosophy of Money.* 2nd ed. London: Routledge.

Singer, Natasha. 2014. "When No One Is Just a Face in the Crowd." *New York Times,* February 2.

Sklair, Leslie. 2002. *Globalization: Capitalism & Its Alternatives.* Oxford, UK: Oxford University Press.

Sklar, Kathryn Kish. 1998. "'The Consumers' White Label of the National Consumers' League, 1898–1918," in *Getting and Spending: American and European Consumption in the Twentieth Century.* Edited by Susan Strasser, Charles McGovern, and Matthais Judt. New York: Cambridge University Press.

Slade, Giles. 2006. *Made to Break: Technology and Obsolescence in America.* Cambridge, MA: Harvard University Press.

Slater, Don. 1997. *Consumer Culture & Modernity.* Cambridge, UK: Polity Press.

Slaughter, Sheila, and Gary Rhoades. 2004. *Academic Capitalism and the New Economy.* Baltimore: Johns Hopkins University Press.

Smith, Adam. 1776/1976. *The Wealth of Nations.* Edited by Edwin Cannan. Chicago: University of Chicago Press

Smith, Mick, and Rosaleen Duffy. 2003. *The Ethics of Tourism Development.* London: Routledge.

Sommer, Jeff. 2012. "The War against Too Much of Everything." *New York Times,* December 23.

Sorenson, Helen. 1941. *The Consumer Movement: What It Is and What It Means.* New York: Harper & Bros.

"Special Report: Universities Excellence v Equity." 2015. *Economist,* March 28.

Spector, Robert. 2005. *Category Killers: The Retail Revolution and Its Impact on Consumer Culture.* Boston: Harvard Business School Press.

Sperber, Murray. 2004. "College Sports, Inc.: How Big-Time Athletic Departments Run Interference for College, Inc." in *Buying In or Selling Out? The Commercialization of the American Research University.* Edited by Donald Stein. New Brunswick, NJ: Rutgers University Press, pp. 17–31.

Srinivas, Alam. 2008. *The Indian Consumer: One Billion Myths, One Billion Realities.* Singapore: John Wiley.

Staudenmeier, William. 2012. "Alcohol-Related Windows on Simmel's Social World," in *Illuminating Social Life.* Edited by Peter Kivisto. Thousand Oaks, CA: Sage, pp. 95–124.

Steenland, Sally. 2013. "Forgive Us Our Debts." *Huffington Post,* February 26.

Stern, Paul, et al., eds. 1997. *Environmentally Significant Consumption.* Washington, DC: National Academies Press.

Stich, Amy. 2012. *Access to Inequality: Reconsidering Class, Knowledge, and Capital in Higher Education.* Lanham, MD: Lexington Books.

Stone, Brad. 2013. *The Everything Store: Jeff Bezos and the Age of Amazon.* New York: Back Bay Books.

Strasser, Susan. 1989. *Point of Purchase.* New York: Pantheon.

Strasser, Susan. 1999. *Waste and Want: A Social History of Trash.* New York: Metropolitan Books.

Streitfeld, David. 2013. "Sales Are Colossal, Shares Are Soaring. All Amazon Is Missing Is a Profit." *New York Times,* October 21.

Strom, Stephanie. 2012. "Has 'Organic' Been Oversized?" *New York Times,* July 8.

Strom, Stephanie. 2014. "Multinational Corporations Court Lower-Income Consumers." *New York Times,* September 17.

Tabuchi, Hiroko. 2015. "Stores Suffer from a Shift of Behavior in Buyers." *New York Times,* August 13.

Tackett, Chris. 2012. "Can Pinterest and Svpply Help You Reduce Your Consumption?" *Atlantic Monthly,* January.

Tam, Daisy. 2008. "Slow Journeys: What Does It Mean to Be Slow?" *Food, Culture, and Society* 11(2): 207–18.

Tarlow, Peter. 2005. "Dark Tourism: The Appealing Dark Side of Tourism and More," in *Niche Tourism: Contemporary Issues, Trends, and Cases.* Edited by Marian Novelli. Oxford, UK: Elsevier, pp. 47–58.

Taylor, Jacquline Sanchez. 2000. "Tourism and 'Embodied' Commodities: Sex Tourism in the Caribbean," in *Tourism and Sex: Culture, Commerce and Coercion.* Edited by Stephen Clift and Simon Carter. London: Pinter, pp. 41–53.

Terranova, Tiziana. 2000. "Free Labor: Producing Culture for the Digital Economy." *Social Text* 18(2): 33–58.

Thain, Greg, and John Bradley. 2012. *Store Wars: The Worldwide Battle for Mindspace and Shelfspace, Online & In-stores.* Chichester, UK: John Wiley.

Thompson, Craig, and Gokcen Coskuner-Balli. 2007. "Enchanting Ethical Consumption: The Case of Community Supported Agriculture." *Journal of Consumer Culture* 3(7): 275–303.

Thoppil, Dhanya Ann. 2015. "India Is One of the Least E-Commerce Friendly Markets Says U.N. Body." *Wall Street Journal India,* March 30.

Thorne, Deborah, and Leon Anderson. 2006. "Managing the Stigma of Personal
Bankruptcy." *Sociological Focus* 39(2): 77–97.

Tolbert, Lisa C. 2009. "The Aristocracy of the Market Basket: Self-Service Food
Shopping in the New South," in *Food Chains: From Farmyard to Shopping Cart.*
Edited by Warren Belasco and Roger Horowitz. Philadelphia: University of
Pennsylvania Press, pp. 179–95.

Torres, Stacy. 2014. "Old McDonald's." *New York Times,* January 21.

"Trend #2: Pre-Selling the Future." 2013. *Trends E-Magazine,* July, pp. 8–13.

"Trend Briefing: Presumers." 2012. November. http://trendwatching.com/
trends/presumers/

Trentmann, Frank. 2009. "Crossing Divides: Consumption and Globalization in
History." *Journal of Consumer Culture* 9(2): 187–220.

Trentmann, Frank. 2011. "Consumers as Citizens: Tensions and Synergies," in *Beyond
the Consumption Bubble.* Edited by Karin Ekström and Kay Glans. London:
Routledge, pp. 99–111.

Trop, Jacyln. 2013. "Secret Weapon in Mall Battle: Parking Apps." *New York Times,*
November 26.

Truong, Thanh-Dam. 1990. *Sex, Money, and Morality: Prostitution and Tourism in
Southeast Asia.* London: Zed Books.

Tsang, Eileen Yuk-Ha. 2014. *The New Middle Class in China: Consumption, Politics
and the Market Economy.* New York: Palgrave Macmillan.

Turnbull, Emanwel. 2013. "Account Stated Resurrected: The Fiction of Implied
Assent in Consumer Debt Collections." *Vermont Law Review* 38: 339–84.

Turner, Victor. 1969. *The Ritual Process: Structure and Anti-Structure.* Chicago:
Aldine.

United Nations. 1998. *Human Development Report.* Oxford, UK: Oxford University
Press.

United Nations World Tourism Organization (UNWTO). 2013. *International Tourism Receipts Grew by 4% in 2012.* New York: UNWTO.

United Nations World Tourism Organization (UNWTO). 2016a. *International Tourism Arrivals Up 4% Reaching a Record 1.2 Billion in 2015.* New York: UNWTO.

United Nations World Tourism Organization (UNWTO). 2016b. "Why Tourism?"
http://www2.unwto.org/content/why-tourism. Accessed April 15, 2016.

Unruh, Gregory. 2011. "Sustainability Holism vs. Green Tokenism." *Huffington
Post,* May 25.

Urry, John. 2002. *The Tourist Gaze.* Thousand Oaks, CA: Sage.

U.S. Department of Education. n.d. http://www.ed.gov/college-affordability/
college-ratings-and-paying-performance.

U.S. Senate, Hearing of the Committee on Health, Education, Labor, and Pensions.
2011. *Drowning in Debt: Financial Outcomes of Students at For-Profit Colleges.*
Washington, DC: Government Printing Office.

Vague, Richard. 2014. *The Next Economic Disaster.* Philadelphia: Pennsylvania State Press.

van Binsbergen, Wim. 2005. "Introduction," in *Commodification: Things, Agency, and Identities.* Edited by Wim van Binsbergen and Peter Geschiere. Munster, Germany: Lit.

Van Wessel, Margit. 2004. "Talking about Consumption: How an Indian Middle Class Dissociates from Middle-Class Life." *Cultural Dynamics* 16(1): 93–116.

Varman, Rohit, and Russell Belk. 2009. "Nationalism and Ideology in an Anticonsumption Movement." *Journal of Consumer Research* 36: 686–700.

Veblen, Thorstein. 1899/1994. *The Theory of the Leisure Class.* New York: Penguin.

Voase, Richard. 2006. "Creating the Tourist Destination: Narrating the 'Undiscovered' and the Paradox of Consumption," in *Tourism, Consumption & Representation.* Edited by Kevin Meethan, Alison Anderson, and Steve Miles. Oxfordshire, UK: CABI, pp. 284–99.

Vyse, Stuart. 2008. *Going Broke: Why Americans Can't Hold On to Their Money.* Oxford, UK: Oxford University Press.

Waldman, Steven. 1999. "The Tyranny of Choice," in *Consumer Society in American History: A Reader.* Edited by Lawrence Glickman. Ithaca, NY: Cornell University Press, pp. 359–66.

Walia, Shelly. 2015. "Why India's E-Commerce Boom Will Look Nothing Like China's." *Quartz India*, April 23.

Wallerstein, Immanuel. 1979. *The Capitalist World-System.* Cambridge, UK: Cambridge University Press.

Wang, Ying, and Vanessa Fong. 2009. "Little Emperors and the 4:2:1 Generation: China's Singletons." *Journal of the American Academy of Child Adolescent Psychiatry* 48(12): 1137–39.

Wapner, Paul. 2010. "Sacrifice in an Age of Comfort," in *The Environmental Politics of Sacrifice.* Edited by Michael Maniates and John Meyer. Cambridge, MA: MIT Press, pp. 33–60.

Warde, Alan. 1997. *Consumption, Food and Taste.* London: Sage.

Warde, Alan. 2000. "Eating Globally: Cultural Flows and the Spread of Ethnic Restaurants," in *The Ends of Globalization.* Edited by Don Kalb, et al. New York: Rowman and Littlefield, pp. 299–316.

Warde, Alan, and Lydia Martens. 2000. *Eating Out: Social Differentiation, Consumption, and Pleasure.* Cambridge, UK: Cambridge University Press.

Warde, Alan, Lydia Martens, and Wendy Olsen. 1999. "Consumption and the Problem of Variety: Cultural Omnivorousness, Social Distinction and Dining Out." *Sociology* 33(1):105–27.

Waters, Malcolm. 2001. *Globalization.* London: Routledge.

Watson, James. 2000. "China's Big Mac Attack." *Foreign Affairs* 79(3): 120–34.

Watson, James. 2006. "Transnationalism, Localization, and Fast Food in East Asia," in *Golden Arches East: McDonald's in East Asia.* Edited by James Watson. Stanford, CA: Stanford University Press, pp. 1–32.

Watson, Matthew, and Elizabeth Shove. 2008. "Product, Competence, Project, and Practice: DIY and the Dynamics of Craft Consumption." *Journal of Consumer Culture* 8(1): 69–89.

Wearing, Stephen, Deborah Stevenson, and Tamara Young. 2010. *Tourist Cultures: Identity, Place and the Traveller.* Thousand Oaks, CA: Sage.

Weber, Lauren. 2015. "Retailers Are under Fire for Work Schedules." *Wall Street Journal,* April 12.

Weber, Max. 1992. *The Protestant Ethic and the Spirit of Capitalism.* London: Routledge.

Weissman, Adam. 2006. "The Revolution of Everyday Life." In *Igniting a Revolution: Voices in Defense of the Earth.* Edited by Steven Best and Anthony Nocella. Oakland, CA: AK Press, pp. 127–36.

Weissman, Jordan. 2012. "Why Don't Young Americans Buy Cars?" *Atlantic Monthly,* March 25.

Welch, William. 2014. "Amazon Says It Can Ship Items before Customers Order." *USA Today,* January 18.

White, Harold. 2008. *Consumption and the Transformation of Everyday Life: A View from Southern India.* New York: Palgrave Macmillan.

Wiedenhoft, Wendy. 2006. "Consumer Tactics as 'Weapons': Black Lists, Union Labels, and the American Federation of Labor." *Journal of Consumer Culture* 6: 261–85.

Wiedenhoft, Wendy. 2008. "The Politics of Consumption: The Tactics of the National Consumers' League during the Progressive Era." *Social Movement Studies* 7: 281–303.

Wiedenhoft Murphy, Wendy. 2010. "Touring the Troubles in West Belfast: Building Peace or Reproducing Conflict?" *Peace & Change* 34(4): 537–60.

Wilk, Richard. 2001. "Consuming Morality." *Journal of Consumer Culture* 1(2): 245–60.

Williams, Colin. 1996. "The New Barter Economy: An Appraisal of Local Exchange and Trading Systems." *Journal of Public Policy* 16(1): 85–101.

Williams, Jeffrey. 2001. "Franchising the University," in *Beyond the Corporate University: Culture and Pedagogy in the New Millennium.* Edited by Henry Giroux and Kostas Myrsiades. Lanham, MD: Rowman & Littlefield, pp. 15–29.

Williams, Jerome, Geraldine Henderson, and Anne-Marie Harris. 2005. "Counting Customers: Assessing Consumer Racial Profiling and Other Marketplace Discrimination." *Journal of Public Policy and Marketing* 24(1): 163–71.

Williams, Rosalind. 1982. *Dream Worlds: Mass Consumption in Late Nineteenth-Century France.* Berkeley: University of California Press.

Willis, Paul. 1978. *Profane Culture.* London: Routledge.

Wilson, Alexander. 1992. *The Culture of Nature.* Cambridge, UK: Blackwell.

Wilson, Julee. 2012. "Target Launches Specialty In-Store Boutiques, 'The Shops.'" *Huffington Post,* January 12.

Wilson, Patrick. 2010. "Fair Trade Craft Production and Indigenous Economies," in *Fair Trade and Social Justice.* Edited by Sarah Lyon and Mark Moberg. New York: New York University Press, pp. 176–97.

Winch, Donald. 2006. "The Problematic Status of the Consumer in Orthodox Economic Thought," in *The Making of the Consumer.* Edited by Frank Trentman. Oxford, UK: Berg.

Witkowski, Terrence. 2010. "A Brief History of Frugality Discourse in the United States." *Consumption, Markets, and Culture* 13(3): 235–58.

Wolf, Marco, and Shaun McQuitty. 2013. "Circumventing Traditional Markets: An Empirical Study of the Marketplace Motivations and Outcomes of Consumers' Do-It-Yourself Behaviors." *Journal of Marketing Theory and Practices* 21(2): 195–209.

Woloson, Wendy. 2009. *In Hock: Pawning in America from Independence through the Great Depression.* Chicago: University of Chicago Press.

Wood, Roy. 1995. *The Sociology of the Meal.* Edinburgh, UK: Edinburgh University Press.

World Tourism Organization. 2014. *UNWTO Annual Report 2013.* Madrid: World Tourism Organization.

Woyke, Elizabeth. 2014. *The Smartphone: Anatomy of an Industry.* New York: New Press.

Yan, Yunxiang. 2006. "McDonald's in Beijing: The Localization of Americana," in *Golden Arches East: McDonald's in East Asia.* Edited by James Watson. Stanford, CA: Stanford University Press, pp. 39–76.

Young, Dannagal Goldthwaite. 2005. "Sacrifice, Consumption and the American Way of Life: Advertising and Domestic Propaganda during World War II." *Communication Review* 8: 27–52.

Yu, LiAnne. 2014. *Consumption in China: How China's New Consumer Ideology Is Shaping the Nation.* Cambridge, UK: Polity.

Zamwel, Einat, Orna Sasson-Levy, and Guy Ben-Porat. 2014. "Voluntary Simplifiers as Political Consumers: Individuals Practicing Politics through Reduced Consumption." *Journal of Consumer Culture* 14(2): 199–217.

Zelizer, Viviana. 1997. *The Social Meaning of Money.* Princeton, NJ: Princeton University Press.

Zimmerman, Eilene. 2013. "A Web Site That Helps Shoppers Find Brick-and-Mortar Stores." *New York Times,* October 16.

Zukin, Sharon. 2005. *Point of Purchase.* New York: Routledge.

Zwick, Detlev, Samuel Bonsu, and Aron Darmody. 2008. "Putting Consumers to Work: 'Co-Creation' and New Marketing Govern-mentality." *Journal of Consumer Culture* 8(2): 163–96.

Index

Absolut Vodka, 151
Active agents, 41, 42–48
Activism. *See* Consumer movement;
  Environmental movement;
  Political consumerism
Adbusters, 151
Adbusters Media Foundation
  (Canada), 151–152
Adidas, 125
Adorno, Theodor, 48
Advertisement:
  culture jamming, 151–152
  in culture industry, 50
  mass consumerism development, 5
  subvertisements, 151–152
Affluent Society, The (Galbraith), 13
African Americans, 6–7, 13, 73–74, 145
Agribusiness, 81–82, 83
Agricultural subsidies, 81–82
Airbnb, 190
Alar, 82
Alibaba, 207
Amazon.com, 69–70, 71, 72, 74
American Federation of Labor (AFL),
  144–145
Americanization, 201, 203
Anheuser-Busch, 145
Antibiotics in food, 81, 85–86
Anti-chain store movement, 96
Anticipatory shopping, 74
Appropriation process, 28–30
Arcades, 61
Asceticism ideology, 8–9
Associative good, 130–131

AT&T, 112
Austerity measures:
  as consumption alternative, 181
  in credit and debt, 175–176
Australia, 86

Bankruptcy, 165–166
Bankruptcy Prevention and
  Consumer Protection Act (2005),
  165–166
Bankruptcy Reform Act (1978), 165
Barcodes, 67
Barnes & Noble, 70
Barthes, Roland, 79
Bayh-Dole Act (1980), 126
Beef industry, 81
Bell Telephone, 112
Benjamin, Walter, 48
BerkShares, 185
Best Buy, 64–65
Bezos, Jeff, 69, 70
Big-box stores, 64–67, 70
Birmingham School, 46–48
Bitcoins, 186–187
Black-listed manufacturers, 144
Blasé attitudes, 60–61
Blockbuster, 70
Bloomingdale's, 64
Bon Maché (Paris), 61
Borders, 70
Bottom of the pyramid (BOP)
  consumers, 213
Bourdieu, Pierre, 44–46
Boutiika, 71

Boycotts, 142–145
Brands:
  consumers and, 43
  in global marketplace, 200, 205–206, 209–210
  mass consumerism development, 4, 5
  sign value, 28
Brave New World (Huxley), 33
Bricolage, 46–48
British Petroleum (BP), 154–155
Brominated vegetable oil (BVO), 86
Bureau of Consumer Financial Protection (BCFT), 147, 177
Burger King, 50
Buycotts, 143–145, 148

Cabela's, 73
Calculated hedonism, 58
Campbell, Colin, 56–58
Cap and trade program, 157
Capitalist culture:
  commodities in, 26, 29, 30–31
  consumption in, 8–9, 12, 13
  consumption locations, 60
  gift exchange, 30–31
  in global marketplace, 198–200
  of consumers, 50
  political ideology of, 12, 13
  production-consumption relationship, 8–9
Cargill/Monsanto, 81
Caribbean, 103
Cascadian Farm, 83
Cast Iron Palace (New York City), 61
Category-killers, 65, 66, 70
Cell phones, 34, 36–37, 49
Certification revolution, 148
Chapter 7 bankruptcy, 165
Chase, Stuart, 146
Chevrolet, 112
Chicken industry, 80, 83
Chick-fil-A, 145
Children as consumers, 51–52
China:
  brands, 205–206
  e-commerce, 207

in global marketplace, 201, 203–207
multinational corporations (MNCs), 205, 206
National Products Movement, 204–205
one-child policy, 205–206
Choice of consumers, 11–12, 13, 53–56
Citizen consumers, 158
Civilizing process of manners, 88
Civil rights movement, 145
Climate change, 154, 157
Clopening requirement, 68
Coca-Cola, 145, 200, 209
Co-creation, 191–194
Coffee, 150
Colgate, 5
Collaborative consumption, 188–191
Collaborative lifestyles, 189
Collective selection, 47
Collective tourist gaze, 106
College of New Jersey, 121–122
Columbia University, 121–122
Commodities:
  appropriation process, 28–30
  as spectacles, 28
  biography of, 32
  commoditization, 37–38
  commodity aesthetics, 28
  commodity chain, 24
  commodity fetishism, 26
  cradle-to-cradle perspective, 35
  craft production, 23–25
  cultural intermediaries, 24
  de-fetishized commodities, 32
  defined, 21
  Diderot effect, 27
  disposability of, 29, 32, 33–35
  environmental pollution, 34–35
  e-waste, 34
  exchange value, 25–26
  extended producer responsibility (EPR), 35
  extended-self construction, 28–30
  flexible accumulation process, 24
  flexible specialization methods, 23
  Fordist mass production, 22–23, 25

gift exchange, 30–32
hazardous waste, 34–35, 36
in capitalist culture, 26, 29, 30–31
in global marketplace, 21–22, 24, 32
meaning of, 28–32
niche consumption, 23–25
obsolescence of, 33–35
planned obsolescence, 33–34
positional good, 27
post-Fordist production, 23–25
production of, 22–25
recycling, 33, 35
scientific management techniques, 22
semiotics of, 27–28
sign value, 26–28
social impact of, 29–32
social media impact, 24
socioeconomic disparities, 27
time-space compression, 24
tragedy of culture, 39
use value, 25
value of, 25–28
waste, 33–35
waste management, 34–35
zero waste perspective, 35
Commoditization, 37–38
Commodity activism, 13, 14
Commodity aesthetics, 28
Commodity chain, 24, 199–200
Commodity de-fetishization, 32, 84
Commodity fetishism, 26
Communist Manifesto, The (Marx &
    Engels), 198–199
Communitas development, 109–110
Community-supported agriculture
    (CSA), 84–85
ConAgra/Dupont, 81, 83
Concentrated animal feed operation
    (CAFO), 81
Condition of Postmodernity, The
    (Harvey), 24
Confederate flag (South Carolina), 145
Conquest of Cool, The (Frank), 48
Conspicuous consumption, 8,
    42–43, 1079
Conspicuous leisure, 8, 42–43

Consumer confidence index, 158–159
Consumer cooperatives, 187–188
Consumerist bias, 2
Consumer movement, 142, 146–147
    See also Environmental movement;
        Political consumerism
Consumer Product Safety Act
    (1972), 147
Consumer racism, 73–74
Consumer Reports, 147
Consumers:
    active agents, 41, 42–48
    brands, 43
    bricolage, 46–48
    calculated hedonism, 58
    capitalist culture of, 50
    children, 51–52
    collective selection, 47
    conspicuous consumption, 42–43
    conspicuous leisure, 42–43
    consumer sovereignty, 53–56
    coolhunt, 47
    co-optation process, 48
    critical theory, 48–49
    cultural capital, 44–46
    culture industry, 48–50, 52–53
    desire of, 56–58
    distinction motivation, 42–43, 44–48
    emulation motivation, 42, 43
    false needs, 49
    freedom of choice, 53–56
    habitus, 44–46
    hedonism of, 53, 56–58
    modern self-illusory hedonism,
        56–57
    omnivore taste, 45–46
    one-dimensionality thinking, 49
    passive dupes, 41, 48–50, 52–53
    postmodern consumer, 57–58
    recuperation process, 47–48
    resistance motivation, 46–48
    socioeconomic disparities, 42–43,
        44–46, 55–56
    subcultures, 46–48
    taste, 44–46
    traditional hedonism, 56–57

trickle-down theory, 42
trickle-up theory, 47
upscale spending, 43
utility maximization, 53–56
Consumer sovereignty, 53–56
Consumers' Research Bulletin, 146
Consumers' Research (CR), 146–147
Consumers Union (CU), 146–147
Consumption:
  asceticism ideology, 8–9
  brands, 4, 5
  commodity activism, 13, 14
  conspicuous consumption, 8
  conspicuous leisure, 8
  consumerist bias, 2
  critical consumer studies, 3
  culture industry, 10
  defined, 1–2
  false needs, 11
  freedom of choice, 11–12, 13
  freedom versus coercion, 10–12
  historical context, 2–7
  in capitalist culture, 8–9, 12, 13
  instinct of workmanship, 8
  mass consumption culture, 4–7
  necessities, 11
  needs, 11
  neoliberal ideology, 13–14
  political ideology of, 3, 12–14
  private sphere, 9–10
  production relationship, 2–3, 7–10
  productivist bias, 2
  prosumption, 10
  public sphere, 9–10
  research development, 2–4
  research overview, 14–18
  tensions and contradictions, 7–14
  utility maximization, 8
Consumption alternatives:
  austerity measures, 181
  bitcoins, 186–187
  co-creation, 191–194
  collaborative consumption, 188–191
  collaborative lifestyles, 189
  consumer cooperatives, 187–188
  crowdfunding, 192

degrowth policy, 195–196
  dematerialism, 195
  digital materialism, 194–195
  do-it-yourself (DIY) movement,
    183–184
  expectation economy, 192
  freegans, 194
  freemiums, 190–191
  frugality, 180–181
  global marketplace, 186–187,
    195–196
  Local Exchange Trading Systems
    (LETS), 184–185
  new-normal austerity, 195
  open-source movement, 188–189
  postmaterialism ideology, 180–182
  presumers, 192–193
  product service systems, 189
  prosumer capitalism, 193–194
  redistributive markets, 189
  reputation capital, 190
  sacrifice, 181
  sharing economy, 188–191
  social capital, 185
  voluntary simplicity movement,
    182–183
  waste recovery, 194
Consumption locations:
  Amazon.com, 69–70, 71, 72, 74
  anticipatory shopping, 74
  arcades, 61
  barcodes, 67
  big-box stores, 64–67, 70
  blasé attitudes towards, 60–61
  category-killers, 65, 66, 70
  cities, 59–63
  clopening requirement, 68
  consumer racism, 73–74
  cookie crumbs, 74
  credit and debt, 61
  department stores, 4, 61–63
  discount retailing, 66
  e-commerce, 69–72, 74–75
  emotional labor of service workers,
    68–69
  festival marketplaces, 65

flâneurs, 61
global marketplace, 66–67, 70–71
historical context, 59–65
housing, 73
hyperconsumption, 65–66
implosion technique, 66
in capitalist culture, 60
installment payment plan, 62
Internet shopping, 69–72, 74–75
iron cage of rationality, 75
localization, 75
McDonaldization effect, 60, 64,
    65, 75
Panopticon effect, 72–73, 74
privatization of public space, 72–75
racial disparities, 73–74
redlining policies, 73
service workers, 66–67, 68–69
shopping malls, 63–65, 72–75
showrooming practices, 61–72
socioeconomic disparities, 62, 63,
    66–67, 71, 73
suburbs, 63–65, 72–75
surveillance practices, 72–75
third places, 76
tragedy of culture, 60–61
transaction time of online
    purchases, 70
UPC scanning, 67
upsell technique, 70
Wal-Mart, 65–67, 71
white flight, 73
women's role, 63, 67, 95, 96
worker safety, 68
Consumption tax, 156
Converse One Stars, 47
Cookie crumbs, 74
Coolhunt, 47
Co-optation process, 48
Corinthian, 133
Corn products, 80, 81
Correspondence principle, 129
Costco, 65
Coursera, 123
Cradle-to-cradle perspective, 35
Craft production, 23–25

Credential inflation, 129–130
Credential theory, 128–130
Credit and debt:
    austerity measures, 175–176
    bankruptcy, 165–166
    Chapter 7 bankruptcy, 165
    consumption locations, 61
    credit cards, 161, 163–164, 177
    creditocracy, 176
    debt bondage, 166–167
    debt forgiveness, 174–176
    debtor-creditor relationship,
        166–172
    debtor default, 165–166, 170–172
    debt settlement, 170–172
    financial risk, 169–170
    global marketplace, 174–176
    heavily indebted poor countries
        (HIPCs), 174–175
    historical development, 162–167, 168
    housing, 6, 161, 163
    Jubilee, 174–175, 176
    mass consumerism development,
        5, 6
    medical debt, 176
    morality of, 167–168, 176
    neoliberal ideology, 162–166
    odious debt, 174
    pawn shops, 172–173
    payday loans, 171
    public debt, 174–176
    religious influence, 168
    securitization policy, 162
    socioeconomic disparities, 169–170
    sovereign debt, 174–176
    structural adjustment policy, 174
    student loans, 119, 132–134, 161,
        176, 177
    usury, 168
Credit Cardholders Bill of Rights Act
    (2009), 147, 177
Credit cards, 161, 163–164, 177
Creditocracy, 176
Creolization, 198, 200–201
Critical consumer studies, 3
Critical theory, 48–49

Crowdfunding, 192
Crowd Supply, 192
Culinary pluralism, 79
Cultural cannibalism, 102
Cultural capital, 44–46, 130–131
Cultural-ideology sphere, 197–198
Cultural imperialism, 91, 198
Cultural intermediaries, 24
Cultural memes, 151
Cultural omnivores, 88
Culture industry, 10, 48–50, 52–53
Culture jamming, 151–152

Dairy industry, 83, 85–87
Dark tourism, 107–108
Debt bondage, 166–167
Debt Resistance Operation Manual, 176
De-fetishized commodities, 32, 84
Degrowth policy, 195–196
Dematerialism, 195
Department stores, 4, 61–63
Diderot, Denis, 27
Diderot effect, 27
Digital materialism, 194–195
Diorama context of restaurants, 94
Discount rates, 133
Discount retailing, 66
Disney Channel, 51
Disney World (Florida):
    corporate representation, 112
    Disneyfication, 110–112
    hybrid consumption, 110–111
    hyperreality of, 111
    merchandising, 111
    performative labor, 111–112
    socioeconomic disparities, 111
    theming, 110
    tourism industry, 110–113
Disposability:
    mass consumerism development, 4
    of commodities, 29, 32, 33–35
    See also Waste
Distinction (Bourdieu), 44–46
Do-it-yourself (DIY) movement,
    183–184
Douglas, Mary, 79

Earthbound Farm, 83
Eating-in, 91–93
Eating-out, 93–95
Eco-gastronomy, 87
Eco-label, 155–156
E-commerce. *See* Internet shopping
Eco-tax, 156–157
EdX, 123
Ehrlich, Anne, 153
Ehrlich, Paul, 152, 153
Elisa, Norbert, 79
Embodied actors, 106
Emotional labor of service workers,
    68–69, 94
End the Occupation, 145
Engels, Friedrich, 198–199
Environmental Defense Fund
    (EDF), 154
Environmental degradation, 34–35,
    82, 114, 153, 154, 157
Environmental movement:
    cap and trade program, 157
    climate change, 154, 157
    consumption tax, 156
    eco-label, 155–156
    eco-tax, 156–157
    fuel efficiency, 153
    global marketplace, 153–154
    greenhouse gases, 157
    greenwashing, 154–155
    individualization, 154
    IPAT model, 152–155
    IWAC formula, 155
    Kyoto Protocol (1997), 157
    negative externalities, 157
    Paris Agreement (2015), 157
    population growth, 152–153
    sustainable consumption,
        153–154
    sustainable fisheries, 155–156
Ethnic identities, 90–91
European Fair Trade Association, 150
European Union, 86, 175–176
E-waste, 34
Exchange value, 25–26
Expectation economy, 192

Extended producer responsibility
    (EPR), 35
Extended-self construction, 28–30
Exxon, 112

Facebook, 190, 191
Fair Trade Federation, 150
Fairtrade Labelling Organization
    (FLO), 150
Fair trade movement, 149–151
False needs, 11, 49
Family Dollar, 73
Farmers' markets, 84
Fat, 80–81, 89
Federal Cigarette Labeling and
    Advertising Act (1965), 147
Federal Housing Administration
    (FHA), 73
Federated Department Stores, 64
Festival marketplaces, 65
Field of struggle, 121–123
Flâneurs, 61
Flexible accumulation process, 24
Flexible specialization methods, 23
Flipkart, 211
Florida State University, 127
Food:
    accessible nutritious food, 89–90
    agribusiness, 81–82, 83
    agricultural subsidies, 81–82
    antibiotics, 81, 85–86
    anti-chain store movement, 96
    beef industry, 81
    chicken industry, 80, 83
    civilizing process of manners, 88
    coffee, 150
    commodity de-fetishization, 84
    community-supported agriculture
        (CSA), 84–85
    concentrated animal feed operation
        (CAFO), 81
    corn products, 80, 81
    culinary pluralism, 79
    cultural imperialism, 91
    cultural omnivores, 88
    dairy industry, 83, 85–87

diorama context, 94
eating-in, 91–93
eating-out, 93–95
eco-gastronomy, 87
ethnic identities, 90–91
fair trade labels, 149–150
farmers' markets, 84
fat, 80–81, 89
food deserts, 89–90
foodies, 88
food insecurity, 89
food sovereignty, 84
foodways, 89–90
gastronationalism, 91
genetically modified foods, 86, 147
global marketplace, 90–91
gourmet food, 88
hormones, 81
imagined communities, 90
industrial food chain, 80–82,
    85–86, 89
label campaigns, 86, 91, 147,
    149–150
local food chain, 83–85, 87
locavores, 84
materialist perspective, 79
meal experience, 94
moralistic hedonism, 83
national identities, 90–91
negative externalities, 82
object of consumption, 80–87
omnivore's paradox, 97
organic food chain, 82–83
places of consumption, 91–97
raw milk, 85–87
salt, 80–81, 89
slow food movement, 87
socioeconomic disparities, 87–90
structuralist perspective, 79
subjects of consumption, 87–91
sugar, 80–81, 89
supermarkets, 95–97
women's role, 92, 93, 94–95
Food deserts, 89–90
Foodies, 88
Food insecurity, 89

Food sovereignty, 84
Foodways, 89–90
Foot Locker, 64
Ford, Henry, 22
Fordist mass production, 22–23, 25
Ford Motor Company, 50
Frank, Thomas, 48
Frankfurt School, 48–50, 52–53
Freegans, 194
Free market ideology, 147–149
Freemiums, 190–191
Frito Lay, 191
Frugality, 180–181, 210–211
Fruit Roll-ups, 51
Fuel efficiency, 153

Galbraith, John Kenneth, 13
Gap Kids, 51
Gastronationalism, 91
General Mills, 83
General Motors, 33–34, 66, 190
Genetically modified foods, 86, 147
Genuine progress indicator (GPI), 196
Gift, The (Mauss), 30
Gift exchange:
    commodities, 30–32
    in capitalist culture, 30–31
    monetized gifts, 31–32
    socioeconomic disparities, 30
Gillette, 33–34, 191
Glacier National Park, 113–114, 115
Global consciousness, 199, 200–201
Globalization, 198–201, 203
Global marketplace:
    Americanization, 201, 203
    bottom of the pyramid (BOP)
        consumers, 213
    brands, 200, 205–206, 209–210
    China, 201, 203–207
    commodity chain, 199–200
    commodity production, 21–22,
        24, 32
    consumption alternatives, 186–187,
        195–196
    consumption locations, 66–67,
        70–71

credit and debt, 174–176
creolization, 198, 200–201
cultural-ideology sphere, 197–198
cultural imperialism, 198
environmental movement, 153–154
food, 90–91
global consciousness, 199, 200–201
globalization, 198–201, 203
in capitalist culture, 198–200
India, 200–201
localization, 198, 201, 203
political consumerism, 148–151,
    152–157
production-consumption
    relationship, 9–10
spatial compression, 198–200
unequal exchange relationship, 199
world-system theory, 199–200
See also Internet shopping
Grand Canyon National Park,
    113–114, 115
Grand Depot (Philadelphia), 61
Great Britain, 150, 185
Great Smoky Mountains National
    Park, 114–115
Greece, 175–176
Green consumerism, 152–157
Greenhouse gases, 157
Greenwashing, 154–155

Habitus, 44–46
Harvard University, 121–122, 123
Harvey, David, 24
Hazardous waste, 34–35, 36
Heavily indebted poor countries
    (HIPCs), 174–175
Hecht's, 64
Hedonism, 53, 56–58
Higher education:
    as adulthood benchmark, 134–135
    as associative good, 130–131
    as field of struggle, 121–123
    citizenship role, 135–136
    community college, 122–123
    corporate influence on, 124–127
    correspondence principle, 129

credential inflation, 129–130
credential theory, 128–130
cultural capital perspective,
    130–131
discount rates, 133
economic capital perspective,
    127–128
for-profit institutions, 123, 132–134
historical context, 121–123
human capital perspective, 128
job market, 120
lateral learning experience, 130
massive open online courses
    (MOOCs), 120, 123–124
meritocracy value, 129
object of consumption, 127–132
place of consumption, 121–127
product assessment, 131–132
public sphere context, 125
research sponsorship, 125, 126–127
social capital perspective, 130–131
socioeconomic disparities, 133–134
sports sponsorship, 125–126
student activism, 136–137
student aid, 119
student loans, 119, 132–134, 161,
    176, 177
subjects of consumption, 132–136
Higher Education Act (1972), 119
Holdren, John, 152
Hollywood Video, 70
Home Depot, 64–65, 183
Homespun movement, 143
Horizon, 83
Horkheimer, Max, 48
Hormones in food, 81
Housing:
    consumption locations, 73
    credit and debt, 6, 161, 163
    racial disparities, 6–7, 73
    redlining policies, 73
    white flight, 73
Huxley, Aldous, 33
Hybrid consumption, 110–111
Hyperconsumption, 65–66
Hyperreality, 111

Ikea, 24
Imagined communities, 90
Implosion technique, 66
India:
    brands, 209–210
    conspicuous consumption, 210
    e-commerce, 211–212
    frugality, 210–211
    in global marketplace, 200–201
    multinational corporations (MNCs),
        208–210
    swadeshi movement, 208–210
Individualization, 154
Individualized collective action, 158
Indonesia, 103
Industrial food chain, 80–82, 85–86, 89
InMails, 191
Installment payment plan, 62
Instinct of workmanship, 8
International Monetary Fund (IMF),
    169, 174, 200
Internet resources:
    agricultural subsidies, 81–82
    bitcoins, 186
    community-supported agriculture
        (CSA), 85
    daily garbage production, 34
    Disney World corporations, 112
    farmers' markets, 84
    freegans, 194
    genuine progress indicator
        (GPI), 196
    Kyoto Protocol (1997), 157
    local food chain, 85, 87
    Made in America, 202
    sustainable seafood, 156
    350.0rg, 145
    Wal-Mart shoppers, 67
Internet shopping:
    Amazon.com, 69–70, 71, 72, 74
    anticipatory shopping, 74
    China, 207
    consumption locations, 69–72,
        74–75
    cookie crumbs, 74
    global marketplace, 70–71

India, 211–212
showrooming practices, 61–72
surveillance, 74
transaction time, 70
upsell technique, 70
IPAT model, 152–155
Iron cage of rationality, 75
Italy, 87
Ithaca Hours, 185
IWAC formula, 155

Japan, 86
J.C. Penney, 64
Jubilee, 174–175, 176

Kallet, Arthur, 146
Kaplan University, 123
Kaufman's, 64
Kellogg's, 209
Kentucky Fried Chicken (KFC), 209
Kickstarter, 192
King's College, 121–122
Kraft, 112
Kyoto Protocol (1997), 157

Label campaign:
  cigarettes, 147
  eco-label, 155–156
  fair trade, 149–150
  food, 86, 91, 147, 149–150
  union label, 144–145, 148
  white-label products, 144, 148
Labor movement, 144–145
Landscape management, 114–115
Lateral learning experience, 130
Lazarus, 64
Lesbian, gay, bisexual, transgender
  (LGBT) community, 145
Levi's, 47, 200
Levi-Strauss, Claude, 79
Liminality experience, 109–110
LinkedIn, 191
Local Exchange Trading Systems
  (LETS), 184–185
Local food chain, 83–85, 87
Localization, 75, 198, 201, 203

Locavores, 84
Lowes, 183

Macy's, 61–62, 64
Made in America, 202
Marcuse, Herbert, 48
Marine Stewardship Council (MSC),
  155–156
Marlboro, 200
Marshall Field (Chicago), 61, 62
Marx, Karl, 2, 11, 26, 198–199
Massachusetts Institute of Technology
  (MIT), 123
Mass consumption culture, 4–7
Massive open online courses
  (MOOCs), 120, 123–124
Materialist perspective, 79
Mauss, Marcel, 30
Max Havelaar Foundation, 150
May department stores, 64
McDonaldization effect, 60, 64, 65,
  75, 93
McDonald's, 51, 90–91, 94, 200, 201,
  205, 209
Meal experience, 94
Mecca Cola, 202
Medical debt, 176
Mennell, Stephen, 79
Meritocracy value, 129
Milk, 85–87
Miller Beer, 145
Mitchell's Fish Market, 156
Modern self-illusory hedonism, 56–57
Montgomery bus boycott
  (1955–1956), 145
Montgomery Ward, 4
Moralistic hedonism, 83
Morrill Land-Grant Act (1862), 122
Muller v. Oregon (1908), 144
Multinational corporations (MNCs),
  205, 206, 208–210

Nader, Ralph, 147
National Association for the
  Advancement of Colored People
  (NAACP), 145

National Association for the Advancement of Colored People v. Claibourne Hardware Company (1982), 145
National Consumers League (NCL), 143–144
National identities, 90–91
National parks:
  landscape management, 114–115
  recreational tourism, 113–114
  restoration practices, 116
  sustainability practices, 116–117
  tourism industry, 113–117
National Products Movement, 204–205
National Traffic and Motor Vehicle Safety Act (1966), 147
Native Americans, 102, 115
Necessities, 11
Needs, 11
Negative externalities, 82, 157
Neoliberal ideology:
  consumption, 13–14
  credit and debt, 162–166
  political consumerism, 147–149
Nestle, 112
Netherlands, 150
New moral tourist, 108–109
New-normal austerity, 195
New Zealand, 86
Niche consumption, 23–25
Nickelodeon, 51
Nike, 23, 28, 35, 125
Nordstrom, 73
Northern Ireland, 107
Novartis/ADM, 81, 83
N.W Ayer & Son, 5

Objectification in sex tourism, 103
Obsolescence of commodities, 33–35
Occupy Wall Street (2011), 152, 176
Odious debt, 174
Omnivore's paradox, 97
Omnivore taste, 45–46
One-dimensionality thinking, 49
100,000,000 Guinea Pigs (Schlink & Kallet), 146

Open-source movement, 188–189
Organic Food and Production Act (1990), 82–83
Organic food chain, 82–83

Packard, Vance, 34
Pandora, 195
Panopticon effect, 72–73, 74
Paris Agreement (2015), 157
Passive dupes, 41, 48–50, 52–53
Passive gazers, 105–106
Pawn shops, 172–173
Payday loans, 171
Performative labor, 111–112
Petrini, Carlo, 87
Philippines, 103
Piggly Wiggly, 95–96
Planned obsolescence, 33–34
Political consumerism:
  black-listed manufacturers, 144
  boycotts, 142–145
  buycotts, 143–145, 148
  certification revolution, 148
  citizen consumers, 158
  civil rights movement, 145
  consumer confidence index, 158–159
  consumer movement, 142, 146–147
  cultural memes, 151
  culture jamming, 151–152
  defined, 141–142
  fair trade movement, 149–151
  free market ideology, 147–149
  global marketplace, 148–151, 152–157
  green consumerism, 152–157
  historical development, 142–145, 147–149
  homespun movement, 143
  individualized collective action, 158
  label campaigns, 86, 91, 144–145, 147, 148, 149–150
  labor movement, 144–145
  neoliberal ideology, 147–149
  purchasers as citizens, 158
  social premium principle, 149
  subvertisements, 151–152

union label, 144–145, 148
white-label products, 144, 148
white-listed stores, 144
women's role, 143–145
Population Bomb, The (Ehrlich), 153
Population Explosion (Ehrlich &
    Ehrlich), 153
Population growth, 152–153
Positional good, 27
Positive boycotts, 143
Post-Fordist production, 23–25
Postmaterialism ideology, 180–182
Postmodern consumer, 57–58
Posttourist, 109
Pottery Barn, 24
Presumers, 192–193
Princeton University, 121–122
Private sphere, 9–10
Procter and Gamble, 5
Productivist bias, 2
Product service systems, 189
Prosumer capitalism, 193–194
Prosumption, 10
Protected Designation of Origin
    label, 91
Protected Geographic Indication
    label, 91
    Protestant Ethic and the Spirit of
    Capitalism, The (Weber), 8
Public Citizen, 147
Public debt, 174–176
Public sphere, 9–10, 125
Purchasers as citizens, 158

Racial disparities:
    African Americans, 6–7, 13,
        73–74, 145
    civil rights movement, 145
    commodity activism, 13
    consumer racism, 73–74
    consumption locations, 73–74
    housing, 6–7, 73
    Native Americans, 102, 115
    redlining policies, 73
    tourism, 102, 115
    white flight, 73

RadioShack, 72
Raw milk, 85–87
Recreational tourism, 113–114
Recuperation process, 47–48
Recycling, 33, 35
Redistributive markets, 189
Redlining policies, 73
Reebok, 47
RelayRides, 190
Reputation capital, 190
Restoration practices, 116
Rich's, 64
Rituals of transformation, 106
Romantic Ethic and the Spirit of Modern
    Consumerism, The (Campbell),
    56–58
Romantic tourist gaze, 106

Sacrifice, 181
Safety of workers, 68
Salt, 80–81, 89
Schlink, Frederick, 146
Scientific management techniques, 22
Sears, Roebuck and Company, 4
Securitization policy, 162
Semiotics, 27–28
Service workers:
    consumption locations, 66–67,
        68–69
    emotional labor of, 68–69, 94
    Wal-Mart effect, 66–67
    worker safety, 68
    7–11, 72
Sex tourism, 103–105
Sex trafficking, 104–105
Sexual orientation, 145
Sharing economy, 188–191
Shenandoah National Park,
    114–115
Shopping malls, 63–65, 72–75
Showrooming practices, 61–72
Siemens, 112
Sight sacralization process, 105
Sign value, 26–28
Slow food movement, 87
Smartphones, 34, 36–37, 49

Smith, Adam, 2, 8, 11, 25–27, 170
Social capital:
  consumption alternatives, 185
  higher education, 130–131
  local currency systems, 185
Social media, 24
Social premium principle, 149
Socioeconomic disparities:
  bottom of the pyramid (BOP)
    consumers, 213
  commodities, 27
  consumers, 42–43, 44–46, 55–56
  consumer sovereignty, 55–56
  consumption locations, 62, 63,
    66–67, 71, 73
  credit and debt, 169–170
  food, 87–90
  gift exchange, 30
  higher education, 133–134
  mass consumerism development,
    4, 5–6
  political ideology and, 12
  tourism, 106, 111
Sovereign debt, 174–176
Spatial compression, 198–200
Spectacles, 28
Staged authenticity, 108
Stanford University, 123, 137
Staples, 64–65, 72
Starbucks, 68, 150
Strike Debt, 176
Structural adjustment policy, 174
Structuralist perspective, 79
Subcultures, 46–48
Suburbs, 63–65, 72–75
Subvertisements, 151–152
Sugar, 80–81, 89
Supermarkets, 95–97
Supplemental Nutrition Assistance
    Program (SNAP), 89
Surveillance practices, 72–75
Sustainability practices, 116–117
Sustainable consumption, 153–154
Sustainable fisheries, 155–156
Swadeshi movement (India),
    208–210

Tamagotchi, 29
Target, 25, 65, 68, 71
Taste, 44–46
Taylor, Frederick, 22
Thailand, 103
Theming, 110
Theory of the Leisure Class, The
    (Veblen), 8, 42–43
Third places, 76
350.0rg, 145
Time, 35
Time-space compression, 24
Tourism:
  authentic experiences, 108–109
  collective tourist gaze, 106
  communitas development, 109–110
  cultural cannibalism, 102
  cultural commodification, 101–102
  dark tourism, 107–108
  Disney World (Florida), 110–113
  economics of, 100–101
  embodied actors, 106
  fun experiences, 109–110
  liminality experience, 109–110
  national parks, 113–117
  new moral tourist, 108–109
  objectification in sex tourism, 103
  object of consumption, 100–105
  passive gazers, 105–106
  places of consumption, 110–117
  posttourist, 109
  racial disparities, 102, 115
  rituals of transformation, 106
  romantic tourist gaze, 106
  sex tourism, 103–105
  sight sacralization process, 105
  socioeconomic disparities, 106, 111
  souvenirs, 102–103
  staged authenticity, 108
  subjects of consumption, 105–106,
    108–110
  tourist-cycle model, 101
  traveler-objects, 102–103
  trinketization, 102–103
  tripper-objects, 102–103
Tourist-cycle model, 101

Toyota, 154–155
Toys-R-Us, 51, 65
Traditional hedonism, 56–57
Tragedy of culture, 39, 60–61
Transaction time of online
    purchases, 70
TransFair USA, 150
Traveler-objects, 102–103
Trickle-down theory, 42
Trickle-up theory, 47
Trinketization, 102–103
Tripper-objects, 102–103
Turkey, 200

Uber, 190
Udacity, 123
Ukraine, 107
Unequal exchange relationship, 199
Unilever, 155–156
Union label, 144–145, 148
University of Missouri, 136
Unsafe at Any Speed (Nader), 147
UPC scanning, 67
Upscale spending, 43
Upsell technique, 70
Urban Outfitters, 68
U.S. Environmental Protection
    Agency (EPA):
    Alar ban, 82
    daily garbage production, 34
    national parks, 114
U.S. Federal Trade Commission
    (FTC), 146
U.S. Food and Drug Administration
    (FDA), 85, 86
Use value, 25
Usury, 168
Utility maximization, 8, 53–56

Veblen, Thorstein, 8, 42–43
Victoria Secret, 64
Vietnam, 103–104
Voluntary simplicity movement, 182–183

WALL-E (2008), 35
Wal-Mart, 65–67, 71, 156
Walton, Sam, 66
Wanamaker, John, 61
Waste:
    e-waste, 34
    hazardous waste, 34–35, 36
    in commodities, 33–35
    waste management, 34–35
    waste recovery, 194
    zero waste perspective, 35
Waste Makers, The (Packard), 34
Wealth of Nations (Smith), 8,
    25–26
Weber, Max, 8
Wheeler-Lea Act (1938), 146
Whirlpool, 209
White flight, 73
White-label products, 144, 148
White-listed stores, 144
Whole Foods Market, 83, 88
Women:
    consumption locations, 63, 67,
        95, 96
    food preparation role, 92, 93,
        94–95, 96
    political consumerism,
        143–145
    social reproduction role, 92
Woolworth's, 4–5
World Bank, 169, 174, 200
World-system theory, 199–200
World Wildlife Fund (WWF),
    155–156

Yale University, 121–122
Yellowstone National Park,
    113–114, 115
Your Money's Worth
    (Chase & Schlink), 146
YouTube, 195

Zero waste perspective, 35